The Salt Companion to Carter Revard

Edited By

ELLEN L. ARNOLD is Associate Professor of English at East Carolina University, where she teaches courses in Native American and Ethnic American literatures. She has published critical essays on Leslie Marmon Silko, Linda Hogan, Carter Revard, and Allison Hedge Coke, and edited *Conversations with Leslie Marmon Silko* (University Press of Mississippi, 2000).

The Salt Companion to Carter Revard

Edited by
ELLEN L. ARNOLD

CAMBRIDGE

PUBLISHED BY SALT PUBLISHING
PO Box 937, Great Wilbraham PDO, Cambridge CB1 5JX United Kingdom

All rights reserved

The selection and introduction © Ellen L. Arnold, 2007
individual contributions © the contributors, 2007

The right of Ellen L. Arnold to be identified as the
editor of this work has been asserted by her in accordance
with Section 77 of the Copyright, Designs and Patents Act 1988.

This book is in copyright. Subject to statutory exception
and to provisions of relevant collective licensing agreements,
no reproduction of any part may take place without the written
permission of Salt Publishing.

First published 2007

Printed and bound in the United Kingdom by Lightning Source

Typeset in Swift 10 / 12

This book is sold subject to the conditions that it shall not,
by way of trade or otherwise, be lent, re-sold, hired out,
or otherwise circulated without the publisher's prior consent
in any form of binding or cover other than that in which
it is published and without a similar condition including this
condition being imposed on the subsequent purchaser.

ISBN-13 978 1 84471 090 4 paperback
ISBN-10 1 84471 090 4 paperback

Salt Publishing Ltd gratefully acknowledges
the financial assistance of Arts Council England

1 3 5 7 9 8 6 4 2

Contents

Acknowledgments	v
Introduction	1
Norma C. Wilson, "Star Legacies"	12
Suzanne Evertsen Lundquist, "Carter Revard as Autoethnographer or *Wa-thi'-gethon*"	34
Robin Riley Fast, "Going Home with Carter Revard"	60
Susan Scarberry-Garcia, "'We Sing As the Birds Do': Listening for Bird Song in the Work of Carter Revard"	77
Patrice Hollrah, "'The Voices Still Are Singing': Osage/Ponca Continuance in the Poetry of Carter Revard"	85
Robert M. Nelson, "Ponca War Dancers: Creating a Pan-Indian Circle"	98
Jerry Harp, "'Reading That Part of the Past': Accessing History in the Poetry of Carter Revard"	110
Robert Bensen, "To Make Their Bodies of Words"	128
Janet McAdams, "Carter Revard's Angled Mirrors"	143
Ellen L. Arnold, "'Present Myth': Old Stories and New Sciences in the Poetry of Carter Revard"	160
Márgara Averbach, "Translating Carter Revard: An Adventure among Mixed and Fertile Words"	183
Susan Berry Brill de Ramírez and Peter G. Beidler, "Scholarship and Stories, Oxford and Oklahoma, Academe and American Indians: The Relational Words and Worlds of a Native American Bard and Storytelling Medievalist—Carter Revard"	202
Susanna Fein, "Trail-Tracking the Ludlow Scribe: Carter Revard as Translator-Scholar-Sleuth of Medieval English Poetry"	219
Author Notes	237
Index	241

Acknowledgments

It has been a great privilege to participate in the making of this volume. I am grateful to all the contributors who gave so generously of their time, scholarly expertise, and personal support to make this project possible. Special thanks go to Janet McAdams, who introduced me to Carter Revard's work and to Carter Revard himself when we were both graduate students at Emory University in the 1990s, and without whom this volume would never have come to be. Bob Bensen, much appreciation for your personal and editorial encouragement throughout. Many thanks as well to Chris and Jen Hamilton-Emery and everyone at Salt Publishing for their patience and dedication in bringing this volume to fruition. Most of all, we all give thanks to Carter Revard for his inspiring and challenging poems and essays, which have brought us all together in celebration, for his kind and good-humored support to all of us in our work, and for his permission to quote from and reprint his work.

We gratefully acknowledge Frank Parman and Arn Henderson of Point Riders Press for the use of poems from *Ponca War Dancers* and *Cowboys and Indians, Christmas Shopping*, and the University of Arizona Press for permission to quote from and reproduce Carter Revard's poems (in *An Eagle Nation*, by Carter C. Revard. ©1993 Carter C. Revard; and *Winning the Dust Bowl* by Carter Revard. ©2001 Carter Revard. Reprinted by permission of the University of Arizona Press) and to reprint Janet McAdams' essay, "Carter Revard's Angled Mirrors" (from *Speak to Me Words: Essays on Contemporary American Indian Poetry* by Dean Rader and Janice Gould, ©2003 The Arizona Board of Regents. Reprinted by permission of the University of Arizona Press).

Versions or portions of essays in this volume by Ellen L. Arnold, Márgara Averbach, Suzanne Evertsen Lundquist, and Susan Scarberry-Garcia appeared in *Studies in American Indian Literatures* 15.1 (2003).

Introduction

Carter Revard was born in 1931 in Pawhuska, Oklahoma, of Osage, Ponca, Irish, and Scotch-Irish heritage. He grew up in the Buck Creek Valley on the Osage Reservation, where he worked in the fields, trained greyhounds, and janitored with his twin sister in the one-room schoolhouse where he and his six siblings completed their first eight grades. After graduating from Bartlesville College High School, Revard won a radio quiz scholarship to the University of Tulsa, where he earned his B.A. in 1952. One of the first American Indian Rhodes Scholars, Revard took an M.A. at Oxford in 1954 and a Ph.D. at Yale in 1959. He taught at Amherst College before beginning a distinguished and prolific 36-year career (1961–1997) at Washington University in St. Louis, Missouri, as a scholar and teacher of medieval English literature specializing in Middle English, history of the English language, and linguistics. (Bibliographies of Revard's scholarly publications on medieval literature appear in the special issue of *Studies in American Indian Literatures* [2003] in his honor and in the appendix to Susanna Fein's essay in this volume.)

The same year Revard graduated from the University of Tulsa and was named Rhodes Scholar, he was given his Osage name, Nompehwahthe ("Fear-Inspiring," relative of Thunder [1998: 139]) by his grandmother, Mrs. Josephine Jump, in a traditional Osage naming ceremony. As he recalls in the preface to his essay collection *Family Matters, Tribal Affairs*, it was not until 1973, amidst growing national awareness of American Indian peoples awakened by the political events of the early 1970s—the Trail of Broken Treaties and the takeover of the Bureau of Indian Affairs building in 1972, the Wounded Knee occupation of 1973—that he began to teach courses in American Indian literatures and cultures. Revard became an organizer in the St. Louis Indian community, helped found the American Indian Center of Mid-America, joined a Gourd Dancers group, and began to publish poetry with American Indian themes (1998: xiii–xvi). Two chapbooks—*My Right Hand Don't Leave Me No More* (1970) and *Nonymosity* (1980)—were followed by *Ponca War Dancers* (1980), *Cowboys and Indians, Christmas Shopping* (1992), *An Eagle Nation* (1993), which won the 1994 Oklahoma Book Award, and most recently, *How the Songs Come Down: New and Selected Poems* (2005), part of Salt Publishing's Earthworks Series. In addition, Revard has published a collection of essays, *Family Matters, Tribal Affairs* (1998) and a multi-genre memoir, *Winning the Dust Bowl* (2001). In 2001 Revard was named Writer of the Year in Autobiography by the Wordcraft Circle of Native Writers for *Family Matters, Tribal Affairs*. In 2005, he received the Lifetime Achievement Award from the Native Writers' Circle of the Americas.

Carter Revard's complex and beautifully crafted poetry has been widely anthologized in collections of American and American Indian literature, and his poems and essays on Native traditions and literatures have inspired two generations of Indian poets and helped to shape contemporary literary theory about Native American literatures. Revard's interests in languages and storytelling cross multiple cultural traditions and histories in ways that challenge cultural boundaries. In her book *The Nature of Native American Poetry* (2001), Norma Wilson says of Revard, "No other Native poet demonstrates so thorough a knowledge of British and American poetic traditions . . . No other Native poet has been able to so fully articulate in English words the relationship between ancient tribal myth and modern life" (15).

Although there are many accomplished and widely published American Indian poets (Simon Ortiz, Maurice Kenny, Duane Niatum, Joy Harjo, Ofelia Zepeda, Wendy Rose, and Luci Tapahonso, to name a few), in addition to many of the most popular contemporary American Indian fiction writers who are also poets (Leslie Marmon Silko, N. Scott Momaday, James Welch, Louise Erdrich, Linda Hogan, and Sherman Alexie, for example), poetry has for a long time been neglected in critical studies and teaching relative to fiction. Only recently have three important books devoted exclusively to Native American poetry begun to define and focus critical approaches to this large body of work: Robin Riley Fast's *The Heart as a Drum: Continuance and Resistance in American Indian Poetry* (1999), Norma Wilson's *The Nature of Native American Poetry* (2001), and Dean Rader and Janice Gould's edited volume of essays, *Speak to Me Words: Essays on Contemporary American Indian Poetry* (2003). As

Norma Wilson points out, poetry as a written form was foreign to American Indians, but it shared similarities with the oral songs and chants that have always been central to their daily lives and spiritual practices; Wilson states, "Contemporary Native poetry has its roots in the land, in the oral tradition, and in history... [W]hen Native poets evoke traditional literature, they are continuing in the oral tradition, drawing from cultural memory the words and images that have sustained their people and sharing parts of their cultural heritage" (2001: ix).

Though Native American literature arises from the vastly diverse languages, traditions, homelands, and histories of several hundred distinct cultural groups, that literature is described by many critics as sharing some essential elements: a rootedness in oral narrative and storytelling traditions; a respect for the sacred power of language both to create and destroy; a deep reverence for the earth and the interconnectedness of human beings with all the living beings and elements of the natural world; a refusal of Western dichotomizing and objectifying epistemologies; and a "reinvention" of the English language, which was imposed on American Indians as a tool of conquest, to empower it to express indigenous worldviews and realities. Though Native poetry shares these characteristics with Native literature in general, Dean Rader and Janice Gould observe that poetry is also distinctly different from other genres. Rader finds that the structure of poetry most effectively "mirrors Native oral potential and Native worldviews" (2003: 11) through its "transform[ation of] the lyric moment into a dynamic narrative event," its resistance to "linear constraints," its use of "creative typography to emulate spoken diction" (8), and its fusion of disparate elements, such as "present and past, poetry and prose, the lyric 'I' and the communal 'we'" (11). Gould argues that many Native poets do in fact work within the constraints of dominant literary forms, and that many of these qualities—storytelling, play with form and typography, etc.—are also found in the work of other American poets; what she finds unique about American Indian poetry is "in the particular truth telling it embodies, in the particular kinds of insights Indians bring to this question of who we are or what we are about as a nation ... [O]ne function of American Indian poetry has been to 'resist cultural erasure,' to question the dominant narrative ... , to remember our histories," to "reclaim and rebuild the identities that the Euro-Americans wanted to annihilate," and to restore balance to Indian people and to a damaged world (10–11).

Carter Revard exemplifies what Rader terms "engaged resistance"—a resistance to "the imperial colonizing thrust of contemporary culture through participation in it" (12). While all of Revard's poetry is deeply informed by and continues Osage and Ponca histories and traditions, as many of the essays in this volume so beautifully elucidate, he is also concerned with building pan-tribal connections and with reclaiming "what's worthwhile in Europe for our people" (1998: 24). In his frequently referenced essay "Herbs of Healing: American Values in American Indian Literature" (1998: 161–83; Rader and Gould 2003: 172–92), Revard compares some of the modern "classics" to poems by contemporary American Indian writers—Wallace Stevens' "Anecdote of the Jar" to Simon Ortiz's "Speaking," John Milton's "On the Late Massacre in Piedmont" to Wendy Rose's "I Expected My Skin and My Blood to Ripen," Robert Frost's "Never Again Would Birds' Song Be the Same" to Louise Erdrich's "Jacklight"—to demonstrate how these "undiscovered" poets correct, enrich, and balance narrow or distorted EuroAmerican visions of history and reality (Dean and Rader 2003: 192). By examining his own use of the Old English riddle form in poems such as "What the TV Said" and "What the Eagle Fan Says," Revard shows how he adapts Anglo-Saxon poetics "for American Indian themes and purposes" (190), bringing those old forms to life, making them "blossom and fruit" (188) with revelations for the present world.

Revard's poetry portrays American Indians not as culturally isolated victims resisting pressures from the outside, but as agents of global history. Interspersed with the more personal and local poems for which Revard is best known—"Coyote Tells Why He Sings," "An Eagle Nation," "What the Eagle Fan Says," "Aunt Jewell as Powwow Princess," etc.—are "scientific and political" poems, such as "Transactions," "Making Money," "November in Washington DC," "Postcolonial Hyperbaggage," "Columbus Looks Out Far, In Deep," or "Transfigurations," poems that, in Revard's words, "connect the Oklahoma, rural, Indian with the national and international political scenery" and "lift the local chiaroscuro into the national sunlight" (28 September 2000: E-mail to author). As Janet McAdams observes, many of Revard's poems are reprinted in multiple collections, making it difficult and not very useful "to characterize Revard's body of work in a linear fashion" (Rader and Gould 2003: 194). Rather, Revard arranges his poems as "angled mirrors, so that full-face, profile, and rear-view versions of their subjects may be seen at the same time" (2001: xiii; qtd. in McAdams 2003: 194), creating a fluid, multifaceted, interactive poetics. Yet, Revard is always, ultimately, a storyteller. This is especially evident in his most recent book, *How the Songs Come Down*, which Revard intends as "a coherent body of work, with a story that comes clear from the way the old and new poems are juxtaposed, grouped, and sequenced," a story whose "grand theme is singing"—the revelations embodied in song, the power and community that song builds (17 December 2005: E-mail to author). Revard's "conversive" blending of Western literary and Native oral traditions (Brill de Ramirez 1999) demand equally conversive, multilayered critical approaches that can address the ways his poems can both epitomize European conventions and interrogate and transform those conventions, can examine how his poems work toward indigenous sovereignties as well as for pan-tribal and global community.

The critical essays in this volume explore Revard's poetry from a variety of perspectives, meeting this challenge by forming their own intersecting, interacting field of "angled mirrors." Norma C. Wilson (University of South Dakota) and Suzanne Evertsen Lundquist (Brigham Young University) provide detailed biographical, cultural, and historical contexts for Revard's work. In "Star Legacies," Norma Wilson draws on his published work and her personal correspondence with Revard to locate the foundations of Revard's writing in the details of family, community, and tribal histories, to show how it expresses the continuity of centuries of indigenous Osage and Ponca tradition. Highlighting the way that Osage origin stories and naming ceremonies relate individual and community to the stars from which the Osage people descended, Wilson concludes, "For his poetry and his life, Carter Revard finds meaning in looking to the sky. Awe in the face of creation is one of his gifts to those who read his poems. His Osage and Ponca ancestors prepared him well to sing with a gift that can help others rise." Suzanne Evertsen Lundquist, also making use of extensive personal communication with Revard, takes a somewhat more theoretical approach to his family, literary, and philosophical genealogies in "Carter Revard as Autoethnographer or *Wa-thi'-gethon*." Using Mary Louise Pratt's definition of "autoethnography" as life-writing produced in cultural "contact zones" where subjects "describe themselves in ways that engage with representations others have made of them," Lundquist examines Revard's essays and poetry as autoethnography that explores differences between Native and Western conceptions of identity and elucidates a theory of mixedblood identity as a dynamic "third space."

Robin Riley Fast's essay, "Going Home with Carter Revard," explores the centrality of "home" as both theme and poetics in Revard's work. In detailed readings of numerous "poems of home" such as "To the Muse in Oklahoma," "Homework at Oxford," "Wazhazhe Grandmother," "My Right Hand Don't Leave Me No More," and "Paint and Feathers," Fast (Emerson College) demonstrates how deeply Revard's poetry is grounded in the knowledge and values of home, and how his examination of the multilayered linkings of home, language, and survival articulate "an ethics and esthetics of relationality." In "'We Sing as the Birds Do': Listening for Bird Song in the Work of Carter Revard," Susan Scarberry-Garcia (Arizona State University) similarly traces a single theme through many poems to show how the "music instinct" that bonds humans and birds helps to form a basis of his poetic sensibility. For Revard, Scarberry-Garcia observes, the Bird People have given their songs to humans so they can better communicate with the spirit world, and his "strategy of intimately knowing and 'naming the birds' is a means of recognizing the cosmic forces that animate, shape, and travel the natural world." The carefully detailed catalogues of bird names and bird song in north central Oklahoma that appear in Revard's poems, she argues, also position him as a teller of "a collective communal history" who passes on local knowledges and thus continues oral traditions.

In "'The Voices Still Are Singing': Osage/Ponca Continuance in the Poetry of Carter Revard," Patrice Hollrah (University of Nevada-Reno) considers Revard's poem "Given" and three of his "Aunt Jewell" poems—"How the Songs Came Down," "An Eagle Nation," and "Aunt Jewell as Powwow Princess"—in which his Ponca Aunt, Jewell McDonald Camp Farmer, is a key figure of intergenerational transmission of traditional Ponca values. Hollrah studies Aunt Jewell's lessons to Revard and his passing on of her teachings to younger generations through his poems to suggest that they are acts of decolonization and self-determination, affirmations of Ponca/Eagle Nation sovereignty that help the people "live more fully." Robert Nelson (University of Richmond) begins from a similar consideration of tribal continuance to examine Revard's creation of pan-tribal community in his stanza-by-stanza close reading of a single poem in "'Ponca War Dancers': Creating a Pan-Indian Circle." Looking first at the Ponca ceremonial dances of the *Helushka* Society and Revard's Uncle Gus's performance of the war dance as a kind of "hub" where "emic and etic perspectives gather," Nelson demonstrates that Uncle Gus clears a space amidst an etic tourist audience for Native traditionalism, thus modeling "a positive strategy for coming to terms with the forces of cultural assimilation." Next, Nelson focuses on the coalescence of an "emic" Pan-Indian "circle of vision" that emerges in the space between Uncle Gus's performance and the white audience, where a "third variety of Indian community, not reserved to any one tribe or geographically fixed setting" is united by the "warrior spirit" of activism, born of AIM resistance in the 1970s, to protect and preserve intra-cultural communities and beliefs.

In "'Reading That Part of the Past': Accessing History in the Poetry of Carter Revard," Jerry Harp (Lewis and Clark College) draws on theorizations of the permeability and mutability of boundaries in American Indian poetry by critics such as Robin Riley Fast and Janet McAdams to examine ways that Carter Revard's poetry "articulates moments of fluidity in which one encounters parts of the past that otherwise remain inaccessible." In such poems as "A Sun Dance Story," "Rock Shelters," and "A Cardinal, New Snow, and Some Firewood," Harp demonstrates how shifts in perception open into moments of reading the past in "strikingly intimate terms," weaving strands of the present and past with cultural meanings and personal discoveries. Similarly, Robert Bensen's "To Make Their Bodies of Words" considers Revard's poems as sites of the intersection of the moment and what is beyond the moment—in Bensen's case, the spirit-world. While Harp writes about the permeability among geographical, spiritual, and historical spaces, Bensen (Hartwick College) focuses on "extraordinary moments [that] depend upon the coincidence or confluence of the Seen and the Unseen," as in the apparition of Revard's Uncle Gus dancing in "Aunt Jewell as Powwow Princess." Interpreting "Looking Before and After" as an early work of visionary experience that informs Revard's "Aunt Jewell poems," including "An Eagle Nation" and "How the Songs Come Down," Bensen shows how Revard's poetics are developed from Osage creation stories and the Naming Ceremony.

Janet McAdams' essay "Carter Revard's Angled Mirrors" (reprinted from *Speak To Me Words*) begins with Revard's advice in *Winning the Dust Bowl* that his poems should be read as "angled mirrors" (2001: xiii). Similar to Lundquist, McAdams (Kenyon College) draws on Pratt's notion of cultural "contact zones" to demonstrate ways that Revard's poetry performs a "third space"; whereas Lundquist addresses cultural identity, however, McAdams focuses on the textual mapping of a "new world" that is always in flux, always transforming. Through detailed examinations of Revard's poetics, particularly the complex trope of voice, in three divergent poems—"Coyote Tells Why He Sings," "What the TV

Said," and "Homework at Oxford"—McAdams demonstrates how Revard destabilizes received binaries without collapsing them by showing their interrelationships or transforming one into its other. Ellen L. Arnold (East Carolina University) takes a somewhat similar approach in "'Present Myth': Old Stories and New Sciences in the Poetry of Carter Revard" by exploring the dynamic interplay of postmodern science and traditional worldviews in poems such as "ESP," "Transfigurations," "The Poet's Cottage," and "Nonymosity." By weaving creation stories and ceremonies from Osage tradition with images and concepts from science, Arnold suggests, Revard creates a contemporary mythology of wholeness that negotiates the borders between nature and culture, myth and history, spirit and matter.

The final three essays in this collection further expand cross-cultural and trans-historical considerations of Carter Revard's work by examining it in global contexts. In "Translating Carter Revard: An Adventure among Mixed and Fertile Worlds," Argentine scholar and translator Márgara Averbach (Universidad de Buenos Aires) shares with readers her process of translating four of Revard's poems—"Coyote Tells Why He Sings,": "To the Muse, In Oklahoma," "Driving in Oklahoma," and "Postcolonial Hyperbaggage"—from English into Spanish for her college students in Argentina. Starting with basic issues of translation across linguistic and cultural borders, Averbach demonstrates how the process of careful translation (especially with the generous participation of the author in e-mail dialogue!) can enrich and illuminate readings of poems in two languages and cultures, as well as contribute to extra-textual intercultural exchange. Two essays, one co-authored by Susan Berry Brill de Ramírez and Peter Beidler and a second by Susanna Fein, break new ground by examining the interrelationships between Revard's medieval scholarship and his American Indian heritage. Beidler (Lehigh University), trained as a medievalist, and Brill de Ramírez (Bradley University), trained in literary theory and criticism, are both also scholars of Native American literature. In "Scholarship and Stories, Oxford and Oklahoma, Academe and American Indians: The Relational Words and Worlds of a Native American Bard and Storytelling Medievalist," Brill de Ramírez and Beidler demonstrate how Revard's roots in Native storytelling traditions offer him unique insights into the orally-informed literatures of medieval England and Europe. In their analysis of Revard's translation and contextualization of the Anglo-Norman poem *Gilote et Johane* in "The Wife of Bath's Grandmother," they argue that Revard's combination of scholarly rigor and storytelling strategies creates a distinctive methodology, a "conversive scholarship," that "welcomes his readers into the worlds within his books, essays, and notes" and offers a valuable alternative model of literary scholarship that "bridg[es] the gap between literature and scholarship through their connective heritage in relational storytelling."

Medievalist Susanna Fein (Kent State University), who shares Revard's scholarly interests in the fourteenth-century Harley Lyrics Manuscript, gives us a detailed glimpse of this creative methodology at work in "Trail-Tracking the Ludlow Scribe: Carter Revard as Translator-Scholar-Sleuth of Medieval English Poetry." Fein explores the work for which Revard is best known among medieval scholars, which she terms "the stuff of legend": his patient pursuit of the fragmentary clues that have enabled him to locate the anonymous scribe in a particular place and window of time, in medieval Ludlow from 1314 to 1349. Fein shows us how Revard's pioneering work, including his lively translations of French works recorded in the Harley Manuscript (such as the bawdy comic interlude *Gilote et Johane* and four even bawdier and funnier fabliaux), and his edition with commentary of the satiric *Papelard Priest*, has rescued excellent but little-known poetry for the general as well as the academic reader. Attributing the success of Revard's scholarship to his "sense of the past as a living, colorful presence, a sense that owes ... much to his American Indian roots," Fein invites those who love Carter Revard's poetry to discover his medieval translations as well, which are "delightful and exceptional in their own way."

Carter Revard tells us that "good language, in both talk and writing, builds a small community in which people can live a little more completely and joyously than solitude allows" (2001: xvi). Revard's good language has provided the opportunity for this community of scholars to lift their own voices in "harmonies and counterpoints" that echo Carter's own (xvi). These essays open multiple entries into Revard's work, and it is our hope that they will provide occasions for lively new conversations about his poems, about Native American poetry, and American poetry in general. Like good poetry, these essays also help us "develop [our] sense of how miraculous the world is" (Revard 2003: 5). I will close with lines from Revard's "Songs of the Wine-throated Hummingbird," the final poem of *How the Songs Come Down*, which traces how song finds its way into the written words that stimulate our human minds to hear the music of the universe anew:

> ... What are sounds,
> and what are songs, that we can make them,
> that we have ears to hear,
> that on these tiny waves
> of air, of water, even of magnetism, we have made
> the smaller ripples that we call Meaning
> when sounds are words—or which, rising
> like Aphrodite from the foam
> of dance and song and love, come through as Music. Deep
> in the blue Antarctic seas, high
> in the green Guatemalan jungle, here
> in these cracked English words,
> can you hear them sing,
> the hummingbirds, the humpback whales,
> a neutron star, a human soul? (2005: 160)

Ellen L. Arnold
December 19, 2005

Works Cited

Brill de Ramírez, S. B. 1999. *Contemporary American Indian Literatures and the Oral Tradition*. Tucson: University of Arizona Press.
"Carter Revard: A Selected Bibliography." 2003. *Studies in American Indian Literatures* 15.1: 142-49.
Fast, R. R. 1999. *The Heart as a Drum: Continuance and Resistance in American Indian Poetry*. Ann Arbor: University of Michigan Press.
Rader, D. and J. Gould, eds. 2003. *Speak to Me Words: Essays on Contemporary American Indian Poetry*. Tucson: University of Arizona Press.
Revard, C. 1998. *Family Matters, Tribal Affairs*. Tucson: University of Arizona Press.
——. 2000, 28 September. "Hello." E-mail to E. Arnold.
——. 2001. *Winning the Dust Bowl*. Tucson: University of Arizona Press.
——. 2003. "Some Notes on Native American Literature." *Studies in American Indian Literatures* 15.1: 1-15.
——. 2005. *How the Songs Come Down: New and Selected Poems*. Cambridge, U.K.: Salt Publishing.
——. 2005, 17 December. "How The Songs Come Down." E-mail to E. Arnold.
Wilson, N. C. 2001. *The Nature of Native American Poetry*. Albuquerque: University of New Mexico Press.

Star Legacies

Norma C. Wilson

Carter Revard writes about "star stuff" (1993: xi). Like his Osage ancestors, who imagined coming from the stars, Revard looks for the higher and deeper meanings of all he has received. Introducing *An Eagle Nation*, he says, "The creation of language, of writing, is less astounding than the invention of water, but not much less, and we each re-create, as we go, all that has been given us... Under the old names, new beings gather; within the new beings, old ways survive" (1993: xi).

From his childhood in rural Oklahoma, among Osage, Ponca and Euro-Americans who lived close to the land, Revard learned to see by the light of a spiritual, philosophical and social perspective that had developed over centuries of life in the middle of North America. In *Family Matters, Tribal Affairs*, he says, "It may well be that myths are like the stars: we see by their light, even though they may have 'died' centuries ago" (1998: 153). His indigenous traditions and the experience of rural life formed the foundation for his poetry.

Living in Community

Born March 25, 1931, Carter Revard grew up in Oklahoma on the Osage reservation, in the town of Pawhuska and on farm land between Pawhuska and Bartlesville, near Buck Creek. Raised by his mother Thelma Louise Camp, of Irish and Scotch-Irish ancestry, and his full-blood Osage stepfather Addison Jump, the author does not recall ever seeing his father McGuire Revard, who was part Osage. Though he is only a small part Osage, Revard grew up with four half-brothers and sisters who were half Osage (17 July 1976: Letter to author). Thelma's brother Woody Camp was married to Jewell McDonald, a Ponca. Carter, his twin sister Maxine, and their older brother Antwine often stayed with their Aunt Jewell, Uncle Woody, and family at the Ponca village of White Eagle; and Jewell and her children often stayed with Carter's family. Over the years the extended Osage-Ponca family members have maintained their relationships.

By 1910 when Addison Jump was born, the Osages had been forced to accept individual allotment of their reservation lands, their ancient ceremonies were being devalued and discarded, and their language was under assault in boarding schools. Revard has written that in these schools Addison and his younger siblings were beaten for speaking Osage. Yet Osage was still spoken in their homes. In *Family Matters, Tribal Affairs*, Revard recalls a feast to mark the first anniversary of his brother Jim's ceremonial naming, indicating that despite forced assimilation, his family continued to follow their Osage customs (1998: 10).

Revard describes in his writing a childhood rich with the experience of Oklahoma farm life in the Buck Creek rural community on the Osage Reservation. In 1934, Addison and Thelma bought an eighty-acre meadow with house, garage, hay barn, cow barn and chicken house between Pawhuska and Bartlesville. Carter's Cousin Roy taught him to read. Carter helped his Grandpa Camp with the milking and other work, and watched with him the innocent kittens. With friends he played under rocks that had sheltered Indians in ancient times, and outlaws during the early twentieth century. He got to know the animals and birds, their tracks and their songs, and also neighbors like Mrs. Josephine Parks, a "rare practicing Christian." Revard remembers eating at her house as "like eating in an Indian household, where the gift of life and friends and relatives is kept quietly in mind" (2001: 48-49). A mile east of Revard's home was the one-room Buck Creek school that he attended from 1936 to 1944. He and sister Maxine served as janitors there in the eighth grade. His fifth, sixth and seventh-grade teacher, Miss Letha Conner, was Osage. When he spent an evening with her in July 2004, she told Revard that both her grandparents were killed during a buffalo hunt in Kansas in the 1870s (12 July 2004: E-mail to author).

Revard's book *Winning the Dust Bowl* surrounds his poetry with the multifaceted dimensions of living in community. For telling his life, Revard says he followed the "planless plan of Mark Twain" (2001: xvi).

The writing of Osage author John Joseph Mathews, who grew up in Pawhuska, Oklahoma, a generation earlier, was another influence. Like Revard, Mathews was a graduate of Oxford, and also like Revard, Mathews respected the common people living on the land. Revard writes, "[I]f you really do know any people like us, my folks and me, you've noticed that they're as smart as rich people, probably less selfish on the average, just as funny and decent—or, I suspect more so—and you know they are on the average a good kind of people to grow up with" (2001: 133).

Entering the Circle of Being

Revard worked at a variety of jobs as a teenager, including grooming and training greyhounds for racing. He attended high school in Bartlesville, just east of the reservation. A radio quiz scholarship enabled him to enter the University of Tulsa in 1948. In 1952, after Carter completed a B.A. in English there, Osage elders sponsored a ceremony in which he was given the name *Nonpehwahteh* (Makes Afraid or Fear Inspiring, a reference to the Thunder Being of Osage creation stories). Revard explains in an essay, "Traditional Osage Naming Ceremonies: Entering the Circle of Being," that ceremonial naming brought him to a "fuller consciousness" of the "mythic dimension" of life and place in the universe (1983: 460). The Osage inscription in his book *An Eagle Nation* "for the Wazhazhe and Ponca Nations and all our Relations" (1993: n. pag.) translates into English:

> I chose the good way,
> you chose *Noⁿ-peh-wah-theh*.
> In literary studies when I had done well
> my grandmother was pleased,
> and the name *Noⁿ-peh-wah-theh*
> she gave to me.
> (4 April 2001: Personal communication to author)

The Osage naming ceremony, like thunder preceding the rain, seems to have been a catalyst for the poems that would follow. This honoring strengthened his ties to the Osage people and ensured the obligation to be a good relative, an obligation which Revard has tried to honor.

As Mathews explains in "People from the Stars," the first chapter of *The Osages: Children of the Middle Waters*, language and naming were of primary importance to the Osage: "Not even the earth and sky had names until the Children of the Middle Waters came" (1961: 7). He says that one of the first things the Osage did was to name the animals, birds, and insects in order to use symbolically the powers that the creator *Wah-Kon-Tah* had given the non-humans, and had not given the humans. They "named themselves *NI-U-Ko'n Ska*, Children of the Middle Waters" (1961: 7). Mathews called those who came from Europe and took over the Osage land, the Amer-Europeans. Revard sometimes refers to the invaders as "Ameropeans."

Revard's writing is consistent with his tribal legacy in both its emphasis on ceremonial naming, and in its profusion of names. Following in his own way the tradition by which land or water clans married into the sky clans, Carter, a member of the Wazhazhe or water people, married Stella, whose name means star, and he thanks her for starlight (1993: xii). Stella Hill Purce was born in New York City and like Revard has Irish ancestry. Both were studying English literature when they met at the Yale University Graduate School in January 1956. They married that year and continued their studies, both completing Ph.D.s in English. Stella Revard became a premier scholar in Milton/Neo-Latin Studies. The Revards have four children.

While studying at Yale, Revard taught at Amherst College. In writing his sonnet "The Coyote" at Amherst, Massachusetts, in 1958, Revard discovered his natural rhythm, meter and subject matter. And he also gave voice to an endangered animal native to his childhood home. While the sonnet has remained the same, Revard later changed its title to "Coyote Tells Why He Sings." He described writing the poem in the first chapter of *Winning the Dust Bowl*. Waking before daylight and listening to the rain, he remembered being caught in an Oklahoma thunderstorm with his brothers and sisters and seeking shelter under rocks in "almost a cave" (2001: 6). Among the rocks they could read the names scratched there in the 1890s. It was a place where outlaws hid. In an interview with Joseph Bruchac, Revard said, "I never thought of the coyote other than as something that was trying to get our calves or our chickens. Then, when I needed the Oklahoma voice, the coyote gave it to me. So it isn't the beings you pick, but those that come to you, who give you earth-time" (1987: 242).

Looking for the poet who would write with a unique American voice, Ralph Waldo Emerson said in his 1844 essay "The Poet," "the poet is the Namer" and "Language is fossil poetry" (1998: 1653). "I look in vain for the poet whom I describe," he wrote (1998: 1659). Whitman answered Emerson's call, but it took another century for America's indigenous authors to reinvent the English language to serve their purpose. Certainly Revard exemplifies the poet as namer that Emerson described. Revard's poems bring fossils to life and give words wings. His use of indigenous words and concepts has provided him with the means to achieve the freedom of expression that Emerson sought for American poetry.

Revard's new poems extend the meanings of those written earlier. While "The Coyote" gave voice to an animal, "Geode," gives voice to a stone, explaining that a geode may begin as an oyster shell and that it takes millions of years for a geode to form. People who buy these beautiful stones at rock shops and use them for paperweights or bookends are reminded in this poem of the long process that went into the geode's formation. Revard's making of this stone with his words exemplifies respect for the beauty of creation and his own sense of obligation to provide a vehicle for this marvel's voice.

Echoing Old English alliterative verse, Revard describes the capacity of the word to give life to stone, now used as bookends:

> I let them separate my selves and set them heavy
> on either side of a word-hoard, whose light
> leaves rustled with heavy thoughts between
> the heavier, wiser, older lines of all
> my residual selves, the wave marks made
> by snowflake-feathery amethyst ways of being,
> by all these words,
> by the Word,
> made slowly into Stone. (1993: 92)

It is significant that Revard, a Wazhazhe, was inspired to give voice to a stone whose formation began in water.

As Emerson suggested, poets speak for cultures. Their words leave a record to symbolize what life was/is for those who will live in the future. Revard wants future readers to be aware of the Osage perspective. Such knowledge can expand their consciousness of what it means to be a human being, a relative to all that lives. Relating the ancient Osage mythology, according to which the people came from the stars to live on Earth, Revard accentuates in poems like "Wazhazhe Grandmother" the contrasts between our ancient and modern environment.

"Wazhazhe Grandmother" begins with an epigraph defining the Osage word *Ho-e-ga*, from Francis La Flesche's dictionary. The definition illustrates the many associations such a word evokes in the minds of

Osage people. The word, which literally means "bare spot," is further defined as "the center of the forehead of the mythical elk," "an enclosure in which all life takes on bodily form, never to depart therefrom except by death," "the earth which the mythical elk made to be habitable by separating it from the water," "the camp of the tribe when ceremonially pitched," and "life as proceeding from the combined influences of the cosmic forces" (1980: 46).

According to an Osage myth recorded by Alice Fletcher and Francis La Flesche, when the ancestors came down from the sky, the elk provided them with a place to live by dropping into the water that covered the earth and calling the winds from the four directions, which evaporated the water. The elk then rolled joyfully on the soft, exposed earth; and his loose hairs stuck in the soil—"The hairs grew, and from them sprang beans, corn, potatoes and wild turnips, and then all the grasses and trees" (1911: 63). Revard's "Wazhazhe Grandmother" conveys his personal perspective on the creation, extending the Osage mythology by adding his own family's story within its literary, historical, geographic and social contexts.

Historical Displacement

The Osage people were able to maintain control of their lands until 1808, when they ceded large areas to the United States. In 1825, by treaty, the government forced them to leave their land in Missouri and move to a reservation in Kansas. In 1870, they were uprooted by an act of Congress, after which the Osage nation bought land from the Cherokees and moved to Indian Territory. With the General Allotment Act, which became law in 1887, the government paved the way for the breakup of tribal lands throughout the U.S. After inducing tribes to parcel out their communal lands to individual families, usually in the amount of 160 acres, the government opened "unassigned" lands to white settlement. The Osage did not accept allotment until 1906 when they obtained two arrangements that differed from those that the United States had forced on most tribes. First, their entire reservation was parceled out to members of their nation; so instead of 160 acres per family, they received over 600 acres per person. Second, the U. S. government was designated trustee, which guaranteed supervision through an arrangement with the elected Osage Tribal Council of the income from subsurface minerals on Osage land. All income from leasing and production was to be paid to the Tribal Council for distribution to each Osage holder of a headright. These arrangements were safeguards, though not guarantees, against cultural and individual losses of fortune.

The government allowed individuals to choose their homesteads from land allotted the entire Osage nation. "Wazhazhe Grandmother" tells of Revard's grandparents, Josephine Strikeaxe and Jacob Jump, choosing to build their homestead during the first decade of the 20th century "where the Osage hills begin" (1980: 46). A century earlier when their ancestors lived in Missouri, along the Osage River valley, they regarded the hills around them as sacred because their ancestors' remains were there. Revard describes the "timbered hollow" on Bird Creek, where his grandparents lived, as a quiet place that "seemed waiting for us" (1980: 47). He remembers it as abundant with a variety of life—prairie chickens, deer, kingfishers, and "deep pools" of water, like the land the elk made habitable. But Bird Creek was dammed in the 1950s, and the land is now "at the bottom of Lake Bluestem" (1980: 47). Revard's record of this beautiful land, so carelessly destroyed to fulfill the desires of townspeople for green lawns and swimming pools, is more than nostalgic. By attempting to give a full account of nature that was a given when he was a child, Revard allows the reader to confront the extent to which Osage history and land have been exploited and obliterated. Of course, by implication the poem relates to the general history of rural life in the United States.

Revard dedicated a related poem, "Rock Shelters," to John Joseph Mathews. Revard knew the older Osage author, who also left words as a record of his life and time with Osage relatives in the shelter of the natural world. During his childhood in the 1930s, Revard's family lived between Doe Creek and Buck Creek. "Rock Shelters" names the animals who had lived there; however, by the 1930s, many of them, including the deer, turkey, antelope, cougar, and bear had been almost wiped out by professional white hunters who had arrived in 1890:

> Here, the winter
> surrounded deer and turkeys, here lived plenty
> of beaver, muskrat, mink and raccoon, fox and
> bobcat and cottontail, coyote slinking, quail
> and squirrels, mice and weasels all with
> small birds watching from the bush or grapevine, berry
> tangles, juncoes, waxwings, cardinals like blood on
> snow, all sheltered here from
> the prairie blizzards north.

> And southward, in the bend of
> Buck Creek level to the southern ridge a valley
> of bluestem grass thigh-deep under
> sunflowers nodding, meadowlarks flying and singing with
> grazing buffalo, red wolves and coyotes trotting watching
> with pricked ears a hunter crawl with
> bow and arrows for a shot. (1993: 10)

This past abundance contrasts with Revard's home place more than fifty years later at the end of the twentieth century:

> Now crossed
> by asphalt road, wire fences, lanes to white farmhouses
> where no farming's done, grapes and lettuce and
> bananas on the polished table from Texas, from
> California, Nicaragua, the orange-fleshed
> watermelons that once lay in sandy fields by
> Doe Creek gone as truckloads of melons rumble
> past from Louisiana into town where food is
> kept. To plant here, you buy. This land
> was needed, we were told, it would be used. So oil is
> pulsing from beneath it, floats dead
> rainbows on Buck Creek and draws its brief trails
> straight as a Roman road across the sky..." (1993: 10)

The poem names not only the changes Revard has witnessed on Earth, but also in the sky. What is a star? Revard provides a broad definition that indicates the difference between what we now see above us and what we now think of as our Earth and the early 20th century perspective of his mixed-blood Osage, Ponca, Irish and Scotch-Irish family who lived on the land. No longer is the focus on natural surroundings:

> ... The small stars now
> move fast and send down messages of war
> to speech machines or pictures of
> pleasure to our living rooms, inviting us out into
> a larger endlessness with many
> centers. Galaxies, before long, may
> be sold for profit, once the first space ship has
> claimed one and the next has
> come to kill all those before... (1993: 11)

The satellites beam down images of Russian missiles, of Near Eastern armies, of items that can be bought at shopping malls. Instead of feeling at the center of the Earth and connected to the cosmos by looking up at the stars, an individual looking up at the stars can feel alienated and fearful. Revard's poem shows how the quest for power and possessions has replaced the human search for meaning and higher forms of truth. Ending with a description of life as the Osage experienced it before the arrival of the Ameropeans, Revard reflects upon their feeling of the wonder and meaning of life on the land:

> ...Think
> of walking on blue
> stars like this one, new
> plants, new beings, all the rock
> shelters where we'll crouch and see
> new valleys from.
> Here is my
> mussel shell. Here is the charcoal.
> We were here. (1993: 11)

Osage myths associate the shell with the introduction to life on earth when all was covered with water (Fletcher and La Flesche 1992: 457). This recent poem moves from description of the place in the present to a memory from Revard's childhood past, to the changes brought by exploiting the land and sky, and finally back to imagine the ancient past, also spiraling into the human exploration of other galaxies. This way of seeing beyond the limited perspective of a single moment or of planet Earth further elaborates a theme introduced in earlier poems like "Wazhazhe Grandmother." Yet, more consciously in later poems like this one, Revard the poet is making his mark.

Myth and Prehistory

Birds prepare for humans in "Dancing with Dinosaurs," suggesting the continuum between the evolution of reptile or dinosaur to bird and the subsequent and related development and continuum of Osage philosophy and ceremony. Revard imagines the journey through space and time as small reptiles begin to sing and to fly and eventually rise "to / twenty thousand feet on swirling / winds of a passing cold front" (1980: 60). They fly above Bermuda, Tobago, and Venezuela before descending "to perch on South America's shoulder, having become / the Male and Female Singers, having / put on their feathers and survived" (61). Revard compares this transformation to his personal naming ceremony:

> When I was named
>   a Thunder person, I was told:
>   here is a being
>   of whom you may make your body
>   that you may live to see old age . . . . (61)

His memory of the ceremony comes during a later ceremony in which a little girl is "being brought in / becoming one of us / as once was done for me" (61). Feathers of small birds flutter on the gourd rattles of the dancers. Revard's song in this poem is a kind of winter count, acknowledging all that has preceded the indigenous dance that continues. The winter count was a visual way of representing the events important to tribal history. Instead of painting images on hide, Revard has here painted the ceremony with words, as part of its entire historical context. Again, as in "Wazhazhe Grandmother," Revard shows his personal experience as part of community and cultural life.

The autobiographical and scholarly essays in *Family Matters, Tribal Affairs* provide insight into Native concepts integral to Revard's poetry. For example, alluding to the Osage and Hebrew creation stories, Revard asks, "[W]here does this earth come from, if not from the stars?" (1998: 153). In the poem "People from the Stars," whose title is taken from Mathews' chapter title, the contrast between past and present evolves from an opening reference to the Wazhazhe coming down "from the stars / by their choice, not by falling / or being thrown out / of the heavenly bars like Satan / into Europe" (1980: 45). The opening lines highlight the difference between the Judeo-Christian view of humanity as fallen and the Osage view of humanity as having chosen their own destiny on the Earth and as also capable of rising above it again, to live among the stars.

Joining the People of Death

Revard mentions in this poem that after joining the "people of death," the Osage "moved to another village / (we call it, *Ho-e-ga*) / where time began" (1980: 45). Readers unaware of the Isolated Earth People who merged with the Osage tribe (Mathews 1961: 15) would understand the "people of death" to be the Ameropeans who killed many Osage people, destroyed their habitat and way of life, and brought clock time to this continent. The ambiguity of Revard's choice of words suggests the possibility of Ameropeans taking on the Osage world view, like the Isolated Earth People of their mythical past.

But Revard also recognizes the ways in which the Osages are caught in the web of modern technology. Significantly, "People from the Stars" calls the people who pay "royalties" to the Osages for oil "Europeans." Osages trade their "royalties" for flights to Las Vegas. Revard remembers looking down like a king, "enthroned / on wings of shining metal" at the "midnight highways," lighted by the automotive "star-strings through the night" (1980: 45). The plane lands in the desert. And the Osage scholar wheels off "to shoot craps at the Stardust Inn / and talk of Indians and their Trickster Tales, / of Manabozho up / in Wounded Knee" (1980: 45). It has come to this, the poem suggests. Las Vegas, a city of artificial light, seems the supreme example of the trickster, a tawdry place for a person from the stars to land.

A later poem, "Close Encounters" tells in two parts much the same story with more detail. The first part leaves out the "people of death" and describes the Osage coming down as eagles, "who let us take their bodies" (1993: 25). The poem is set in the era before the invasion of the Ameropeans when the Osage were surrounded by dancing leaves and sunlight: "Nothing's lighter than leaves, we sang" (26). And yet the leaves were those of the massive oaks, and the songs created a solid society.

In the poem's second part Revard describes the experience in Las Vegas:

>   ... At the Stardust Inn deep
> within that city of dice and vice and Warhead Testing,
>   I was to give a paper
>   to the Rocky Mountain Modern Language Association
>   on Trickster Tales. (1993: 26)

At dawn, the traditional time for prayer, he walked:

>   to a vacant lot under
>   its desert willows
>   where lived a wren, some vivid orange flowers
>   papery on thornleaved stems hugging the sand,
>   and one empty billfold
>   with its credit cards spread around a sole
>   identity card that pictured
>   a security guard from San Diego ... (27)

This description conveys the tenuous and small hold of very few species of animal and plant life near this city. Nature is the setting for a robbery or some worse crime. The poem ends with reference to Revard's "singing" (at the conference) of Columbus, the Pilgrims and Cortez as tricksters who "brought / this krypton iris here and made / the desert bloom, / how they raised / the great light-sculptured houses / of cards and dice on sand," and of how the "rainbow ghosts of waterfalls / are pulsed into the sockets of / Las Vegas light flashing . . . / . . . its humongous word, / VACANCY, / VACANCY, / up to the dancing stars" (28). Ending the poem with pulsing irony, Revard exposes the gambler trickster's concept of this place as vacant of meaning, or purpose, or life. Las Vegas, Revard suggests, is the ultimate "city of God"; and the gambler's house, built on sand, has no foundation. Revard's walk to a vacant lot underscores the disconnect between the gambler's construct and the natural place—an orange flower and a wren make their home, at the edge of a city environment, re-designed to steal our resources. The title "Close Encounters" alludes to the movie *Close Encounters of the Third Kind* that was filmed at a place sacred to the indigenous Kiowa nation, and known as *Tsoai* to them, but dubbed Devil's Tower by the Ameropeans.

Many of Revard's poems satirize the abuse of indigenous cultures. His early poem, "Discovery of the New World," places the Ameropeans in the moccasins of Native Americans, suffering dreadfully as little green men from the stars colonize the Earth. Satirizing the notion of Manifest Destiny, the persona speaks with the voice of a creature from another planet describing human beings to his commander. The poem exposes the arrogant thinking of the exploiting colonizer:

> The creatures that we met this morning
>   marveled at our green skins
>   and scarlet eyes.
> They lack antennae
>   and can't be made to grasp
>   your proclamation that they are
> our lawful food and prey and slaves . . . (1980: 43)

Like the indigenous people before them, Ameropeans are seen as "helpless creatures," subjugated by beings come from afar. The creatures from outer space are superior in their technologies, though lacking empathy. Despite its sharp criticism, the science-fiction premise of this poem written in the 1970s elicits a smile, but as corruption and greed have grown more pervasive, Revard's satire has sharpened. In "Postcolonial Hyperbaggage," a wealthy persona looks for ways to make his crimes disappear into some kind of reversible black hole in a Vuitton suitcase.

Revard names Nixon, Reagan and Bush, and suggests that "several American presidents could be considered perfect Godfathers" (2003a: 1). These Godfathers would like the indigenous people to disappear, though their images could be useful on money. Using the Spanish term *desaparecidos*, Revard connects disappeared victims of violent torture and killing in Latin American dictatorships like Chile and Guatemala with the marginalization of North American Indians: "All Indian Reservations could be *desaparecidos* / into Death Valley, yet accessible through / its golden icon, the Sacajawea Dollar" (2).

An Eagle Nation

Separating his work from that of confessional, elitist, and individualistic poets, Revard says in "Some Notes on Native American Literature," "[M]y literary theory is based on what literature does and can do within and for a community, rather than on what it does for the writer and a coterie of friends in ratholes and patrons in penthouses" (2003b: 11). The history and community of his Ponca relatives is just as essential to Revard's poetics as the Osage mythology and world view. According to their tribal stories, the Ponca and Osage were earlier part of one people, and they might have never separated if a fog had not risen behind the group that crossed the Mississippi first. This group that would become the Osages followed its tributary, the Osage River, south. They later made their home in the area that is now Missouri and Kansas (Calloway 2003: 60).

The group that became the Poncas moved farther northwest, up the Missouri, and settled on its tributaries in Iowa and eastern Nebraska where they continued raising corn, squash, and beans as well as hunting buffalo and other big game. As both groups moved, they sometimes reunited with other Dhegihan-speaking peoples, as evidenced by an Osage clan among the Poncas and a Ponca clan among the Osages. The Osages were also influenced by the Mississippi and Oneota cultures. And the Poncas and Omahas were influenced by the Caddoan-speaking Pawnees and Arikaras (Calloway 2003: 60–61). A close association between Osage and Ponca people has existed for hundreds of years.

Although by an 1865 treaty, the U.S. government had guaranteed the Ponca a reservation in northeastern Nebraska, the government deeded these lands to the Sioux three years later and forced the small tribe of 681 persons to move to Indian Territory in 1877. Many Poncas died on the journey. Their leader, Standing Bear, and thirty of his people left Indian Territory in 1879 after the death of Standing Bear's son, whom they intended to bury in their homeland. When the Secretary of the Interior ordered their arrest, and General Crook took them into custody, many non-Indians sympathized with the Ponca. Omaha journalist Thomas Henry Tibbles publicized the case, and Nebraskans raised money to employ lawyers who filed suit against General Crook, for Standing Bear's release on a writ of habeas corpus. The government argued that Indians were not eligible for the writ because they were not "persons" within the meaning of the Constitution. The judge filed a decision declaring that an Indian is a person entitled to the same constitutional protection as any other person. Standing Bear and his friends were then permitted to continue on their journey back to their home. Standing Bear said at the trial that he might go back to his homeland and "work until he was blind, but that would not change his color; that he would be an Indian in color," but that he wanted "to go and work and become a citizen" (Tibbles 1972: 89). In his decision filed on May 12, 1879, Judge Dundy interpreted Standing Bear's words to mean that "he and his followers had finally, fully, and forever severed his and their connection with the Ponca tribe of Indians, and had resolved to disband as a tribe" (Tibbles 1972: 104). Thus, the judge indicated that to become a "person" entitled to a citizen's rights, an Indian had to renounce his tribal identity.

In 1879 White Eagle, a respected Ponca leader, who had remained in Indian Territory, dictated a letter, thanking the lawyers and those who had taken pity on Standing Bear, but also detailing the wrongs that had been done to the Poncas when they were removed from their homelands. They had been taken from houses built by their own hands, their possessions had been confiscated, their livestock had all died from the hard journey, and their possessions had not been replaced. Like their Osage neighbors they were living in dire poverty. He asked the people of the United States to right the wrongs (Tibbles 1972: 118–21).

By 1880 for the first time since their removal, a larger number of Poncas were born in Indian Territory than died. In 1881 Congress appropriated money to compensate the Poncas for their losses and to establish them in their new home in Indian Territory or to allow them to return to the Nebraska reservation if they wished. Along with White Eagle, the majority of Poncas decided to remain in Indian Territory. But 170 left to join Standing Bear in Nebraska.

It was not Standing Bear's intention to cut his ties to his people. The dual citizenship of American Indians would not be guaranteed until the passage of the Indian Citizenship Act of 1924. According to Vine Deloria, Jr., this Act

> ... gives all Indians born within the territorial limits of the United States full citizenship but adds that such status does not infringe upon the rights to tribal and other property that Indians enjoy as members of their tribes. A dual citizenship exists here, which is not to be hindered in either respect: Indians are not to lose civil rights because of their status as members of a tribe, and members of a tribe are not to be denied their tribal rights because of their American citizenship. (1984: 3-4)

However, Deloria notes that this "distinction has not often been preserved" and that Congress attempted in the 1920s and the 1950s to "sever unilaterally the political relationship between the Indian tribes and the United States, using the citizenship of individual Indians as its excuse" (4).

Revard's book *Ponca War Dancers* (1980) features on its cover a photograph of White Eagle, for whom the Poncas in Indian Territory named their new community. Within both the Ponca and Osage communities and ceremonies, Revard has actively experienced his ancestral traditions. The book's title poem, "Ponca War Dancers," honors Revard's Uncle Gus McDonald and his cousin, Carter Camp. Set in 1974, a year after the occupation of Wounded Knee, the poem describes the community life and spirit of Poncas as they gathered for a memorial feast in Ponca City, Oklahoma. His Irish relatives called Carter Revard "Mike," distinguishing him from his cousin Carter Camp in his community and in this poem, as well.

The four-part poem shows the various ways that Gus McDonald, whose Ponca name was *Shongeh-Ska* (White Horse), still followed Ponca customs. The first part illustrates his respect for the avoidance custom of not speaking directly to his nephew's wife. That such careful respect can be easily misunderstood as sexism in the modern world is illustrated by the poem. Revard describes Gus McDonald as a champion dancer in the imagery of the second part of the poem,

>   spinning light as
>   a leaf in a whirlwind
>   the anklebells shrilling, dancing
>   the Spirit's dance

>   in a strange land where
>   he had gone and fasted
>   and found his vision
>   to lead his people ... (1980: 54)

However, Revard says there was "nowhere to lead them except / into white ways" (54).

In the third part of the poem, Revard recalls driving to the memorial feast with his Ponca cousins "all strong in AIM" (55). Though they were followed by a state trooper, they arrived safely at the auditorium, "where all the Ponca and Osage women / had fixed the frybread, boiled beef (sure tastes / like slow elk, we all said), lots of fruit / and Jello and all" (57). It was ordinary all-American family reunion food, except for the frybread and the Indian joke about the meat. The poem describes the integrated community of Ponca and Osage:

>   They'd brought the Osage drum
>   out of mourning to honor Uncle Gus,
>   and the Osage War Dancers
>   had come to dance for him,
>   then when the Ponca singers
>   sang the McDonald song his
>   nephews and nieces danced round
>   tall and straight and proud. (57)

Later, after the dancing, the focus shifts to a contemporary leader when Revard recalls sitting with Carter Camp in a Ponca City Bar: "Uncle Gus was the best all right. / - Mike, they'll nail me some time or other / for Wounded Knee... / But I'm back with my people now" (58).

In the fourth part of the poem, Revard mentions that his Uncle Gus's niece put his Osage name *Shongeh-Ska* on her Indian Crafts shop in California to honor him. And Revard says,

>   I've set down this winter-count for a kind
>   of memorial song
>   to Shongeh-ska, one
>   of the greatest of Ponca dancers
>   to dance once more. (59)

The poem's last lines allude to his cousin Carter Camp as a political prisoner and clarify why Revard thinks the dancing and singing are so important, even in modern times:

> We know that even
> where Poncas are in prison
> the songs are with them,
> how can the bars stop singing
> inside their heads? (59)

Since the songs are a way of feeling and being free, this too, is an important reason for Osage and Ponca to sing and for Revard to sing as a poet.

Although long before Europeans came to North America there had been a great deal of inter-tribal contact, it has been essential to survival for tribes to assert their separate identities. Yet, assertions of sovereignty and calls for justice such as the 1973 AIM and Oglala Civil Rights Organization takeover of Wounded Knee, in which Carter Revard's Ponca relatives participated, fostered closer relationships among tribes. Revard pictures the contemporary, pan-tribal experience in the poem "Aunt Jewell as Powwow Princess" from *Winning the Dust Bowl*. His record of the 1995 event at Cahokia Mounds, where indigenous people lived in the largest city north of Mexico from 1000 to 1400 A.D., gives a sense of the ways in which the ghosts of the past are constantly interacting with contemporary life. At the powwow Revard saw his Uncle Gus, who had died twenty years earlier, dancing. And when he mentioned this to his eighty-year-old Aunt Jewell, she told him to listen carefully. An honoring song for his uncle, *Shon-geh-skah*, was being sung. She told Revard of having gone a month earlier to the Sun Dances on the Rosebud Reservation in South Dakota where "there were so many / of the Old People who would want / to come to the circle and dance" (2001: 180).

Although the Princess is usually a young woman, the organizers of the powwow chose to honor Aunt Jewell to show their regard for elders. The arrival of 400 bikers on Harley Davidsons bringing "food for the elders and for / the children, for all the people" is a dramatic example of renewal brought by the positive interaction that can happen between indigenous people and other marginal groups in American society. Together everyone recognized the beauty of generosity: "Rusty and the singers and the dancers / called those bikers back into the Circle / and they came on foot, over four hundred strong, and stood / behind them in the Circle, all the spectators stood" (2001: 183). After the honoring ceremony, Revard "did not see / Uncle Gus again that evening" suggesting that perhaps the singing and the good feelings of community at that sacred place had made it possible for *Shon-geh-Skah* to return to the world of the spirits. As the sacred staff was posted, clouds "sent a few small drops" and later on the way home "briefly" a "heavy rain" came down, with the healing touch of the sky (183).

In the title poem of *An Eagle Nation*, the story of a family excursion to Oklahoma City, Revard's beloved Aunt Jewell addresses a caged eagle in the zoo as *Kahgay*, or brother, apologizing "for all of us" (1993: 33). According to their cosmology, before the ancestors of the Osage and Ponca came down from the stars, they sent scouts to Earth as messengers. Eagles and other animals met the scouts and offered themselves as guides. Of his Aunt Jewell McDonald Camp, who seems to have been the strongest cultural influence on Revard, the poem says, "Now she's the eldest in her clan, but still the fastest / to bring the right word, Ponca or English, sacred or / profane, whatever's needed to survive she brings it" (31). The same statement could be made of Revard as an elder in the circle of Native poets.

The family's visit to the Red Earth powwow juxtaposes contemporary dancing with the memory of a story told by Revard's Uncle Woody about the first time he saw Jewell, the woman he would marry, at the Osage dances. Musing about the past and present circles that had brought his relatives to "this huge alien floor" in Oklahoma City where the powwow was happening, Revard recognizes that though "it all has changed and the ways are strange," "the voices still / are singing, the drum-heart / still beating here" (1993: 34). Though he identifies his people who are imprisoned or caged, with the eagle they saw in the zoo, Revard, nevertheless ends the poem on a hopeful note. His final lines assert that whether or not the United States government acknowledges their right to freedom and justice, the Osage and Ponca maintain their cultural pride and identity: "whatever the placards on / their iron cages may have to say, we the people, / as Aunt Jewell and Sun Dancers say, / are an EAGLE NATION, now" (34).

That identity, now as always, has to be fought for, as the Ponca and Osage, along with other indigenous people, are increasingly ignored and marginalized. In "Starring America," Revard remembers going back to the Osage Reservation, "wheeling around with my one / surviving uncle of six" and being "shaken" by seeing that the hospital where he was born had been torn down and had become only a "vacant lot" (1993: 112). The bricks hauled from St. Louis by Revard's Grandpa Alex and the family history of work, births and injuries are now "Dissolved into thin air" (112), an allusion to Prospero's speech in *The Tempest* regarding the ephemeral nature of human lives. The Osage now have a new hospital "down / in Indian camp," (113) at which, Revard suggests, the nation has been isolated into a "Limbo" and expected by the Ameropeans to "*vanish: to be forever deaf / to all salvation's song*" (115). With this allusion to Dante's

Divine Comedy, Revard suggests an ironic parallel between Virgil, Dante's pagan guide through Hell and Purgatory, and the Osages, neither of whom are allowed to enter Heaven.

The difficulties still posed by American society today sometimes make it necessary for Indians to travel long distances to maintain their spiritual life. In chapter four of *Winning the Dust Bowl*, entitled "White Eagle, Later," Revard remembers going back to the Ponca reservation to visit Aunt Jewell in the 1970s. Symbolic of their relationship with the Lakota, she and her husband had planted fruit trees there, and a cottonwood tree brought from Crow Dog's Paradise near the Little White River on the Rosebud Reservation in South Dakota, where the family had gone to participate in the sun dance.

The poem "Paint and Feathers" juxtaposes in two columns the ancient and contemporary life of a Ponca child. In the old society the child would be ceremonially touched with crimson to "move upon the path / of life as does the young / sun at dawn surging / upward in scarlet" (2001: 17). Eagle plumes would be fastened into his hair, so he could "have the sun's power / and travel with him" (17). A "disc of mussel shell" would be fastened around his neck so he might "stand and see / all life" within his vision (17). Buffalo fat would be touched on his hair to fill his "deepest hungers," and he would be prepared to take his name "in the House of Mystery" (18). But in the contemporary world, the traditional community seems to have neglected or lost the child who falls prey to toxic influences. In the second column of the poem, the boy is told, "Now put your face into / this brown paper bag filled / with aluminum spray-paint / breathe in" (17). After paint-huffing, the child staggers and stumbles, with eyes "wide / and blank, white paint across" his face (17). Jamming the feathers of a dead scissortail flycatcher bird into his hair, the boy becomes the apparition of death, as ants crawl across his eyes. He climbs into a car and drives, "northward / without headlights, straight / into the other car" (17). Though his relatives loved this child, the destructive influences of poverty and hopelessness overwhelmed him, isolating him from his traditional community. Later at the Sun Dance, relatives will dance for the child "who will not live / to see old age" (18). Only after four years of dancing are completed, and the sacrifices have been made by his extended family, will their collective grief be released as the spirit of the child is renewed: "At the Sun Dance, Little Brother, / we will dance for you, the feather / will fly, *xu-be*, up past the knot, / to where we hear you laughing" (18).

The juxtaposition of the two very different experiences of childhood confronts the reader with the harsh reality of many children on today's reservations, where traditional ceremonies and customs are not fully integrated into their daily life. Revard's juxtaposition of columns in "Paint and Feathers" exemplifies his mastery of formal poetics. This and other poems emphasize the essential importance of relatedness to personal and social cohesion. Revard achieves similar effects in riddle poems, utilizing the Old English form of alliterative half lines as a means of expressing indigenous perceptions. For example, "Birch Canoe" reveals that Revard can be a vehicle for his Wazhazhe people only because they transformed him into a means of conveying their perspective through space and time. He is able to sing their vision because they "embraced" his "body's whiteness" (1993: 83) and brought him into the center of Osage life.

The riddle poems give mysterious names to objects or beings, showing them as more than ordinary. "What the Eagle Fan Says" allows this ceremonial object to mirror the motion and meaning of the dance. Even the shape of the poem gives the reader a sense of the circling eagle and the needle threading beads. The fan reminds the dancer holding it of his part in the continuing spiral of creation:

now I move lightly	in a man's left hand
above dancing feet	follow the sun
around old songs	soaring toward heaven
on human breath,	and I help them rise" (1993: 35).

Revard dedicated this poem to the Comanche family (Wah Kinney), to the St. Louis Gourd Dancers, and to friend Dale Besse, who beaded the fan, to thank them for honoring him with the eagle feathers that were set into his beaded fan. For his poetry and his life, Carter Revard finds meaning in looking to the sky. Awe in the face of creation is one of his gifts to those who read his poems. His Osage and Ponca relatives prepared him well to sing with a gift that can help others rise.

Works Cited

Bruchac, J. 1987. *Survival This Way*. Tucson: University of Arizona Press.

Calloway, C. 2003. *One Vast Winter Count*. Lincoln and London: University of Nebraska Press.

Deloria, V., Jr., and C. M. Lytle. 1984. *The Nations Within: The Past and Future of Indian Sovereignty*. Austin: University of Texas Press.

Emerson, R. W. 1998. "The Poet." *The Heath Anthology of American Literature, Vol. 1*, Ed. P. Lauter, et al. Boston: Houghton Mifflin.

Fletcher, A.C. and F. La Flesche. 1911. *The Omaha Tribe*. 27th Annual Report of the Bureau of American Ethnology, 1905-6. Washington, D.C.: Government Printing Office.

Fletcher, A.C. and F. La Flesche. 1992. *The Omaha Tribe, Vol. II*. Lincoln and London: University of Nebraska Press.

La Flesche, F. 1973. "Right and Left in Osage Ceremonies." *Right and Left: Essays on Dual Symbolic Classification*. Ed. Rodney Needham. Chicago and London: University of Chicago Press.

Mathews, J. 1961. *The Osages: Children of the Middle Waters*. Norman: University of Oklahoma Press.

Revard, C. 1976. "From The Old Manor, Sunningwell, near Abingdon, Oxfordshire, England, July 17, 1976." Letter to N. Wilson.

———. 1980. *Ponca War Dancers*. Norman, Oklahoma: Point Riders Press.

———. 1983. "Traditional Naming Ceremonies: Entering the Circle of Being." *Recovering the Word: Essays on Native American Literature*. Eds. B. Swann and A. Krupat. Lincoln: University of Nebraska Press. 446–66.

———. 1993. *An Eagle Nation*. Tucson: University of Arizona Press.

———. 1998. *Family Matters, Tribal Affairs*. Tucson: University of Arizona Press.

———. 2001. *Winning the Dust Bowl*. Tucson: University of Arizona Press.
———. 2003a. "Postcolonial Hyperbaggage." *Studies in American Indian Literatures* 15.1: 1–2.
———. 2003b. "Some Notes on Native American Literature." *Studies in American Indian Literatures* 15.1: 1–15.
———. 2004, 12 July. "Re: Essay." E-mail message to N. Wilson.
Tibbles, T. H. 1972. *The Ponca Chiefs: An Account of the Trial of Standing Bear*. Lincoln: University of Nebraska Press.
Wilson, N. 2001. "The Mythic Continuum: The Poetry of Carter Revard." *The Nature of Native American Poetry*. Albuquerque: University of New Mexico Press. 14–29.

Carter Revard as Autoethnographer or Wa-thi'-gethon

Suzanne Evertsen Lundquist

Midway through his "autobiographical" essay "Walking Among the Stars," Carter Revard asks: "Well, so that isn't very Indian, is it?" (1987: 73). Revard's question, of course, is more than rhetorical. It is a way of acknowledging or suggesting that readers might want or expect something more "authentic" or "traditional" by way of an "Indian" autobiographical sketch. In his foreword "To the Reader" in *Winning the Dust Bowl*, Revard tugs again at genre expectations: "All of those prose settings [for the poems in *Winning the Dust Bowl*] were newly written for this book," writes Revard; "I wrote them down because, at readings, people would ask how certain poems grew as they did and why in those particular [hybrid] forms—so I would talk of how Coyote came into a sonnet, how greyhound racing was origami-folded into a sestina, why a birch Canoe spoke Anglo-Saxon, why walking on the Isle of Skye brought me out of blank verse into free verse" (2001: xiv). From the 1987 statement in "Walking Among the Stars" to the 2001 statement in "To the Reader," Revard demonstrates his concern with ethnographic and genre complexity. Throughout his works, Revard challenges, collapses, merges, or juxtaposes the boundaries between Native and Anglo/European artistic forms and world views—Indian voices adapting, translating, transposing, or gainsaying English forms.

Revard is keenly aware of the differences in ethnographic approaches to self-life writing. Revard claims that: "Something strange appears when we look at certain autobiographies of Indian people: the notion of identity, of how the individual is related to world, people, self, differs from what we see in 'Euro-american' autobiography" (1998: 126). Revard differentiates between Native and Western conceptions of identity by explaining that: "In 'Western Civilization,' an *identity* is something shaped between birth and death" (126). On the other hand, Native "autobiography" or identity-formation has a long pre-history in myth, arises within and contends with particular historical events, and is shaped markedly by ethnic inheritance.

In observing Geronimo's autobiography, for instance, Revard supports his assertions about Native self-life writing by noting that, "Geronimo does not even get around to mentioning his own birth until the book's third chapter" (1998: 126). Geronimo begins his life story with the creation narrative of the Apache under the direction of the Creator, *Usen*. Usen established the Apache homeland, foods for the sustenance of the people, and abundant materials for clothing and shelter. Such a context, it must be noted, underscores the sorrow of having the Apache's land of inheritance taken away from them by the American government. Revard explains: "Whatever the order of importance among such facts might be for a Euroamerican autobiography, Geronimo ranked them from the cosmic through geologic to tribal, subtribal, family and then only, last and in full context, the 'individual' self that was Geronimo" (127). Given such a context, remarks Revard, "every *name* in [Geronimo's] narrative, whenever he speaks it, has its symbolic meaning that resonates in this deeper context, can be rightly understood only in light of that part of the people's history which he is then telling" (127). Revard concludes that: "'History' and 'Myth' and 'Identity' are not three separate matters . . . but three aspects of one human being" (141).

This difference—between Euroamerican autobiographies and Native self-life writing—is ontologically significant. This difference is predicated upon the distinction between individualism and communalism as primary expressions of humanity. Arnold Krupat explains the difference in terms of figures of speech. When "personal accounts are strongly marked by the individual's sense of herself predominantly as different and separate from other distinct individuals, one might speak of a *metonymic* sense of self." By comparison, when "any narration of personal history is more nearly marked by the individual's sense of himself in relation to collective social units or groupings, one might speak of a *synecdochic* sense of self" (1992: 212). Editor of *The Norton Book of*

American Autobiography, Jay Parini, suggests that, "Autobiography inherently involves a challenge to social and personal norms; writers put themselves forward as exemplary, with the implication that they are doing something different from their fellow citizens" (1999: 17). In a country grounded on the democratic assumption that "individual liberty" is fundamental to the "pursuit of happiness," communal ways of claiming a self could even be construed as contrary to democratic ideology. And yet, as American history so clearly exemplifies, *amendments* to self-evident truths have been multiple. Amendments to genre considerations have been underway from the late twentieth through the early twenty-first century. The move, in terms relative to Revard's works, is from life writing as auto-biography (the self viewed as independent from or resistant to cultural contexts) to auto-ethnography (the self as possible only within cultural contexts).

Genre considerations are no small matter in today's critical marketplace. Nor is positionality. E.D. Hirsch, for example, claims that: "All understanding of verbal meaning is necessarily genre bound" (1965: 76). This means that readers understand what "truth claims" are being made by a text based on genre formation. A treatise by Einstein, for instance, is approached with different expectations than biblical narratives or the cartoon page in the Sunday news. Traditionally, college literature courses attend to poetry, drama, and fiction—with attention paid to the "invented" perceptions of reality composed by authors. Jose Ortega y Gassett argues that genres "are broad views of the cardinal directions of the human." What is more, "Each epoch brings with it a basic interpretation of man. Or better, it does not bring such an interpretation with it as much as it is that interpretation" (in Beebee 1994: 272). The classic genres, for instance, are myths (stories of the intervention of the Gods into human affairs); epics (long narratives about heroes whose character and actions exemplify the values of an entire nation); tragedies (dramas about a good person who, through some imperfection in character, makes choices that bring about his/her demise—not, however, before some dramatic character revelation); and so forth.

Autoethnographic texts, however, are literary as well as ethnographic in terms that are particularly significant to Postmodern studies. Sally Cole, for example, explains the nature of ethnographic texts—texts that are "experiential," "interpretive," and "dialogic"; contemporary ethnographic texts are *reflexive*, not only about the "anthropological self but also about context—about the subjectivity and historical specificity of the field experience as well as the social and political realities of the lives of anthropological subjects, the traditional Other" (1992: 125). In autoethnographies, it must be noted, the *auto* (self) is both anthropologist and Other. Revard as autoethnographer, notwithstanding, does not simply recount his "field" experience (the personal/cultural experiences that have shaped his ethnic *self*), Revard develops a theory of ethnic identity throughout his various works. Furthermore, he does so in recognition that his various roles in life—a hyphenated (mixed-blood, multi-ethnic, multi-cultural) son, grandson, brother/twin, cousin, husband, father, teacher, scholar—inform his perceptions.

Revard also acknowledges that a "change of 'style' comes from a real change in 'life'—that is, in how I am related to the world that lives in and around me, and how I use language to deal with it" (2001: xiv). Such awareness is also in keeping with Postmodern thought. David Porush maintains that: "Postmodernism places the self-conscious activities of the human observer/scientist/teller—and consequently the making of narratives—in the center of things" (1989: 377). Revard's works continually reference his *self* as both the creator of *experience* (self-conscious and self-reflexive) as well as creator of his *expressions* of experience (the telling, interpretation, and writing of experience). Anthropologist and ethnographer Victor W. Turner, in his study of the etymology of the English word *experience*, discovered that *experience* derives from the Indo-European *per-* "to attempt, venture, risk." Turner notes that other cognates—Germanic, Greek, and Latin—relate the word *experience* to the phrase: "'I pass through,' with implications of rites of passage" (1986: 35). Other possible links indicate that "*experience* is also related to *experiment*" (Turner 1986: 35). Revard, it must be noted, is likewise abundantly aware of *positionality*. He believes that life-changes alter consciousness and that consciousness alters verbal expression. Autoethnography, it must be noted, is also both a process (an epistemology or way of locating a self within multiple ethnic parameters) as well as a product (literary work with genre particularities).

Throughout *Winning the Dust Bowl*, Revard is conscious of the balancing act between process and product. For example, Revard's balancing act includes his *positioning* himself within his "red-and-white" heritage. In "Buck Creek to Oxford by Birch Canoe," for instance, Revard says:

> Even with a voice, a song, and one kind of name, there was the matter of 'placing' the voice—*locating a self*. Maybe a good piece to illustrate how this worked at times for me, in my mixed red-and-white heritage, is the piece

using an Old English poetic form (the 'riddle,' a dramatic monologue in alliterative half lines) to let an American Indian 'space ship'—alias birch-bark canoe—tell how it gets around in this world. (2001: 19)

Revard explains that he "picked up the riddle form" when he was "getting the B.A. in English at Oxford university, and years later when I used it to let a Birch Canoe tell its story, I came to understand that this was also my story: the bringing into being of a mixed self, afloat between cultures and times, between heaven and earth, between North America and Europe—another way of being 'transported' into and through time" (2001: 19).

Within Revard's "contextualizing" of "Birch Canoe," come further ethnographic insights. Revard takes time to instruct readers in the formal elements of the riddle. However, the idea of a *riddle* moves beyond genre distinctions to identity considerations as the *real riddle*. After explaining the creation of the canoe from the "white bark off a birch tree" sewn together with "tamarack roots," Revard says: "I hope the reader will see that these words create red men who take white bark and make it into a way of moving in this stream, whatever heaven or earth it may be; and that my being a mixed-blood Osage and white person is part of the double vision which the riddle allows" (2001: 21). In other words, Revard uses the genre of a *riddle* to speak of his inherited mixed-blood identity as not only a mixed blood/mixed ethnic identity but as a way of seeing the world through multiple perspectives or "double vision."

This kind of "double vision" is characteristic of Native autoethnographies. In such works, Native authors are doing for themselves what anthropologists have formerly done. And yet, Native authors are not attempting to speak for entire tribes. They have become anthropologists of their own Native-American-European experience—each formulating a theory of ethnic identity particular to their life experiences. Numerous Native authors are composing works which demonstrate how myth, ethnicity, ancestry, gender, historical moment, geographical local, education, life-stages, and economic status have shaped their identity. For example: N. Scott Momaday's *The Way to Rainy Mountain* and *The Names* (Kiowa); Leslie Marmon Silko's *Storyteller* (Laguna Pueblo); Janet Campbell Hale's *Bloodlines* (Coeur-d'Alene); Gerald Vizenor's *Interior Landscapes* (Ojibwa); Louise Erdrich's *The Blue Jay's Dance* (Ojibwa); Diane Glancy's *Claiming Breath* and *Cold and Hunger Dance* (Cherokee); Paula Gunn Allen's *Off the Reservation* (Laguna Pueblo); and Louis Owens' *I Hear the Train* (Choctaw) join with Carter Revard's *Family Matters, Tribal Affairs* and *Winning the Dust Bowl* in the growing number of works that are more autoethnographic than autobiographic. Their works, while admitting to a sense of self in relation to collective social unites, are dynamic. For example, in *The Names*, Momaday is a Kiowa of mixed ancestry who records his experiences living among the Jemez Pueblo people as an outsider during a particular stage in his life and during a particular evolutionary period in the Jemez ritual calendar. Momaday's sense of an Indian self has been informed by that particular geographical locale and historical moment.

In her essay, "Arts of the Contact Zone," Mary Louise Pratt (one of the first scholars to identify autoethnography) defines an autoethnographic work as:

> ... a text in which people undertake to describe themselves in ways that engage with representations others have made of them. Thus if ethnographic texts are those in which European metropolitan subjects represent to themselves their others (usually their conquered others), autoethnographic texts are representations that the so-defined others construct *in response to* or in dialogue with those texts. Autoethnographic texts are not, then, what are usually thought of a autochthonous forms of expression or self-representation ... Rather they involve a selective collaboration with the appropriation of idioms of the metropolis or the conqueror. These are merged or infiltrated to varying degrees with indigenous idioms to create self-representations intended to intervene in metropolitan modes of understanding. (1999: 3)

In *Imperial Eyes*, Pratt locates autoethnographies in the "contact zone"— "the space of colonial encounters, the space in which peoples geographically and historically separated come into contact with each other and establish ongoing relations, usually involving conditions of coercion, radical inequality, and intractable conflict" (1992: 6).

Contemporary autoethnographers have not only appropriated the conquerors' idioms, they *are*, in many respects, the "contact zone." Their "self-representations" *are* often "intended to intervene in metropolitan modes of understanding,"—no matter how fully the Native author participates in the practices of the dominant culture (as college professors, novelists, poets, short story writers, political figures). This contact zone is identified variously in Revard's works: "I grew up poor," writes Revard, "in a mixedblood family on a reservation among people like ourselves, trying to resist and survive the incoming flak from people who thought they were not like ourselves, hitting us with loud or silent messages that everything happening to us was our fault"—like living in the Dust Bowl and surviving the Depression (2001: xv). The title, *Winning the Dust Bowl*, is an appropriation of a historical American epoch as a metaphor for the Osages' mode of surviving naturally or politically imposed desolations. The Dust Bowl refers to a period in United States History (1931 through 1939) when severe drought hit the Midwestern and Southern plains and spread through seventy-five percent of the country. Thirty-five million cultivated acres of crops were destroyed and two-hundred and twenty-five million acres of topsoil were lost. Fifty percent of the herds of cattle had to be destroyed because they were unfit for consumption. The rest of the cattle were slaughtered and distributed to poor families throughout the nation. Farmers and cattlemen tried to avoid bankruptcy, often without success. "Black blizzards" (dust storms) were common during the era. One third of the population of the U.S. were adversely affected by the drought; numerous social programs were instigated to help victims of the Dust Bowl survive ("Surviving," 2005: 1–5). And yet, the Osage and Okies, as Revard claims, not only survived but *won* the Dust Bowl—perhaps due to their mixed-blood, and cooperative, heritage.

The title *Winning the Dust Bowl* also alludes to winning the "rose bowl." The term Rose Bowl entered the English language at the same time Dust Bowl entered, Revard explains. Winning the dust bowl, therefore, becomes somewhat analogous to winning the Rose Bowl. The title poem, "Winning the Dust Bowl," is contextualized in the chapter "Okie Survival." Revard explains that this chapter is about how his cousin, Roy Camp,

> ... himself not an Indian, caught a freight train from Oklahoma to California and not only survived but was able to create [a] new home and family and life out there—a life beyond what Steinbeck had pictured in 1938-9 in *The Grapes of Wrath* . . . My book's title poem celebrates our survivors from that time and place which non-Indian journalists had christened the 'Dust Bowl' . . . The whole Great Plains during the great drought of 1931–1939 became a great 'Bowl of Dust' instead of the 'Fruited Plain' of the song 'America,' or the cornucopia into which the great land runs took place when the U.S. Congress had taken away the land from the Indian nations and given it to surrounding white people who 'knew how to farm it.' (4 May 2005: E-mail to author).

Many of Revard's poems in *Winning the Dust Bowl* are survival poems; the chapter titles contextualize these poems variously: Indian Survival One,

Two, Three, Four and so forth. These chapters refer to Indian veterans surviving wars; contemporary survivors of those people who left the Cahokia Mounds; Revard surviving a visit to Las Vegas; Indians surviving the massacre at Sand Creek, among other survivals.

Revard's genealogical background is mixed Osage, Scotch-Irish, and Irish with Ponca folks mixed in. "I am of Osage descent on my father's side," writes Revard; "[I] had a fullblood Osage stepfather and five part-Osage half-brothers and sisters, as well as (by marriage) a Ponca aunt and six half-Ponca cousins." *Fullblood* Osage, *part-*Osage, *half-*brothers and sisters, *half-Ponca* cousins are not terms that Revard would now use, he says, "because to use them accepts and implies a lower status and character for the person described, who has only an inferior 'half-breed' identity" (3 May 2005: E-mail to author). However, when they appear in Revard's earlier works, they are terms denoting an ironic, rather schizoid or tentative delineation of relationships. In reality, for Revard, relationships are based on kinship behaviors (care) rather than on full (pure)/empty (flawed) metaphors. Revard's attention to mixed-blood, mixed-ancestral metaphors does not reflect the schizoid identity imposed by outside observers. Revard's designation of mixed identity is used ironically. For him, Indian identity is more than a matter of blood-quantum; it is a matter of communal acceptance, a preferred or mythological way of approaching experience, an ancestral heritage, a way of relating to place, and so much more.

Revard's retelling of the experience he had when his Irish and Scotch-Irish grandfather (James Alexander Camp) said, "You ought to go to college, Mikey," exemplifies Revard's understanding of his mixedblood (one complex word) kinship. Revard discloses that his grandfather was a semi-literate man who had a hard time reading, "was paid about seventeen and a half dollars a month at the beginning," but used "some of this money to get reading glasses" (1998: 60). Revard explains that his grandfather received this money monthly from Social Security. Revard's grandfather Camp "turned sixty-five in 1935, so he was among the first people to be enrolled in the New Deal's Social Security program," Revard notes (4 May 2005: E-mail to author). Such meager means coupled with devoted labor for his family prompted Revard to write:

> So for Grandpa to say I should go to college was full of meaning to me. And of course I listened, because even though I was annoyed at having my private thoughts interrupted I could see he was serious. And he had helped raise me from a baby, too. I never knew him to lie, and I knew him

to be as fair and just a man as there was. I knew he had worked all his life, and I knew he was here with no money and in poor health, and he was working every day to keep this place livable. (1998: 60–61)

Several of Revard's poems are about his grandfather's diligent everyday work: "Pure Country," "My Right Hand Don't Leave Me no More," and "Homework at Oxford."

Revard's grandfather died three weeks after the above conversation. Revard records that:

Just three days before he died he had got up early, on the birthday of my twin sister and me, and put together the makings of a birthday cake: my mother was down with a flu that day, and he did it in place of her. The cake fell, and its two layers—I remember there were two, and I think he said it was a cake for twins and that was why he made two layers—the two layers were very heavy, and very sweet as if soaked in honey, probably because he had used white Karo syrup, sugar being already rationed because of the war. But it was a delicious cake and I am as glad of it as of his telling me to go to college. (1998: 61–62)

Revard was, at that time, the second member of his family to attend college. The other was Revard's "fullblood Osage uncle, Kenneth Jump, who had got to Notre Dame for a short while before Pearl Harbor, but was taken into the Army after that" (1998: 61).

This identity by *halves* and *wholes* further illuminates the complexity of being in the contact zone. The issue of "pure" blood is also challenged by the mixedblood metaphor (ironically, humans can't survive without both red and white blood cells). The communal effort to get Revard launched on his way through college, or anywhere for that matter, is often acknowledged by Revard. The key to his development seems to be kinship ties: "I made choices, or thought I did," Revard explains, "but I hardly chose such body and mind as got wrapped around me, or to have had the sisters and brothers, mother and stepfather, uncles and aunts and grandmother and grandfather, who set me on this path and walk beside me. Odd or even, chosen or given, grandpa, we've made it this far," Revard attests (1998: 75). Revard's Anglo teachers are also touted—for their kindnesses, support, and belief in Revard's possibilities. Individualism (the self-made man), the stuff of autobiography, is anathema to Revard.

The year Revard received his Rhodes' Scholarship to attend Oxford, he also received his Osage name. "In September 1952, I was given my Osage name in a ceremony arranged by tribal elders and my fullblood grandmother Josephine Jump, in Pawhuska, Oklahoma (The Agency town of the Osage Reservation where I was born and raised)" (18 June 2004: E-mail to author). Revard's Osage name is *Nompehwahthe*, which means *Fear-inspiring man*. Osage myth narrates that in primordial times:

> [W]hen the Osages were trying to come down from the stars to earth, their messenger was sent ahead to find a place where they might become a people. Having passed through three divisions of the heavens, the messenger had found no habitation for them, but in the Fourth Division he saw the 'Man of Mystery, the god of the clouds'—and turning to his brothers, he said: 'Here stands a *fear-inspiring man*!' His name, I verily believe, is *Nom-peh-wah-the* . . . !' Thereupon this mysterious and terrible man addresses the messenger and other Osages: 'I am a person of whom your little ones may make their bodies. When they make of me their bodies, they shall cause themselves to be deathless.' (1998: 140)

In this myth, *Nom-peh-wah-the* is identified as a spiritual being who renders his substance (spirit/matter) to the Osage so that they might have existence, a habitation, and also be able to transcend mortality and death. Revard suggests that a "valid way to 'translate' the Osage term that La Flesche renders as 'make bodies of' is 'if they will *incarnate* this great and powerful being'" (4 May 2005: E-mail to author).

"The name *Nom-peh-wah-the* therefore embodies and recalls this part of the people's sacred history, as well as that part of its chronicle—history when certain famous men bore this name in the memory of the elders," Revard explains (1998: 139). The Osage rite of giving a name entitles the initiate to recognition as a person integrated into tribal stories and histories. However, the story of the original *Nom-peh-wah-the* imparts a particular dynamic identity to Revard. With Revard's Osage name comes the recognition of identity as evolutionary—through time, space, and matter. Revard's name perpetuates the mythic narrative. His name, it must be noted, arises out of a pre-Osage or primordial time; endures through Osage traditional eras; and continues into a post-traditional epoch.

Revard explains that traditionally,

> . . . an Osage would have had his personal identity carefully, explicitly, unmistakably linked with that of his people, with the symbolic arrangement of his village, with the marriage arrangements and hunting encampments and choosing of chiefs and war and peace ceremonies, with the animals whom he could hunt or whose feather he could wear, the plants he would eat, the earth and sky he dwelt within. (1998: 141)

Revard affirms that the Osage were "tied to land, people, origins and a way of life, by every kind of human order we can imagine" (1998: 141). And yet, in a post-traditional epoch, colonial incursions, biracial marriages, Allotment, drought, the Depression, and a plethora of other natural/historical events have continually modified traditional Osage life-ways. Revard's identity is generated within a post-traditional time frame.

Revard's educational narrative further illuminates post-traditional notions of an ego/self. Revard received a B.A. from the University of Tulsa (1952), an M.A. from Oxford University (1954), and a Ph.D. from Yale (1959). He earned his way in life teaching at Amherst College (1956–1961) and Washington College, St. Louis (1961–1997) where Revard taught Middle English Literature, History of the English Language, English Grammar and Word Histories, Shakespeare, and Mark Twain, as well as American Indian Literature, Trickster Tales, and other similar courses. As a scholar/creative writer, Revard has published eight books, twenty-two essays on Medieval Literature, seven essays on linguistics, twenty-two articles on Native American/American Literature, contributed poetry to thirty-two anthologies and forty-three journals, and published short stories in six journals. Revard's honors, conference addresses, and readings are too numerous to count (18 June 2004: E-mail to author). (In reality, Revard has not kept a thorough account of his speeches or conference addresses; on Vitae, university committees favor publications over face to face encounters with real humans, preferring the written over the oral.). In 2000, the Kathryn Buder Center for American Indian Studies, in the George Warren Brown School of Social Studies at Washington University, funded a scholarship named the Carter Revard Scholarship in honor of Revard's distinguished service to Washington University. The scholarship was to be awarded annually to a student of American Indian descent.

It is difficult to comprehend the cross-cultural reticulation of a medieval scholar who is likewise an Osage member of the St. Louis Gourd Dancers. Revard attends powwows, helped found and direct the American Indian Center of Mid-America, while at the same time taking leave from university and tribal duties to do research on Medieval Literature in Europe. Revard's literary expressions, however, partake of these multiple traditions. Kenneth Lincoln speaks of "cultural fusions" to discuss the kind of art that Revard produces. While Native aesthetics "premises art as morally, kinetically, even spiritually ingrained in the natural tribal world—a native good, not so much personally made or made up as naturally given and passed through an artist," multicultural aesthetics bespeaks a "reciprocal appropriation" (Lincoln 1999: 155).

Another term for "reciprocal appropriation" is "hybridity." Hybridity, according to Homi K. Bhabha, ". . . displays the necessary deformation and displacement of all sites of discrimination and domination. It unsettles the mimetic or narcissistic demands of colonial power but re-implicates its identifications in strategies of subversion that turns the gaze of the discriminated back upon the eye of power" (1985: 35). In words relative to Revard, this means that his artistic expressions constantly bring traditional power systems into ethical question. Kumkum Sangari contends that these artistic expressions come about because "[T]he hybrid writer is already open to two worlds and is constructed within the national and international, political and cultural systems of colonialism and neocolonialism. To be hybrid is to understand and question as well as to represent the pressure of such historical placement" (1987: 144).

In another essay, Bhabha furthers Sangari's understanding of hybridity by speaking of "a third space." This third space is the place from which writers like Revard interpret experience. This third space "destroys" the "representation in which cultural knowledge is continuously revealed as an integrated, open, expanding code. Such an intervention quite properly challenges our sense of the historical identity of culture as a homogenizing, unifying force, authenticated by the originary past, kept alive in the national tradition of the People" (Bhabha 1988: 208). In this quote, Bhabha is challenging two opposing beliefs: that one's cultural paradigms are not only superior but constantly progressing or developing OR that one's cultural traditions are constant or non-changing. In other words, Bhabha is suggesting that the boundaries of personal/cultural identity are continually imploding. As a result, *fixed* tribal/national/international identities are not possible nor are they desirable. Relativism—the notion that identity is relative to one's personal, cultural, and historical experience—is an outcome that makes those who believe in truth with a capital "T" anxious. And yet, cultural relativism does not forego the ongoing dependence on relationships for identity formation and reformation as a constant—truth with a lower case "t."

While the jargon of contemporary criticism is forbidding, the theory itself is groundbreaking, forward looking, and a movement towards non-violent, multi-cultural, democratic possibility. In Native American critical terms, the "third space" is a trickster pose. Emmanuel Levinas posits that such a pose marks the ability to challenge narcissistic approaches to reality, what he calls *Ipsiety*, while at the same time simultaneously moving towards an enlarged, often conflict-ridden, in-between, critical space, what Levinas calls *Alterity*, which means movement towards the non-conquerable Other (Levinas 42–48). Not surprising, the Osage already have a word for this "third space": *wa-thi'-gethon*. Francis La Flesche explains that in traditional Osage cosmology, "[O]nly humans had the power of *wa-thi'-gethon*, the ability to search with the mind and thus learn. Endowed with this unique ability among living things, humans were sent forth to travel the earth as though it ... [were their] own to occupy" (1932: 33). In other words, travel across boundaries, cultures, and places, informs—in-forms, creates new forms, challenges old forms.

An exemplary model of Revard's "ability to search with the mind and thus learn" dialogically, across boundaries, in the "contact zone," or from the "third space" are three autoethnographic narratives: "How Columbus Fell from the Sky and Lighted up Two Continents," "Report to the Nation," and "Herbs of Healing"—all contained in *Family Matters, Tribal Affairs*. "How Columbus Fell from the Sky and Lighted Up Two Continents" speaks across cultural myths from that "third space." The subtitle, "Columbus, Milton, Shakespeare, and the Osage and Navajo Creation Stories," indicates the vast comparative leaps Revard is able to make. Says Revard, "Perhaps it is worthwhile ... to set down here a few thoughts about the Columbian encounter, as a way to look at future encounters—whether they happen during some glorious voyage out among other stars, or precede a sudden holocaust of humans on the Paradisal world we now inhabit, or lead to assimilation with the little green beings if they should be less murderous than the Europeans proved to be" (1998: 143). In a play on Milton's epic, Revard suggests that Columbus found a Paradise and proceeded to lose it because of his naive misconceptions of the people he encountered—including his criticism that the Taino "*seemed to hold all possessions in common*" and thus had no understanding of private property (Revard's emphasis; 1998: 146). Revard's facility with Milton's works as well as Columbus's journal draws forth the many ironies of conquest, including the idea that: "Europeans projected upon these island peoples the old myths of the Anthropophagi, demonizing the newly discovered humans in order to justify enslaving or exterminating them" (1998: 147).

Revard's analysis of Shakespeare's *Henry the Fifth* shows how Henry's words "succinctly state the standard Renaissance theory of warfare, that where a besieged city has been breached but continues to resist and thus to cost the lives of the besieging soldiers, the besiegers can legitimately take any vengeance they please (as payment more or less) for the unnecessary loss of lives" (1998: 149). The fact that Revard is both Native and Euroamerican—a contact zone—gives his criticism a unique authority. As an American citizen, Revard acknowledges the many products of technology he enjoys—including the laptop on which he writes many of his essays. But, says Revard, "If and when I see a United States where the hungry all are fed, where differences in ability, income, and race are not used to divide us into a wealthy and overfed few on the one hand, and a hungry, ill-fed many on the other, *then* I will agree that the coming of Columbus was not a bad thing" (1998: 151).

Revard suggests that Natives seem to have managed quite well before Columbus arrived—and continue to reclaim identity and survive—because of their mythic approach to life. In fact, mythic approaches to human experience are central to Revard's prose and poetry. Myth not only narrates the sacred time of the beginnings, myth teaches humans about the appropriate and four-fold relationship between the Creators, the cosmos, particular communities, and each individual's potential within what is often called "the sacred circle." Because myth is so significant, cross-culturally, to identity formation, Revard often addresses mythic complexity from that "third space." Revard writes: "Let us, then, compare Adam's apple with Montezuma's papaya, so to speak: let us see how two pre-Columbian societies conceived and dedicated themselves (as Lincoln phrased it) to the proposition that all men are created equal—and to the nobler proposition that all beings are our equals" (1998: 151). In the naming ceremony of the Osage, the myth of creation is recounted so that the children being named can orient themselves within the various elements of the cosmos from which their being has been created. "In the Bible," Revard notes, "Adam and Eve are in one version created together in god's image; in another, Eve is made from Adam's rib, after the animals have been created" (1998: 152). This distinction is significant because the animals are not only created as "subordinate, but subservient, to humans" (1998: 152). In comparison, the "Osages tell of meeting the animals of this world in a sacred dimension, before actually descending into this world—and they are given, by the animals, the wisdom to live here in a good way that will allow them to endure into 'the peaceful days,' a ritual term which implies more than just 'old age'"(1998: 152).

While Revard's analysis of various mythic constructs of reality is more complex than can be illuminated here, he demonstrates that one's mythology creates not only patterns of belief but also of behavior. Furthermore, Revard contends that comparative mythology can be mutually beneficial. Revard asks:

> Is it only "mythmaking" to say that humans come from the stars? Is it more "factually accurate" to say that humans are made out of this earth we live on, as is said in the Hebrew Creation Story? To these questions I respond with another: where does this earth come from, if not from the stars? Not just ordinary stars either, but from supernovas, in whose explosions are produced all the heavier elements in our human bodies; so if we are formed of the dust of the ground, that dust is also star-stuff. And as for this planet Earth, it is certainly among the stars, is it not? We *do* come "from the stars," just as we *do* come "from the earth." The old Hebrews got it right; so did the old Osages. (1998: 153)

This recombination of the elements of heaven and earth is Revard's way of creating a "third space" from which his readers can view his assertions—a space where the disrespect for the earth and her creatures can be exposed for what it is: a crippling disability.

Revard's inclusion of the Navajo creation myth expands his discussion into the origins of scurrilous sexuality and socially destructive behavior with the following insights into the moral implications of the Navajo creation story: "*we are related to the evils we must destroy: they come from our own behavior*" and "*these evils can be turned to good things*" (Revard's emphasis; 1998: 159). In the Navajo cosmology, men and women separated because of gender inequities—the men hunted merely for sexual self-gratification rather then for mutual survival and affection. Such a separation brought about the stasis of the earth: no creation or procreation was possible. It took the intervention of Changing Woman to re-establish harmony in the world. Revard uses Paul Zolbrod's translation/interpretation of the Navajo myth to discuss the enormity of gender issues to human ontogeny. Elsewhere, Zolbrod suggests that "the basic theme of the Navajo creation story is that solidarity must be maintained between male and female if there is to be harmony in the world" (1987: 14).

In a June 19, 2004 e-mail, Revard wrote about his perceptions of myth. In his delineation, Myth becomes those narratives—both sacred and secular—which create paradigms of reality upon which humans have generated their most impressive advances. Myths, in this regard, become those narratives which address and explain issues of ultimate human concern:

> [A] myth is a story composed by the most careful and profound human thinkers in a given era that provides a plot and characters for their understanding of how we and the world came to be the way we are. Some myths now, of the most persuasive and most widely believed kind, are "scientific" the Big Bang, String Theory, Brane Theory, Evolution, Molecular Genetics, Plate Tectonics, Electro-Magnetism, Particle Theory, and so on. Some are "literary": *King Lear, Paradise Lost,* the collected poems of Emily Dickinson. Some are "historical": Europe, China, Japan, India, Catholicism, Islam, Athens, Rome, New York City. Some are "sociological": Race, Law, Logic, Grammar maybe.
>
> For writing poems, the point is to try to cage or bottle or mummify a given myth within a small set of words that appear to make statements or ask questions in a natural language. For "Dancing with Dinosaurs" I tried to link the stories of Indians and of dinosaurs who survived in brilliant feathery disguise as birds. For "Another Sunday Morning" (in *Ponca War Dancers*) I wanted to put World War Two into the lane between my childhood home and U.S. 60; and for "Starring America" (in *An Eagle Nation*) I wanted to get New York City and the Ponca Reservation tied together, as it were, 'entangling' them the way quantum teleporting works by entangling atoms, so to speak, with Dante as the unifying force for that entanglement; and something of the same entanglement I tried in "Homework at Oxford" and "Sea-changes." For "Earth and Diamonds" (in *An Eagle Nation*) I tried to parallel the creation stories of our mythic "earth"—dull, dead, mundane, but then seen as product of supernova explosions and cosmic togethering—and of 'diamonds' as once thought to be produced by the sun's fruitful rays getting down into the pre-earthly materials and transforming them. For "And Don't Be Deaf to the Singing Beyond" (a quote from Dante's *Purgatory*), I wanted to parallel the deaf 'faith' of my Uncle Arthur with the 'blind faith' of my very religious friends and neighbors, in contrast to our own prudent retreat from a tornado. (19 June 2004: E-mail to author)

Revards quips, "whether these ruminations are of use or interest to your mind I don't know." Yes, they are of interest, and profoundly so. They show a mythic understanding of "entanglement" that speaks to Revard's "third space" or vantage point: at once literary, scientific, multi-cultural, ecological, and personal.

Revard's notions of *place* are also both cosmological and particular. Speaking of the Osage reservation, Revard says: "This is not a country whose citizens stay put, and much of the vital energy in its major cities flows from country people who have moved there" (1998: 55). Revard, in the typical tradition of a *wa-thi'-gethon*, suggests that there is a

> ... secret that has been kept from the media mutts and money-mongers: in a small town way out there like Pawhuska now, or even along the road through Buck Creek, you may be passing lawyers flying in and out of Washington, D.C., women who have picnicked on the Lake Isle of Innisfree, men who've worked in the Alaskan or Arabian oil field, soldiered in Saigon, pubbed in London, swamped grapes in California camps, taken doctorates from Heidelberg or law degrees from Harvard ... (1998: 55)

Revard comments, "If Hannibal's Huck and Tom were to light out for the Territory now, they might do well to knock first in Osage country, if only to find a good Interpreter" (1998: 56). Revard explains that in the 1880's, when Mark Twain used the term *territory*,

> ... everybody understood that "the territory" meant "Indian territory." Twain's Huck Finn was supposed to be about the same age as Twain, born—that is—in 1835, so that when Huck was about twelve or so and wanting to "light out for the territory," it would have been in the late 1840's, or at most early 1850's. My Osage great-grandmother, Mrs. St. John, was born in 1851 when the Osages were on the Kansas reservation—in what was then still part of "the territory." Even when Twain published *Huckleberry Finn*, in the mid-1880's, Allotment had not been forced on the Indian Nations still living on their reservations in what is now Oklahoma and what was then "Indian Territory." So my comment was intended to remind readers in the 1980's, or in the 21st Century, that there are still a lot of Hucks and Toms who want to "Light out for the Territory." (4 May 2005: E-mail to author)

Incidentally, Pawhuska means "White Hair, a name gained by an eighteenth-century chief who took a white wig from a British officer in lieu of a scalp," explains Revard; and Oklahoma "means Land of the Red Man, a name given [ironically] to indicate that it was forever Indian Territory" (1998: 93).

If, however, Huck and Tom were to meet Carter Revard, they would be shown how their creator was an "Indian hater." In a scholarly article, "Why Mark Twain Murdered Injun Joe—And Will Never Be Indicted," Revard exposes Mark Twain as "a writer as deep and humane as Henry James or Joseph Conrad," and yet as a writer who also "hated Indians" and "expressed this hatred quite viciously in books that remain very popular ... " (1999–2000: 643). Revard claims that "no one in the American literary and cultural establishment has looked closely at this hatred in its violently racist expression" (1999–2000: 643).

Revard's lengthy critical essay shows how and why Injun Joe was a creation of Twain's racism. Apparently Revard's argument has proved persuasive enough that it will be reprinted in the forthcoming Norton Critical Edition of Mark Twain (to appear in 2006). Injun Joe is a scapegoat—the one who takes on the sins of a nation. Injun Joe is Twain's "shadow self," explains Revard. It wasn't until "Twain left America for a trip round the world by which he hoped to pay off the creditors he owed," that he made his "great discovery that the American takeovers of Indian Territory and of the Spanish Empire were closely related, which led him to realize that what he thought he hated about Indians was what he actually hated about Americans, and still more what he hated about 'the damned human race'" (1999–2000: 670).

"Herbs of Healing: American Values in American Indian Literature," further demonstrates Revard's "third space" or trickster pose—his position as teacher/scholar/creator of both mainstream and minority American Literatures. "There are some big Guns of American culture and politics who aim to shoot down 'Minority Literature,' claiming that it is trash unworthy of our classrooms, that conversing with it corrupts and keeps students from the uplifting morality of the 'classical' books they ought to be spending time with," Revard contends. For the sake of the "next generation of Americans, to whom we stand *in loco parentis*," Revard sets "certain 'classic' poems beside others by contemporary American Indian writers, hoping this critical look will prove the true values of America are just as vividly and richly present in 'ethnic' as in the classic poems" (1998: 162).

To illustrate his thesis, Revard examines three "classic" American and English poems alongside three by contemporary American Indian poets. First he compares the family values in Wallace Stevens' "Anecdote of the Jar," alongside those apparent in "Speaking," by Simon Ortiz of Acoma Pueblo. Next he explores the violent nature of the classic "Us versus Them" mentality by comparing John Milton's "On the Late Massacre in Piedmont" to Hopi Wendy Rose's poem of protest against the Wounded Knee Massacre. Then Revard moves to gender issues through a discussion of Robert Frost's "Never Again Would Birds' Song Be the Same," set beside "Jacklight," a poem by the Ojibwa poet Louise Erdrich. The outcome of such exegesis is remarkable as both epistemological exercise and philosophical exploration of timeless concerns: kinship, gender, war. The balance between 1) Revard's voice as analyst; 2) the subjects that matter; and 3) the perspective attained at the juncture between ethnic boundaries and borders intensifies the dialogic implications of Revard's experiment.

Revard's poems and essays are a marvelous example of how various disciplines and ethnic identities converge in narratives that also combine poetry, short stories, mythologies, and references to the multiple voices and experiences that have made Carter Revard. And yet, his brand of being personal is always in relationship to social groups—be they family, faculty, students, tribes, or various authors within and without Native America. Revard is clear, in his prose and poetic narratives, that he is the teller, the observer. And yet Revard plays with his own persona, especially in his chapter "Report to the Nation: Repossessing Europe." In this "epistle," Revard calls himself *Special Agent Wazhazhe No. 2,230*. Revard explains: "*Osage* is an Anglicized version of the Osage word *Wazhazhe*" (2001: 112). Furthermore, in 1906, explains Revard, "when the Osage roll of all tribal members was drawn up . . . it listed 2,229 Osages; so my parodic narrative is spoken by an apocryphal additional member" (4 May 2005: E-mail to author).

"Report to the Nation: Repossessing Europe" begins: "When I claimed England for the Osage nation, last month, some of the English chiefs objected. They said the Thames is not the Thames until it's past Oxford: above Oxford, it is two streams, the Isis and the Cherwell. Forked tongue, forked river I suppose" (1998: 76). In this report, Revard composes a stunningly ironic commentary on the violent illogic of colonization, all the while playing Coyote, hoping that he won't be cheated, arrested, hanged, or assassinated for his efforts like Cortez, Balboa, Pizarro, and the conquistadores. One caution that Revard makes in his report is that Europe, "being secondhand and pretty badly used, ought not to be priced so high as Louisiana when Jefferson bought it from a French dictator the land on which, as he knew and did not know, our Osage people happened to exist" (1998: 89). "Europe," writes Revard, "won't be worth things of serious value. So don't any of us offer language, traditions, beadwork, religion or even half the Cowboy and Indian myth, let alone our selves, this time" (1998: 89).

Revard/Special Agent Wazhazhe No. 2,230 hypothesizes: "Maybe instead of sending people over to take the land, and drive people off and starve those that won't leave into submission, and show them how to live and worship by force if need be, we'd do better just to transport Europe over to us, and not try to counterpunch Columbus" (1998: 80). Wazhazhe knows a better way to conquer Europe: "I saw how we can cram most of Europe into a computer and bring it back to deal with on our own terms, far more efficiently and cheaply than by trying to load all that geography on our backs the way Ameropeans have done. We can turn everything of theirs into electrons dancing around at our fingertips, words or corporations or whatever" (1998: 81). Wazhazhe has a little trouble, however, "processing Greece" (1998: 84). He would be "for claiming all the Peloponnese, including Argos as well as Olympia, because it could be useful to us—what the hell, we might as well have pastoral as well as epic and tragedy if we want to claim Europe for our kids" (1998: 87). The question Revard is actually posing is this: why not claim what various cultures have to offer in terms of creative contributions to humanity—the humanities: pastorals, epics, tragedies—instead of lands upon which Other peoples have inherited their identities?

"These words"—myths, epics, dramas, comedies—are what we have to pass on to our children, continues Revard: "[W]hatever has evaporated will give its aftertaste, enough for anyone wanting to steal a culture from under the noses of its guardians; they wouldn't let me take the gold mask of Agamemnon, but I did sneak out with his story" (1998: 89–90). Then Revard turns particularly tricksterish: "Wonder how things would have gone if it had been Coyote not Oedipus up against that Sphinx. Europe with a Coyote Complex . . . hey, maybe it WAS Coyote!" (1998: 90). This essay, finally, rests upon genre concerns: "Comedy is worth more than tragedy any time where survival is at stake" (1998: 90). In this auto-critical trickster narrative, Revard speaks of an intellectual "conquering" and not a conquering of lands and peoples; this conquering comes through an appreciation of cultural offerings (which, by definition, are portable).

Much of *Winning the Dust Bowl* is founded on Revard's family lines and chronologies. Pictures of extended family members enhance the poetry about times, places, losses, and musings: about how life begets such particular complexes of intimate relationships. In "Walking Among the Stars," (*Family Matters, Tribal Affairs*), Revard tells us: "I try now to think of each poem as a giveaway talk, one honoring that relative, the way at the end of a dance there will be a time when the Indians ask the MC to call up certain people, and the women will be given a shawl, the men a blanket, or some such gifts, and through the MC it will be told why the persons are being called to receive this" (1998: 16). "That Lightning's Hard to Climb" is a *giveaway* elegy to Revard's mother, Thelma Louise Camp. In this poem, Revard likens the loss of the tallest catalpa tree in his "old front yard at Buck Creek" to the loss of his mother; the tree where "sun-lucent leaves" sheltered the running laughter of children and other "nestlings" as well as the "dancing spatter" of rain and now is gone, "and only / some green shoots with their heart-shaped leaves / now mantle where the / living tree once stood" (2001: 107–108). Revard says that he "hoped the story of Elijah, transported up by the 'Lightning U-Haul,' but leaving his mantle to Elisha, will be evoked by that final reference to the leaves that 'mantle' where the living tree once stood." Revard intends for readers to recognize the elegy for his mother as part of the same biblical narrative that the old spiritual "Swing Low, Sweet Chariot" was grounded upon (4 May 2005: E-mail to author).

Or there is *"Wazhazhe* Grandmother" written for Revard's Osage grandmother, Mrs. Josephine Jump—the grandmother who sponsored Revard's naming ceremony. Revard laments his grandmother's passing in memories of the times through which she lived on the homestead along Bird Creek—times, like Bird Creek, whose existence is quashed by the creation of a dam. And yet "Bird Creek's old channel under Lake Bluestem" finds "big catfish" slowly groping in darkness "up over the sandstone ledge of the drowned / waterfall," or scavenging "through the ooze of/the homestead and along the road where / an Osage bride and her man came riding one special day / and climbed down from the buggy in all their / best finery / to live in their first home" (2001: 111). The losses of James Alexander Camp—Revard's Irish and Scotch-Irish grandfather (who told him to go to college)—of Revard's twin sister Maxine, of Revard's bankrobbing Uncle Carter accompany his poems about survival: of dinosaurs (in the form of birds); of the Dust Bowl, foreign wars, or even survival from speaking at a literary convention in Las Vegas.

To whom, but Aunt Jewel, could Revard have told that he saw his dead Uncle Gus, her brother,

> there at Cahokia where the great city
> of Indian people once had been,
> her brother dancing, Uncle Gus,
> left us twenty years before,
> and I don't see such things, but I saw him there
> twice, dancing with
> the hawk's wing he carried ... (2001: 181)

In "Aunt Jewell as Powwow Princess," Revard brings together his mythic and logical imagination. "I was AGHAST at what I saw," he writes. "I've got no way of seeing things like that"—the spirit body of his uncle (2001: 179). Revard suggests that such an experience is like sitting on a rock that is labeled uranium: "Sometimes it's super-real, you see into things, / I mean you see / what isn't there, but yet it makes / the things you CAN see have a different meaning" (2001: 179). Some Indian people, claims Revard, are like "physicists who figure how / to look inside some distant star, it's possible / to see how each thing, deep inside, / is something else" (2001: 179). In this instance, however, the "something else" is a spirit being. To counterbalance his assertions, Revard does a study of the word he uses to introduce the poem AGHAST:

> Well hell, for instance right
> here in that word 'aghast' which I just used, there lives
> a 'ghost'—because one thousand years ago, inside
>   those Anglo-Saxon warriors, the soul
> that spoke and danced, they didn't call that
> a SPIRIT but a GAST—so when they said AGHAST,
> they meant something was walking in their SOUL. (2001: 179)

Revard then moves on to a typical discerning insight that shows the outcome of conjoining Native and Anglo ways of perceiving:

> So after all, maybe it's just as good to say
> "Ghost Dance," as "Spirit Dance," the way
>   Americans say it, speaking
> of what the people did who are called,
> because of Columbus, INDIANS. Maybe
> inside this English word INDIAN
> there is a GHOST that haunts
> all English-speakers, even in these words. (2001: 179–180)

Genealogical awareness is the bedrock of Revard's poetry; and his readers come to hold dear the members of Revard's family tree. He provides a kind of archeology of family and place that is archetypal: worthy of emulation. Stella Revard—Revard's wife and a renowned Milton scholar—is hidden in various poems; "I will keep those places secret," writes Revard, "perhaps because of the intimacy they communicate" (21 June 2004: E-mail to author). Revard's wife appears in "How the Songs Come Down," "The Man Lee Harvey Oswald Missed," "Planet of the Blue-eyed Cats," "Starring America," and "Songs of the Winethroated Hummingbird," for example. Carter's and Stella's children—Stephen (b. 1956), Geoffrey (b. 1961), Vanessa (b. 1967), and Lawrence (b. 1969)—also appear in various poems: "Dragon-Watching in St. Louis," "Over By Fairfax, Leaving Tracks," "Christmas Shopping," and "Planet of Blue-Eyed Cats" to mention a few.

For those who have tried to assemble a genealogical chart from what Revard has written but got endlessly bogged down, I give Revard's answer to my e-mail inquiry:

> My mother's maiden name was Thelma Louise Camp (1908–81); my uncles—her brothers—all of whom spent time with us when I was a boy, and who were important figures for me, were Arthur (1898–1955), Aubrey (1900–1934), Bertrand Allen (1904–1956 or 1957), Dwain (1906–1982?), Carter (1910–1936), and Woodrow (1914–1994). My blood father was McGuire Revard (1903–1963); his father was Charles E. Revard, who was born in either Tacoma or Olympia, Washington, in the late 1860's, but with his father returned to Oklahoma and joined the Osages after they moved from Kansas to our reservation in Oklahoma in 1872. Charles Revard was one of the Original Osage Allottees in 1907, and had a ranch up near Hulah in the northeastern part of the Osage Reservation until he moved to San Antonio in the 1920's. He was killed there accidentally in the mid 1920's.
>
> On my mother's side, her father was James Alexander Camp (1870–1942), of Scotch-Irish ancestry, and her mother was Margaret Sophronia Bell, of Irish and Scotch-Irish ancestry. Both were born in east Texas not far south of the Red River border of Oklahoma, and moved to southern Missouri about 1874. They grew up near the little town of Doniphan, on the Current River in the Ozarks just north of Arkansas. In 1936, after my Uncle Carter Camp was shot to death, we drove all the way over (along highways 60 and 160) from Buck Creek to Doniphan MO and visited all the relatives still living there, and I remember clearly some parts of that visit, especially going swimming in the Current River, and going up to see the Big Spring there.
>
> My grandfather Camp's father and uncle were in the Civil War, one on each side—the Southern soldier was captured and spent much of the war years in a prison camp in Illinois I think. (28 January 2005: E-mail to author)

Revard clarified his stepfather's genealogy in a January 29, 2005 e-mail:

> My stepfather, Addison Benjamin Jump Sr., was born in 1910, married my mother Thelma Camp about 1933, and died about 1993. He was "full-blood" but not born soon enough to be listed on the 1906 roll of Original Allottees; his share of oil money came by inheritance. His father, Jacob Jump (born in late 1880s I think, died c. 1919), married his mother, Josephine Strikeaxe (born c. 1894), about 1908 and they had four children: Addison (b. 1910), Arita (1912) Louis (1914) and Kenneth (1918). (29 January 2005: E-mail to author)

Revard knew Jacob Jump's mother. Of her, he writes:

[W]hen as a little boy I knew her, in the 1930's, she was in her eighties; she lived to age 90 and died in 1941, when I was ten. Strange to think of her being a small girl when the great herds of buffalo still ranged across Kansas and the Plains, in the decade when the Forty-Niners and the Colorado gold and silver seekers were going across from Missouri west through the Osage territories—and of her living through the John Brown and guerilla days of the 1850s in bloody Kansas, and then the Civil War, and then making the trek down into Indian Territory when Sherman's troopers were out there establishing peace and freedom by wiping out buffalo, antelope, and Indians. (28 January 2005: E-mail to author)

Again, as Revard discusses much of the American history he has lived through, he often comments on that history, with preference given to his Osage heritage.

What is more, Revard suggests that "noticing where we are and how we are in the world"—the people, places, events—might cause us "to give thanks for what has been given," to "maybe leave a few words for the children coming on, in praise of this green world halfway to heaven and just above our heads" (2001: 80). Revard's poetry, in this respect, is not merely for academic communities, but for his children and grandchildren, of which he has ten: Stephen has four children, Geoffrey two, and Vanessa four. What is more, Carter's and Stella's children carry on their parents' influence. Lawrence, for example, has an MFA and is publishing poems. Lawrence is also helping Stella with "her edition of Milton's Shorter Poems for Blackwell's by collaborating with her on translating Milton's Latin and Greek poems" (18 June 2004: E-mail to author).

Revard's autoethnographic enterprise is much like that of Geronimo—attending to mythic, cosmic, geologic, tribal, mixedblood-family, and individual self-positioning. Revard's positioning also involves his "double vision," what is being called hybridity. However, Revard's hybrid or mixedblood vision attains to that "third space" that is critical, philosophically, for commenting on or coming to consciousness about those old, worn-out, often violent, binaries: Us/Them; Native/American; Male/Female; Communal/Individual; Mythic/Logic, and so on. This kind of "contact zone" causes scholars to rethink genre. In this regard, Revard is truly Mythic (in the modern, more positive, sense of Myth): he gathers in relationships: 1) to myth/mystery; 2) to the cosmos/environment/place; 3) to various communities—ancestral, tribal, mixed-heritage family, scholarly; and 4) to his own journey within the cycle/circle of life. However, Revard's Osage heritage (particularity) provides the still point or creates the center for his gaze: he is *Wa-thi'-gethon*. This four-quartered, ever-expanding circle is, as so many Native peoples attest, an expression of the sacred circle.

Works Cited

Bruner, E. M. 1986. "Experience and Its Expressions." *The Anthropology of Experience*. Eds. V.W. Turner and E. M. Bruner. Urbana: University of Illinois Press.
Bhabha, H. K. 1997. "Signs Taken for Wonders." *The Post-Colonial Studies Reader*. Eds. B. Ashcroft, G. Griffiths, and H. Tiffin. London and New York: Routledge. 29–35.
——. 1997. "Cultural Diversity and Cultural Differences." *The Post-Colonial Studies Reader*. Eds. B.Ashcroft, G. Griffiths, and H. Tiffin. London and New York: Routledge. 206–12.
Cole, S. 1992. "Anthropological Lives: The Reflexive Tradition in a Social Science." *Essays on Life Writing*. Ed. M. Kadar. Toronto: University of Toronto Press. 113–27.
Hirsch, E. D. 1965. *Validity in Interpretation*. New Haven, Connecticut. Yale University Press.
Krupat, A. 1992. *Ethnocriticism: Ethnography, History, Literature*. Berkeley: University of California Press.
La Flesche, F. 1995. *The Osage and the Invisible World*. Norman: University of Oklahoma Press.
Lincoln, K. 1999. "Native Poetics." *Fiction Studies*. 45.1: 146–184.
Porush, D. 1989. "Cybernetic Fiction and Postmodern Science." *New Literary History* 20.2: 373–396.
Pratt, M. L. 1999. "Arts of the Contact Zone." *Ways of Reading*. Eds. D. Bartholomae and A. Petrosky. New York: Bedford/St. Martin's.
——. 1992. *Imperial Eyes*. London and New York: Routledge.
Revard, C. 1987. "Walking Among the Stars." *I Tell You Now: Autobiographical Essays by Native American Writers*. Eds. B. Swann and A. Krupat. Lincoln: University of Nebraska Press. 65–84.

——. 1998. *Family Matters, Tribal Affairs*. Tucson: University of Arizona Press.
——. 1999–2000. "Why Mark Twain Murdered Injun Joe—And Will Never Be Indicted." *The Massachusetts Review* 40.4: 643–670.
——. 2001. *Winning the Dust Bowl*. Tucson: University of Arizona Press.
——. 2004, 18 June. "Myth and Stuff." E-mail to S. Lundquist.
——. 2004, 18 June. "C V as Promised." E-mail to S. Lundquist.
——. 2004, 19 June. "Genealogy." E-mail to S. Lundquist.
——. 2005, 28 January. "More Genealogy." E-mail to S. Lundquist.
——. 2005, 29 January. "Genealogy Again." E-mail to S. Lundquist.
——. 2005, 3 May. "Essay for Ellen's Book." Email to S. Lundquist.
——. 2005, 4 May. "Annotated Essay." E-mail to S. Lundquist.
Sangari, K.1997. "The Politics of the Possible." *The Post-Colonial Studies Reader*. Eds. B. Ashcroft, G. Griffiths, and H. Tiffin. London and New York: Routledge. 143–147.
"Surviving the Dust Bowl." 2/22/2005. *American Experience*. http://www.pbs.org/wgbh/ames/dustbowl/timeline/index.html.
Turner, V. W. 1986. "Dewey, Dilthey, and Drama: An Essay in the Anthropology of Experience." *The Anthropology of Experience*. Eds. V. W. Turner and E. M. Bruner. Urbana: University of Illinois Press.
Zolbrod, P. 1987. "When Artifacts Speak, What Can They Tell Us?" *Recovering the Word: Essays on Native American Literature*. Eds. B. Swann. and A. Krupat. Berkeley: University of California Press.

An earlier version of this essay, "Carter Revard as Auto-ethnographer," appeared in *Studies in American Indian Literatures* 15.1 (2003): 67–73.

Going Home with Carter Revard

Robin Riley Fast

The first three essays of *Family Matters, Tribal Affairs* ("Walking Among the Stars," "Buck Creek Community," and "Going to College") serve, among many other purposes, to help define what home means for Carter Revard. Home, as evoked in these essays, is family—each name recalling stories and threads of relationship, and place: "an eighty-acre meadow with some tillable land, prime bluestem hay" (1998: 5), "a blue water pond for cattle, and fish . . . willows . . . elms . . . hackberries" (1998: 9). It is an extensive web of people, land, memory and knowledge, the site and substance of story and song (hence of language). As known and remembered in the present, home partakes of both evanescence and solidity. Revard writes, "I sit typing this in the upstairs of the old garage," yet he writes of "houses" that "did not last," a hospital that "melted into thin air" (1998: 6, 7, 8). Similarly, the languages of home are both lost and speakable, singable: "It never occurred to me to learn the [Ponca and Osage] languages, words plentiful as passenger pigeons . . . All those stories, all that language, all those times, passed over our heads and disappeared" (1998: 19). Yet, "like that mockingbird, I have more than one song, but they are all our songs. It has seemed to me that no one else will sing them unless I do," so Revard dares to place his family, as "Ovid or Virgil or Horace" placed their heroes, "among the stars" (1998: 20). The centrality of home for Revard, and the ways in which he articulates its meanings and realities, is the focus of this essay.

William Bevis has observed that "[i]n Native American novels, coming home, staying put . . . is not only the primary story, it is a primary mode of knowledge and a primary good" (1987: 582). While Revard and his poems do not "stay put," and tell many different stories, they do repeatedly "come home," to knowledge and to the sources of grounding that sustain. Joy Harjo, another Oklahoma Indian writer who has traveled far from home, might speak for Revard, and for the presence of home in his work, when she says, "In a sense we never leave Oklahoma, or maybe it would be better said that Oklahoma never leaves us. The spirit is alive in the landscape that arranges itself in . . . poems and stories" (1981: 43). And Eric Gary Anderson might be building on Harjo's insight when he identifies "a dynamic relationship between grounded, rooted home places and an American Indian . . . intelligence of travel" (1999: 29), such that "Native poetry . . . both travels and maintains . . . a centered but flexible sense of home places" (2003: 49). As all of these writers suggest, and Revard's work substantiates, Native writers are not inclined to agree that "you can't go home again." On the contrary, Revard and others demonstrate, one must go home again and again, whether literally or in spirit, as Revard, in poems, prose, and "real life," often does. Revard's words take him home, and invite his readers to join him: as he says, "American Indians now, with words, make places to live—in poems and novels and essays, as well as on reservations and in cities" (1998: xi); and as words evoke home, they also become a kind of home: "I've made this a home of new and selected poems, and put a meadow around it of history and autobiography" (2001: xiii).

Revard's poems of home are representative of an important complex of issues that infuse the body of his work as a whole, and that concern language, history, community, and place. As well, these poems of home are representative of important elements of Revard's style and poetics. Further, his commitment to home, and his conception of home as communal, securely grounded in family, place, and history (including culture, language, and story) join him to a strong chorus of similarly committed and grounded Native writers. When (Navajo) Luci Tapahonso says, "the place of my birth is the source of the writing," and "[t]his writing . . . is not 'mine,' but a collection of many voices that range from centuries ago and continue into the future" (1993: x, xii), she affirms the vitality and multi-dimensionality of home as her source of language, analogous to what we will see in Revard's "Making a Name." Similarly, Okanagan writer Jeannette C. Armstrong links language, home, and history, when she affirms, "[L]anguage was given to us by the land we live within. . . [T]his N'silxchn [language] . . . embraces me and permeates my experience of the Okanagan land and is a constant voice within me that yearns for human speech. I am claimed and owned by this land, this Okanagan" (1999: 175, 176). As does Revard, these Native writers ground themselves in the particulars of their home places. Thus Nora Marks Dauenhauer evokes the specific realities of her Southeast Alaskan Tlingit culture: "Not only have we always used salmon as our main diet, and ... the mainstay of our subsistence and commercial economies, but the different varieties of salmon are part of our social structure and ethnic identity as well... We need salmon to continue as physically, mentally, and spiritually healthy people" (1992: 3, 6). For Dauenhauer, too, home is the source of art: "This enduring relationship between the Tlingit people, the fish and animals, and the land, and the connection of all of these to our social structure ... are passed down in the oral tradition and visual art of each clan" (1992: 4)—and in her own writing. Acoma Pueblo writer Simon J. Ortiz, too, states that "[l]ike myself, the source of these narratives is my home"; further, he recognizes that "the way out" of the internalized oppressions imposed by colonization "has to do with the consciousness we have of ourselves, the language we use ... and our responsible care for and relationships we have with our communities and communal lands" (1992: 168, 27). Ortiz makes explicit that the discourse of home is also the discourse of survival. As Revard, like the other writers quoted here, participates in an ethics and esthetics of relationality, his examination of the meanings of home contributes, too, to the discourse of survival, a crucial issue for contemporary Native America.

Revard's work demonstrates that home remains a vital source and grounding, however far he may travel. He affirms the centrality of his home place early in two recent books. His prose introduction to "To the Muse in Oklahoma," from *Winning the Dust Bowl*, shows how, paradoxically, traveling away from home (literally and mentally) brings him back home again, and how, conversely, memories of home can also invoke distant places:

> In 1975 ... on a trip to Greece ... we drank from the springs of ... assorted ... gods and muses.
> Remembering, back in St. Louis, those mountain springs in Greece, my mind went back again to the dry blackjack hills around the Buck Creek Valley, and I remembered that there were small springs up there, and ... I thought how, even then [in the "Dust Bowl times"], there was a little water in the pond my folks had made for the cows and horses ... To see them so thirsty, and to help them quench that thirst, in a parched summer or a frozen winter, that was how I remembered those hot dry Grecian mountains with their Muses' springs. (2001: 8)

The poem acknowledges that Revard's Oklahoma "bluestem meadow / is hardly Helicon," but celebrates this place where "the thunder / sent living waters down," and "we / walked upon the water / every winter" (2001: 9). These words associate home with the miraculous; memories of sliding on the ice evoke vitality and delight. Revard again claims home for poetry in the prose poem "In Oklahoma" that introduces *An Eagle Nation*. Again, he begins by referring to canonical cosmopolitan culture, as he reprimands Gertrude Stein and Wallace Stevens for their dismissals of the hinterlands. The poem gives Revard's home both holiness—"a THERE depends on how, in the beginning, the wind breathes upon its surface," and inhabitants—an "Osage man fishing ... [a] bobwhite," and others. It evokes the complexities of life—"His wife in the Indian Hospital with cancer. Children in various unhappiness"—in a vividly concrete place. And it ends with an invitation: "You have to be there before it's a there. Daddy, would you pass them a plate of fish? See friends, it's not a flyover here. Come down from your planes and you'll understand. Here" (1993: 3). These lines close the gap between "there" and "here," as they turn from third-person to second-person address and, in the final "here," both reclaim home as central and offer food. Home is both locally grounded and the basis for a creative relationship with the world beyond home, as "Homework at Oxford" will also demonstrate.

The title of "Homework at Oxford" signals both the distance the writer has traveled from his Oklahoma home, and the conscientiousness (as well as love) with which he will maintain his bonds to that place. In this and other poems, he evokes home as a place of abundance (notwithstanding frequent poverty) and vitality (notwithstanding the knowledge of mortality), a place often of joy and wonder, recaptured in an exuberant and embracing style, with a tone that is at once nostalgic and clear-eyed.

"Homework at Oxford" begins in cold discomfort in the Oxford room where the young Revard has spent the night studying Meister Eckhart's "dark book," and ends in the expectation of returning to that room, to "puzzle out fifty lines of *Beowulf*—that dark poem."[1] But though the poem is framed by his Oxford studies, what it most persuasively demon-

---

[1] I wish to acknowledge my students Matthew Mosher and Jessie Hardy, who, in the course of my study of this poem, also wrote papers on it. I do not believe that I have borrowed from them, but I am sure that my reading of the poem was enriched by the opportunity to study it with them and their classmates.

strates is the power of home to bring the student back and hold him, in the hour between last darkness and first dawn, as he moves through the memories and knowledge that ground him. Prompted, as it seems, by the "shrewd and curious" eye of the rooster in his Breughel print (one detail of the Oxford world that resonates with home), the scholar leaves his study, goes out to the college's "rampart walk," and, hearing the familiar sounds of cattle, is transported: "it might be morning darkness in Oklahoma" (1993: 76).

What follows may or may not reveal homesickness,[2] but it definitely evokes home's density of meaning and the depth of the young man's attachment—an attachment grounded in sensation, in subtly suggested knowledge, and in unstated but transparently evident love for place and family. The body of the poem is a web of memories, evoked by rich and variegated imagery, complicated by shifts in tone and pacing, from the wild exhilaration of children bombarding each other with unripe persimmons, to the awed anticipation of a lone boy awaiting the twilight arrival of a great blue heron, to that same boy delicately robbing sparrows' nests to throw "the naked pulsing bodies / Of young birds hot and tender and blind" to the kittens (1993: 80), and finally to the morning chores shared with his grandfather.

Among the wealth of imagery, variations of light are especially telling. Light is implied when "the pond / would spill a silverlet through red-pebbly clay and down / to the crawdads' pool in a run of clean-gurgling water" (1993: 76). It is vivid in "a windy sunbright sky" and when, of an early morning, "[t]he east shone scarlet and gold, the air was brilliant" (77, 79). In these passages the light contributes to the sense of joy and well-being. It is more complex in the final home-memory lines, at the end of the milking passage. Both here and in the preceding vignette, Revard evokes his childhood awareness of his grandfather's failing heart, and the grandfather's consequent, barely voiced anxiety for the family. In the earlier passage, while making a birthday cake for the children, the grandfather "leaned in the kitchen door ... holding his heart, trying to breathe," while the whole family stopped, waiting, bathed in "warm cake smells" (80). (Note that these images associate home both with nurturance—thus life, and with the knowledge of mortality.) Now, as the milking chores end, "The lantern's light

---

2   Though the poem has seemed to me (and I think to Janet McAdams) to voice homesickness, Revard has noted that "I had not thought of the poem as showing homesickness, but rather, ... home-healthiness" (McAdams 2003: 203).

had shrunk, I raised the hot globe and blew it out... We watched ... the eastern sky dovegray and crimson over the cold March pastures" (82–83). The lantern light has "shrunk" because the light of day is growing, yet the act of blowing out the light inevitably suggests darkness—which is partially lightened by the eastern sky. We have diurnal and seasonal cycles and continuity here; we also have the knowledge of mortality and loss, and the boy's implication in that knowledge. This knowledge, evoked of course as well in the nest-robbing passage, gives depth and completeness to Revard's evocation of home—which embraces all of life, and thus implicitly affords the grounding with which the home-bonded person is able to venture forth and return.

The depth of this grounding, and of the vision that home has given the poet, is further evident when we note that, while the bright images in the Oklahoma passages do contrast to the framing "darkness" of his Oxford readings, these readings are not wholly dark: the "black book" is "filled with images of light," as well as of "the soul's darkness" (1993: 75), and the "dark poem" tells of "a great light" that "[f]lashed like heaven's candle" (83). When we note as well the cumulative complexity of the light images associated with Oklahoma, we may also suspect that the contrast between the two places is not wholly oppositional. Revard subtly connects Oxford and Oklahoma, not only by contrast but also by a kind of oblique resonance of imagery. Still, while in Oxford the simultaneity of light and dark may suggest opposition and paradox, in Oklahoma the blended light/dark imagery is clearly part of a located, relational, and sustaining sense of wholeness, which supports the scholar in his travels away from home.[3]

As Revard anticipates returning to his Oxford room and to the homework of studying *Beowulf*, he again ventures from home. The references to *Beowulf* seem to combine the effects that Revard earlier divided between Meister Eckhart's dark book (antithetical to the sensuous world-grounded realities of home), and the Breughel "Adoration of the Magi"—with its "pigeons, rooster, ramshackle thatch of a roof" (1993: 75) and laughing, glittering infant evoking just that world of sense and wonder and vital mixed-ness that the young man knows as home. Thus the passage in which the student anticipates, and the poet recalls, *Beowulf* offers possibilities without settling on one at the expense of

---

3 Revard frequently uses light imagery with great complexity, often evoking the Osage story of the people's star origins. For example, see "Close Encounters" (1993: 25–28) and "Given" (2001: 80–82).

others. Beowulf's is an alternative story of purposeful adventuring—not Revard's story, but not wholly alien. Both wander in foreign worlds, and Beowulf's undersea voyage might figuratively suggest as well Revard's mental voyage. Both discover "treasures," and both are stories of loyalty, his warriors' to Beowulf, and Revard's to home and family. Provocatively, the poem ends with an image of violence from the saga: "the furious waves grow dark with the blood of those monstrous things" (83). Such an ending seems to suggest two things: grounded in the knowledge of home, the student is prepared, indeed eager, to "puzzle out" what *Beowulf* offers. At the same time, because, unlike those of the saga, Revard's "kings" (his antecedents, the inhabitants of his memories) are *not* "long-forgotten," Revard's final line may turn us back toward the Oklahoma passages, in the knowledge that these "furious waves" and this Anglo Saxon saga are not all.[4]

Revard repeatedly looks back to his Oklahoma home, and though he never makes it as explicit as in "Homework at Oxford," we can imagine that these other returns are similarly sustaining. Home, in these poems, is marked by abundance. While in "Homework at Oxford" Revard exercised a kind of double vision, simultaneously remembering himself at Oxford, (and) remembering himself at home, and evoking the rich density of home's reality through the variety of his memories, in "Making a Name," he conveys that density of multi-layered reality, the wholeness, so to speak, of home, through an abundance of family voices heard, reported, and quoted, as he "direct[s] the movie / made from the story" "author[ed]" by his "Ponca folks, Aunt Jewell and / Uncle Woody" (2001: 12). We hear directly the voices of Revard the "movie" director, of Aunt Jewell, and, quoted by Aunt Jewell, of her great aunt. Indirectly, we know that other family members' voices are part of this story, and we're invited imaginatively to hear the voice of the three-year-old whose words are the story's focus: "That little kid, whoo, LISten to him swear! / Listen, my God it's ME—" (14). His words, Aunt Jewell guesses, interjecting the hint of another story, and the memory of another voice, came

> from your Grandpa Camp when he was plowing
> the garden up that month and you had followed
> with him behind the mules and plow,
> and those were real *lazy* mules! (14)

---

4 For a different view of the *Beowulf* section, see McAdams 2003: 204.

So home, we see (and hear) in this poem, is family, and as such is storied and multi-voiced.

Again, rather like his position in "Homework at Oxford," where he heard the cattle, and remembered Oklahoma, from a slightly elevated position on the rampart walk, here he is "looking down from the sky": distanced and yet at the same time on the ground, "on the back porch... a / small boy... with his foot— / ... *with his foot in* / ... *a SLOP-bucket filled with garbage*" (2001: 13–14). Revard's use of italics in this poem differs from that in "Homework at Oxford," however. There he used italics to separate his home memories from the "present" of Oxford. Here, he is at home both in the telling (though figuratively "looking down from the sky") and in the story itself. As readers we might expect him to use different type faces to distinguish among tellers or between past and present, but he doesn't seem to do that either. Rather, I think, he intersperses passages in italics and roman type so as to remind us that his story (and his knowledge of home) is made of multiple layers, shaped by multiple perspectives, *without* allowing us to draw clear lines between these various elements and thereby simplify what he has given us.[5] The italics *may* identify the movie's key images (laughter, the approach to the scene, the child's foot in the bucket and his swearing, the young Aunt Jewell), but the images need the surrounding (roman type) elaboration to be more than scattered impressions. Home as place, family, memory, and all that they entail, is dynamic, its multiple layers and voices intermingling, recognizably distinct (Aunt Jewell's voice *is* Aunt Jewell's voice), but woven into a single fabric (or "movie").

Revard concludes this poem by explicitly acknowledging home as the source of the language with which he weaves his connections:

> I learned my English words from experts,
> but who knows,
>   the chance to practice ALL of them
> might never have come to me had I not lived
>   for some time in my youth with my feet
> set firmly on an Indian Reservation. (2001: 15)[6]

---

5 This is not to say that he simplifies by using italics in "Homework at Oxford"; that poem's groundings and dynamics create their own complexities.

6 It is intriguing to think that in highlighting language here, Revard might be echoing his recognition of how Charles Eastman's education in "the Santee system of names for animals and plants... tied his sense of personal identity to his sense of tribal identity and relationship to the world" (1998: 132): for both Eastman and Revard, language binds one to home.

That home is at once the source of voice, hence of language, and dependent upon voice, is something Revard reiterates in "Finding a Voice" (2001: 3–7), and in "Buck Creek": "Finally when I . . . discovered how to put Oklahoma sounds into the lines . . . I began to find some ways to write about Buck Creek" (2001: 101).

In "Making a Name," the abundance associated with home is preeminently that of language. In other poems, it is the abundance of the natural world that intrigues, enchants, and engages the poet and his remembered boyhood self. In "Another Sunday Morning" (1992: 14–15), Revard evokes a boy's attentive awareness of the abundant life around him, the tracks, movements, and sounds of all the animals that preceded or accompany his walk to the highway for the Sunday paper. A similar attentiveness is evident in "Behind the Hill," as a group of children go adventuring in the woods. They "felt the animals hiding, the breath of wind," watched a squirrel's "fluid grappling dash / Over supple tree tops," and "little sunperch at play . . . finning themselves and yawning," then "sprawled on the fine heavy sand under shifting elm-shadows" (2001: 40–41). But almost always, in such poems, the natural abundance and the rich vitality and joy of children co-exist with currents of more somber knowledge. Thus the edenic "Behind the Hill" ends with the image of a water-moccasin "slithering and floating" by in the water, "so near we saw elliptic cat-pupils contracted / To slits, his shadow on the sand beneath him," then "crawl[ing] out on a rock" to lie "quiet in the sun" (2001:41), recalling the "darting copper head" that, in "Homework at Oxford," surprised a cousin on his way to get the morning paper in an Oklahoma "August dawn." In "Another Sunday Morning," the boy reads news of World War II, of

> . . . maimed survivors screaming
>   in Japanese or English until
> their gasoline-blistered heads
>   sank down to the tiger-sharks. (1992: 15)

Because the whole poem is one long, intricate sentence, the war news becomes virtually part of the home place and time. In "Where the Frontier Went" (1992: 22–26), home is the place both of abundant, vivid life, imaged in the seasonal cycle, and of death, as the boy stumbles upon the graves of a family whose history is lost. Different kinds of knowledge are again joined in "Communing Before Supermarkets," where Revard recalls poverty as he speculates that his memory of "elephantine loads of melons," "bushels of peaches, / apples and apricots" is so vivid "because we were always trying / to have enough money to eat" (2001: 76). The home of childhood, then, is remembered as both "shelter[ing] and vulnerable" (2001: 107), the place of knowledge of life and also of death, danger, and want.[7]

Not surprisingly, then, home is also a site of loss in some of Revard's poems. "Wazhazhe Grandmother" is an elegy for Revard's Osage grandmother, and also for her first married home, buried now beneath a dam-created lake. Both losses are contained, however, in memories (actual and imagined) of life and of promise: of deer coming "down / at dusk with the stars / to drink from the deep pools" near the homestead where "an Osage bride and her man came riding one special day / . . . in all their / best finery / to live in their first home" (2001: 110, 111). Another double elegy, "That Lightning's Hard to Climb" (2001: 106–108), commemorates "a favorite tree . . . in the old front yard at Buck Creek . . . felled by lightning" (106), and is dedicated to Revard's mother, Thelma Louise Camp. This poem embodies the re-creative power of memory and language, and promises new life in the "green shoots with their heart-shaped leaves . . . where the / living tree once stood" (108). But from the very first line ("—Struck down?"), it is shadowed by the knowledge of vulnerability and loss: the tree, "the swaying giant," held scissortail nestlings "in its arms as / the flashing giant glanced in / flooding silver down on them"; and the "grownups [who] watched" the children's play after the storm "from the / gloominous porch, talking of old / and happy faroff things and laughter long ago" (107–108) are gone, themselves the subjects of the now-grown children's reminiscences of long ago. Most painful of these poems of loss is "My Right Hand Don't Leave Me No More," in memory of Revard's grandfather. His importance in Revard's early life is indicated in the prose section that precedes the poem in *Winning the Dust Bowl*: "He had died of a heart attack in March of 1942" (when Revard was eleven), "and the loss was heavy, not just hard emotionally but also practically, because he was a handy man—the place was falling apart, everything would need fixing, and he was the one who always put things back together" (2001: 98). The poem focuses entirely

---

7 It is important to note that in each poem the bleaker knowledge is to some extent discerned by the children: it is never wholly the adult rememberer's after-the-fact recognition. Rather, Revard is showing us that at least to some degree the child's home-knowledge was mixed, home's multi-faceted abundance and vitality tinged with "other" awareness. This mixed-ness contributes to making home a solid grounding for all of life.

on the grandfather, whom it addresses directly from the first to the last line, and though there are moments of understated humor early on, no mitigating promises of continuance, no green leaves of "dark water turning into / a spilling of light" (2001: 110), soften the knowledge of loss. Indeed the power of grief grows as the poem ends, the tone evolving as the perspective shifts from that of an adult, capable of irony, with the vocabulary and insight of greater experience ("your deprecating hands / And weary eyes"), to that of a child:

> You fixed the broken farm. It was your hands drove
> The shining nail, squeaking under the hammer, into
> Its massive gatepost's new-peeled oaken bulk.
> . . .
> I thought your hands that held off shame and poverty
> From all of us could keep off death himself,
> My grandfather, but I was gone when he came
> And did not help. You died bringing in wood for the fire. (2001: 105)

Only in these final lines is the poem's addressee named as "[m]y grandfather," and the occasion of the poem, his death, explicitly identified. In these lines, too, the knowledge of the dead man's vital role in keeping home afloat converges with the raw grief mingled with a child's sense of guilt—emotions which in the child's experience haven't had time to soften. Here, almost unbearably, knowledge of home is knowledge of grief.

Grief and loss are accentuated by the use of contrast in a poem that addresses the pain of a younger generation. In *Winning the Dust Bowl*, Revard juxtaposes the exuberant "Making a Name" with "Paint and Feathers," in chapters entitled, respectively, "White Eagle, Early" and "White Eagle, Later"—White Eagle being the Ponca Tribal Village where Revard's beloved Aunt Jewell lived, and where Revard and his sister were cared for as young children. The first poem is Revard's only wholly joyous look back to childhood; the second, an adult's response to troubled contemporary youth. As he says in the prose introduction to "Paint and Feathers," "Things were a long way from peaceful or easy at White Eagle" in the 1970s (2001: 16). The poem is constructed of two facing vertical columns of words, and the structure emphasizes the tragic gap between the traditionally grounded ceremonial language of the left-hand column, which echoes the Ki-non, the preliminary ritual of the Osage naming ceremony, and the mostly more mundane language of the right-hand column, which evokes the direction-less, self-destructive lives of youths who have lost the grounding of home.[8] The poem's double opening makes the gap clear:

Into a star	Now put your face into
You have cast yourself,	this brown paper bag filled
have made your body of	with aluminum spray-paint,
the male star who touches	breathe in, reel back,
the sky with crimson	shudder, stagger now.
That I touch now upon	Walk now along this asphalt,
your face so you	stumble, your eyes wide
may move upon the path	and blank, white paint across
of life . . .	your face . . . (16–17)

Revard's left-hand column refers to the four symbolic "decorations"—red paint, eagle plumes, buffalo fat, and a mussel-shell gorget, "which are to be bestowed upon the child with its name," and which represent the powers of dawn and of the sun, and "earth's life-sustaining abundance" (1987: 449, 450). The reference to "the male star" (the sun) and, in the closing lines of the left-hand column, to "the House of Mystery," recall the second stage of the naming ceremony (the Tsi Ta-pe—Approach to the House). This part of the ceremony is a "symbolic prayer, . . . a ceremonial approach to the Eternal Powers," and the literal house where the ceremony is completed becomes "a figure for the ordered cosmos, and . . . the House of Wa-kon-da" (Revard 1987: 451). The right hand column, in stark contrast, recounts the broken life of a child, high on paint fumes, "blinded / by metal paint and headlights / whiting out the stars" (2001: 18), who is killed in a head-on collision while driving "without headlights." Both columns use direct address and a step-by-step present-tense organization that at once instructs and describes, creating the effect of ritual language in the left-hand column, and making the opposite column a discordant and disturbing echo. Thus while the traditional ritual promised to enable a child "to follow . . . the great path of life and power . . . the orderly way of the heavens" (Revard 1987: 447), the contemporary child is killed because he drove in the wrong direction.

The double juxtaposition of the right-hand column to the left, and of this poem to "Making a Name," sharpens the anguish of the lost child's wasted life and of the observer, recognizing the terrible vulnerability of people who have lost the connection and the sustaining meaning of tradition, of the names and ceremonies that would keep them at home

---

8 My source for the Osage naming ceremony is Revard's essay "Traditional Osage Naming Ceremonies: Entering the Circle of Being."

in "the tribal circle of being" (Revard 1987: 458). Revard does not elaborate on why the child was unable to be sustained by the ritual language of the facing column or to be grounded in the communal knowledge such language offers, though allusions to television may suggest something of the alienating lure of mass culture. The fact that in his "slack blinded saunter" he "move[d] towards / the old dance grounds" may imply that he knew, on some level, where the sustenance of home could be found, as might his placing a dead scissortail's feathers in his hair—though Revard's language seems as much to reflect the child's troubled condition as to offer hope: "The dead bird [is] crawling / with ants ... pull / tailfeathers loose and jam them in your hair" (2001: 17).[9] In any case, it is not only children who are vulnerable in this poem, but implicitly, home and community are at risk, dependent as all are on the continuance of interwoven lives. Thus the poem's final promise to the dead child, "At the Sun Dance, Little Brother, / we will dance for you" (18), offers to bring him back into the communal circle, to restore both his spirit and the world of home.

"Paint and Feathers" seems to be Revard's most sustained voicing of grief for the broken lives and the vulnerability of individuals, home, and community. Such grief gives urgency to the need for hope, and for restorative and sustaining "homework," and Revard offers these in all of his books. (His chapter headings in *Winning the Dust Bowl* are indicative: of thirty-eight chapters, five are titled "Losses," and seven, "Indian Survival.") The title poem of *An Eagle Nation*, which gives an adult's perspective on home, family, and community, is particularly powerful. It unambiguously affirms continuance through language and relationship, as Aunt Jewell speaks in Ponca to an eagle; through humor, as a multi-generational family enjoys an outing at the zoo; and through tradition and ceremony, as Revard witnesses his cousins' joy on seeing their oldest son dancing at a powwow, and feels "what the drum did for Aunt Jewell's heart and ours" (1993: 33). This is a poem that could have been fairly bleak: the eagle is caged; Aunt Jewell is in a wheelchair, her heart "alarm[ing] the doctors now and then" (31); contrary to Ponca practice, there is an admission charge at the powwow. But these facts are balanced, and survival is affirmed. The eagle responds to Aunt Jewell's Ponca words, and Revard celebrates the creative, performative, dialogic power of language: "we the people, / as Aunt Jewell and Sun Dancers say, / are an EAGLE NATION, now" (34). (I am using

---

9 For a different reading of this poem see Scarberry-García 2003.

"performative" in a double sense, referring both to language's status as performance, and to a particular quality of efficaciousness, the capacity of language to make real what it says.) The vitality that infuses this poem (not only the powwow dancing, but the family's energy, the stories of travel, and the dance of language) offers hope, as past and future merge and a new generation hears the stories and joins the dance: "the voices still / are singing, the drum-heart / still beating here" (34). "Here," in this poem, is "this Oklahoma time" and place, to which Revard's people migrated (by choice, necessity, or compulsion), where family, memory, story, ceremony, and the knowledge of relationship provide the grounding that makes survival possible.

Many characteristics of Revard's style and poetics are evident in the poems that I have discussed here, suggesting that in this respect, too, his poetry is grounded in the knowledge and values of home. I will draw attention to just a few of these traits, to indicate some of the ways in which we might consider Revard's to be a poetics of home. That language and home are mutually locating, and serve to ground Revard as speaker and poet, is evident in both "Making a Name" and "An Eagle Nation," and implied in the Preface to *Family Matters, Tribal Affairs*, where he states that the collected pieces "make a community of words on Indian ground" (1998: xii). Revard's complex syntax, blending of local and cosmopolitan references, and attentiveness to the concrete details of experience enact a vision of home and the world as alive and dynamic, a rich and interconnected whole—a vision such as is discernible in, among many others, "Another Sunday Morning" and "Homework at Oxford." The narrative quality of all of these pieces (however variously it may appear in, say, "In Oklahoma," "Paint and Feathers," and "That Lightning's Hard to Climb") draws attention to the performative quality of the language, to Revard's commitment to the creative power of the word, and his attentiveness to the dynamics that bind the speaker/writer, the word, and the listener/reader (as, for example, in "In Oklahoma"). Such language is grounded in Revard's embracing knowledge of home and serves thus to remind us, too, of how the language of home is linked to ethics, to spirit, and to survival. "Paint and Feathers" shows how such links are realized in a traditional context, and what the cost may be if the connections fail.

The multi-layered linkings of home, language, ethics, and survival are confirmed in Revard's prose piece "Report to the Nation: Repossessing Europe." When "Special Agent Wazhazhe No. 2,230" recalls the wisdom of the elders at home and turns away from satirical mimicry of the European conquerors and colonists, it is to appropriate the wealth of European languages, and thereby to "bring [Europe] back [to Oklahoma] to deal with on our own terms" (1998: 80). Only after recognizing the possibility of such a creative appropriation—prompted by realizing that the elders would disapprove of his more literal-minded plans for conquest—does he reconnect with home by integrating home-evoking poetry into the account of his European adventures. In this context the importance of the poems' recreations of home ground (for example, in "To the Muse, in Oklahoma") is accentuated, for it is the memory of home, as represented by the elders, that has kept the traveling special agent from becoming just another colonizer.

Revard's is an energetic and embracing poetics and poetry, moved by a serious moral vision and grounded in the complex knowledge of home. He demonstrates that knowing home as community—encompassing land, people, history, and culture—can be life-giving, while he also grieves the loss of home connections that kills the paint-sniffing child of "Paint and Feathers." Home is vulnerable, its web of relationships subject to fraying or breaking. But if the knowledge of home can be maintained or restored, Revard suggests, then home grounding and home grounds can be the basis of hope and survival, and so he also stresses the importance of individual and communal participation in the dynamic life embodied in dance, story, family, and bonds to home places. His knowledge of home infuses his poetry with hope for continuance; and it allows him, too, to respond creatively to both the struggles and the wonders that the world beyond home offers, in ways that can offer sustenance to us all.[10]

---

10. Thus grounded in home, he's able to build connections to other worlds, languages, and cultures—as we have seen, in "Homework at Oxford," and as is also evident in his Anglo-Saxon-inspired riddles.

Works Cited

Anderson, E. G. 1999. *American Indian Literature and the Southwest*. Austin: University of Texas Press.

——. 2003. "Situating American Indian Poetry: Place, Community, and the Question of Genre." *Speak to Me Words: Essays on Contemporary American Indian Poetry*. Ed. D. Rader and J. Gould. Tucson: University of Arizona Press. 34–55.

Armstrong, J. C. 1998. "Land Speaking." *Speaking for the Generations: Native Writers on Writing*. Ed. S. J. Ortiz. Tucson: University of Arizona Press. 175–94.

Bevis, W. 1987. "Native American Novels: Homing In." *Recovering the Word: Essays on Native American Literature*. Ed. B. Swann and A. Krupat. Berkeley: University of California Press. 580–620.

Dauenhauer, N. M. 1992. *Life Woven with Song*. Tucson: University of Arizona Press.

Harjo, J. 1981. "Oklahoma: the Prairie of Words." *The Remembered Earth: An Anthology of Contemporary Native American Literature*. Ed. G. Hobson. Albuquerque: University of New Mexico Press. 43–45.

McAdams, J. 2003. "Carter Revard's Angled Mirrors." *Speak to Me Words: Essays on Contemporary American Indian Poetry*. Eds. D. Rader and J. Gould. Tucson: University of Arizona Press. 193–206.

Ortiz, S. J. 1992. *Woven Stone*. Tucson: University of Arizona Press.

Revard, C. 1987. "Traditional Osage Naming Ceremonies: Entering the Circle of Being." *Recovering the Word: Essays on Native American Literature*. Ed. B. Swann and A. Krupat. Berkeley: University of California Press, 1987. 446–66.

——. 1992. *Cowboys and Indians, Christmas Shopping*. Norman: Point Riders Press.

———. 1993. *An Eagle Nation*. Tucson: University of Arizona Press.
———. 1998. *Family Matters, Tribal Affairs*. Tucson: University of Arizona Press.
———. 2001. *Winning the Dust Bowl*. Tucson: University of Arizona Press.
Scarberry-García, S. 2003. "'I Have More Than One Song': Singing and Bird Song in the Work of Carter Revard." *Studies in American Indian Literatures* 15.1: 53–59.
Tapahonso, Luci. 1993. *Sáanii Dahataal, The Women Are Singing*. Tucson: University of Arizona Press.

"We Sing as the Birds Do": Listening for Bird Song in the Work of Carter Revard

Susan Scarberry-Garcia

As Carter Revard knows, the powerful "music instinct" in humans is also one of the fullest manifestations of bonding between species. A strong link between humans and birds is expressed when someone walking in a field caws back to a crow or whistles to a bobwhite two short notes, followed by a long high-tone. Song composition is a form of musical communication that becomes the language of spirits, voiced in acoustic trills. Osage poet and essayist Carter Revard is a fascinating writer, a poet who delights in the world of sound, in the discovery of ordinary and extraordinary things, a contemporary scop who reveals transoceanic literary connections in his creative work that celebrates birds of two hemispheres.

In Revard's autobiographical book *Family Matters, Tribal Affairs*, the poet explains about the birds peopling his work: "If there are so many birds in the poems that come to me, it is because on the meadow and with the elm, catalpa, poplar trees around a house where birds would have only those trees except for the willows of the pond a quarter mile away, our trees were where the orchard orioles, robins, turtledoves, scissortails, bluebirds, kingbirds, dickcissels came to perch and sometimes nest and sing or shout" (1998: 18). These birds are joined in the dizzying catalog by mockingbirds, shrikes, indigo bunting, yellow-headed blackbirds, flickers, redheaded woodpeckers, yellow-bellied sapsuckers, meadowlarks, bobwhites, sparrow hawks, redtail hawks, Swainson hawks, red-shouldered hawks, turkey vultures, and marsh hawks (18–19). For Revard, it seems, the multiplicity of mellifluous bird songs at home is akin to the diversity of human languages on the planet. And like the miner's canary testing air quality in the mines, the health of birds is a good indication of the health of the planet, and of the health of indigenous human populations. At a time when the loss or extinction of languages parallels the loss of habitat and species in the animal world, Revard, as ornithologist by inclination, proclaims the sense of joy and awe that comes from sighting unusual birds, or even everyday birds, just behaving like birds—soaring, pecking, preening or singing.

The work of the late ornithologist, Luis F. Baptista was recently discussed in *The Los Angeles Times*: "[His] research led to his conclusion that no two species of birds have the same speech pattern and that individuals of the same species—say . . . the white-crowned sparrow—speak or sing a different dialect according to whether they nest in Alaska or Argentina. . . . 'Some birds are bilingual; some are trilingual'" (Oliver 2000). These remarkable observations are supported by studies in Northumbria, on the English/Scottish border, that suggest that even sparrows in adjacent fields sing in different dialects. When reflecting on this uniqueness and diversity of verbal expression, I am reminded of Revard's Uncle Gus in the poem "Ponca War Dancers":

> twirling and drifting
>   stomping with the
>   hawk wing a-hover then
>   leaping
>   spinning light as
>   a leaf in the whirlwind
>   the anklebells shrilling, dancing
>   the Spirit's dance

on the Osage dance grounds as the "grave, merry faces / Osage and Ponca, Otoe and Delaware, / Quapaw and Omaha, Pawnee, Comanche and Kaw" look on (1980: 54). This gathering of tribes is akin to Revard's catalog of multicolored birds, each with its songs and dances mysteriously distinct and radiant. The rainbow necks of pigeons that Revard notices in "Outside in St. Louis" are symbolically akin to the rainbow feathered gourd and the beautiful "rainbow bodies" of small birds who give life to Osage girls that Revard describes and celebrates in "Dancing with Dinosaurs" (1980: 61–62; 1993: 71). It is the Bird People who image the multicultural diversity of the Native People whom Revard knows best, and it is the Bird People who have given their songs to humans to better communicate with the spirit world.

The poet Carter Revard, having been named *Nom-peh-wah-the* for the Thunder Beings, further identifies with Mockingbird who creatively mimics the voices of others. In his essay "Walking Among the Stars," Revard writes: "So, like that mockingbird, I have more than one song, but they are all our songs" (1998: 20). In this statement Revard positions himself, self-effacingly, as an agile teller of tales of a collective communal history. Extending oral tradition by telling and then writing about the life of birds in north central Oklahoma, Revard is a carrier of unusual local knowledges. And as Mockingbird, Revard also carries the voices of Aunt Jewell, Carter Camp, and Addison Jump, among others, far away from their homelands.

In "Brothers" from *Cowboys and Indians, Christmas Shopping*, Revard recounts an incident from his childhood when his brother shot and then killed a wounded male meadowlark. Having been handed the dying yellow bird, the poet recalls the painful intensity of the moment as the "she-bird . . . hover[ed], shrilling." And the poet depicts his sense of helplessness as he questions: "'What'll we do?' 'Maybe he'll live'" to a brother who responds: "his guts are smashed, idiot." The poem concludes with the poignant line: "No one remembers this but me" (1992: 11). Apparently this early sensitivity to the value of the life of birds, which struck Revard at ten, helped to form the basis of his poetic sensibility.

Another poem in the same volume, "A Mandala of Sorts," traces the journey of a feather, perhaps of a sparrow or robin, all the way to the sea and beyond to a distant shore:

> And I watch go riding down the gutter a feather
> That spins and twinkles, left by one of those birds
> Whirled behind summer, down the earth's tilting
> Into the dawn, or across dark seas to shores
> Hushed by their singing, where sunburned lovers lie
> Among stars at dusk, and watch the gold moon rise. (1992: 31)

As Revard contemplates the feather's intercontinental journey, I recall his recent essay, "Beads, Wampum, Money, Words—and Old English Riddles," where Revard states matter-of-factly: "The eagle's feathers are also alive" (1999: 188). Thus, this knowledge that the feather carries its vitality and potential for new life, even if off the bird, is widely shared by Native people. A Navajo friend of mine has disclosed to me that he periodically washes his eagle feathers in the snow to purify and renew them. And a Pueblo elder whom I have collaborated with once told me, "The feather is portraying something that's impossible for man to do, to duplicate, and yet the feather has been separated for some time and yet it's still living. It's still revealing what it's supposed to reveal, the beauty of color" (Toledo 26 October 1991: Personal Communication to author). Revard echoes other Native writers such as Linda Hogan, who in her essay "Feathers," likewise seeks the beauty and mystery of feathers (1995: 15–20).

Wearing feathers is a great honor in Osage country and Revard images this ritual gesture in "Paint and Feathers," a eulogy for a young Osage man whose life was cut short in an automobile accident. When the police find him, "they do not notice feathers / from scissortails blowing in / the midnight wind" (1992: 39). But it is these feathers plucked recently from a dead bird along the road that help define this man's tribal identity as they blow in his hair. Revard mitigates the tragedy by describing the narrator as equipping the man for his journey to the next world as he ties sacred feathers in his hair:

> ... white
> eagle plumes I fasten now
> into your hair, so you
> may have the sun's power
> and travel with him. (39)

This funerary rite is melded into reminiscences of the young man's naming ceremony where he was symbolically identified with a "male star" and thus to the Osage creation story. At once, as the poet paints crimson arcs on the departed man's face and ties eagle plumes into his hair, "present time," the "now" of the poem, transforms into the mythic time of the ancestors. Wearing a sun disc of mother of pearl around his neck, the departed may now:

> ... stand and see
> all life within your vision
> all colors of it in
> horizon's circle, changing
> and still as sun at noon. (39)

This Osage man has been fully prepared for his journey to the spirit world, where his vision has been broadened by the sacred energy of the white eagle plumes, in order that he may see infinitesimally far into the interpenetrating networks of spirit. "Paint and Feathers" ends fittingly with the affirmation that relatives will continue to pray for him: "At the Sun Dance, little brother, / we will dance for you" (39). And in the sky world where "the feather / will fly itself" buoyed by the currents of air, the departed Osage will likewise gain the power of flight, sustaining his journey into the next life, just as the scissortail feather which the young man puts in his hair moments before his death symbolizes the transcendence he will soon achieve through his people's last farewell rites for him (39).

One of Revard's best known poems, "What the Eagle Fan Says," is composed in the form of an Old English riddle, told from the perspective, one guesses, of an eagle spirit embodied in a feathered fan. Long a scholar of Old English and Middle English poetry, Revard models this cryptic Plains poem on alliterative Anglo Saxon verse. Threading through the clouds, hearing the voices of "human relatives" below on earth, Eagle offers his body to Plains dancers once he has been brought down from the sky. Now implanted in buckskin, the eagle feathers "in a man's left hand, / follow the sun/ soaring toward heaven" (1992: 51). Still the eagle, in a new life of the fan, "move[s] lightly / above dancing feet / around old songs / on human breath / of thunder beings/ of spinning flight . . . " to "help them rise" (51). Having been gifted with eagle feathers himself, the poet thanks the spirits of the sky world for allowing this spiritual messenger bird to uplift his people.

Revard's book, *An Eagle Nation*, reinforces this bond between humans and eagles, not only in the title but also in individual poems such as "Close Encounters," where the link between Osage and ancestral eagles is clear. Revard writes of the Golden Eagles, as well as Red Bird, Cedar Tree, and Black Bear, who mythically allowed Osage to "take their bodies," and their own food, "great showers of acorns, seeds for / . . . our daily bread" (1993: 25). And within this same volume, in the title poem, Revard describes an event that occurred when his family visited the Oke City Zoo. A wounded bald eagle impervious to the whistles of "a nice white couple" turned his head and spoke in a "low shrill sound" to Aunt Jewell, who "from her wheelchair, spoke in Ponca to him," calling him "*Kahgay: Brother*" (32). The poet observed: "I knew she was saying good things for us. / I knew he'd pass them on" (33). This power of communication between traditional Native elders and the Bird People seems to be one fundamental means of insuring that the spirit world is beneficent, bestowing blessings upon generations of Ponca and Osage.

In his poetic translation of "The Swan's Song," an Old English riddle from the *Exeter Book*, a tenth century British collection of poetry on mystical themes, Revard establishes the regal dignity of this magnificent bird. If this were merely yet another translation of this thousand year old poem, perhaps it would go unnoticed, but the imagery of this translation is also appropriate for a poet interested in present-day tribal concerns:

The Swan's Song

> Garbed in silence   I go on earth,
> dwell among men   move on the waters.
> Yet far over halls   of heroes in time
> my robes and the high   air may raise
> and bear me up   in heaven's power
> over all nations.   My ornaments then
> are singing glories,   and I go in song
> bright as a star   unstaying above
> the world's wide waters,   a wayfaring soul. (1998: 177–78)

The swan, at home on earth, on land or water, flies over humans, including heroes from oral traditional tales. He is indeed of the earth, in the natural world, but also at home with the spirits above "all nations" (178). The swan describes himself on his flight path: "I go in song / bright as a star," thus symbolically linking himself, likely for Revard, to the Osage, who are intrinsically Star People (178). And in the "Beads, Wampum, Money, Words—and Old English Riddles" essay, Revard calls this "wayfaring spirit," the swan, a "traveling spirit," perhaps a metaphor for ancient Native wanderers singing traveling songs (1999: 182). The swan then becomes an image of humanity in its fullest spiritual expression.

In reflecting upon the origins of the world in "Dancing with Dinosaurs," Revard theorizes that birds were originally dinosaurs that sprouted feathered wings as a survival strategy: "Before we came to earth, / before the birds had come, / they were dinosaurs, / their feathers were a bright idea" (1980: 60). Admitting that he has "mythicized" the dinosaur-bird transformation hypothesized by scientists, Revard continues this mythic revelation in "Walking Among the Stars." He writes: "I have noticed that we Indians put on feathers to survive, as the dinosaurs did, and that we sing as the birds do, when we dance in our feathers to bring the new children into our circle, when we sing the old songs, we are doing just what the old Osage Naming Ceremonies, linked to our Creation Stories, describe" (1998: 25). Since, as the young narrator

Omishto in Linda Hogan's novel *Power* attests, "[E]verything, our words, our intentions, travels by air" (1998: 3), Carter Revard's strategy of intimately knowing and "naming the birds" is a means of recognizing the cosmic forces that animate, shape, and travel the natural world (1998: 108). Carter Revard stands strong among other learned Native American poets such as Scott Momaday, Geary Hobson, and Joy Harjo who join the singers of antiquity in envisioning the sacred grace of birds in flight.

Works Cited

Hogan, L. 1995. *Dwellings: A Spiritual History of the Living World*. New York: W.W. Norton.
——. *Power*. 1998. New York: W.W. Norton.
Oliver, M. 2000, 15 June. "Luis F. Baptista: Ornithologist Mastered the Dialects of Birds." *Los Angeles Times*. 9.
Revard, C. 1980. *Ponca War Dancers*. Norman, Oklahoma: Point Riders Press.
——. 1992. *Cowboys and Indians, Christmas Shopping*. Norman Oklahoma: Point Riders Press.
——. 1993. *An Eagle Nation*. Tucson: University of Arizona Press.
——. 1998. *Tribal Matters, Family Affairs*. Tucson: University of Arizona Press.
——. 1999. "Beads, Wampum, Money, Words—and Old English Riddles." *American Indian Culture and Research Journal* 23.1: 177–89.
Toledo, J. R. 1991, 26 October. Personal Communication to S. Scarberry-Garcia.

"The Voices Still Are Singing": Osage/Ponca Continuance in the Poetry of Carter Revard

Patrice Hollrah

Family Stories

The quotation that introduces the title of this essay is from the end of Osage poet Carter Revard's poem "An Eagle Nation." The poem was first published as "Eagles, Drums, and a Ponca Elder" in *Indian Youth of America Newsletter*, and later included in the collection of the same title, *An Eagle Nation* (Revard 1993: 31–34). The Ponca Elder of the original title is Revard's Aunt Jewell McDonald Camp Farmer. The poem is now included in Revard's most recent collection *How the Songs Come Down: New and Selected Poems* (2005: 40–44), and speaks to the survival of Revard's Osage and Ponca family members and the continuity of tribal culture. In fact, the poem's dedication is similar to the one for the entire *An Eagle Nation* collection. The collection's dedication reads, "*This book / is / for the Wazhazhe* [Osage] *and Ponca Nations / and all our relations*" (1993: dedication page), and the poem's dedication reads, "For the Camp/Jump brigades," the family names of Revard's Ponca and Osage relations (1993: 31). The poem's dedication also telescopes from the larger community of the collection's dedication to Revard's family relations. In an inverse way, the poem's love and respect for the family members expands out to include the larger groups of the Osage and Ponca Nations.

The militaristic choice of "brigades" to represent these two Native groups resonates with the idea of the Osages and Poncas as two army regiments or squadrons, trained in the defense of their homelands, nations, and culture, a persuasively accurate description. However, after Revard heard this explication at the 2005 Native American Literature Symposium (held at Mystic Lake Casino and Hotel, April 7–9, 2005), he graciously explained that his mother fondly used the expression to describe the families. Revard fills his poetry with stories of family members, and his Ponca Aunt Jewell in particular is a key figure that represents "someone who is respected for living in good Indian ways" (2001: 175). Describing Aunt Jewell as a "valued and respected" elder, Revard writes about "how important the older people are to [Natives'] survival and to making [their] survival a good one" (2001: 175).

An example of this role of making a good survival for the people is Aunt Jewell as Keeper of the Drum. The note for her photograph on the front cover of *How the Songs Come Down* (2005) reads, "Center: Mrs. Jewell McDonald Camp Farmer (1914–1999). Keeper (through her mother, Julia Fastwalker) of the Pah-Tha-Tau Drum of the Ponca People. . . . The Drum, which dates from the 1880s, continues through her daughters, granddaughters, and great-granddaughters, who still honour the Drum with semi-annual dances" (back cover). Aunt Jewell is shown in the center of two members of the Women's Society, and she holds a place of honor as the Keeper of the drum, a position that will pass down to the women in her family through future generations. This essay considers poems that illustrate how tribal culture passes from one generation to the next. These poems have all been included in the 2005 collection *How the Songs Come Down*: the first poem is "How the Songs Came Down" from the 1980 collection *Ponca War Dancers* and re-titled in the new collection in the present tense as "How the Songs Come Down" (49–52; 2005: 65–69); the second poem is "An Eagle Nation" from the 1993 eponymous collection (31–34; 2005: 40–44); the third poem is "Aunt Jewell as Powwow Princess" from the 2001 memoir *Winning the Dust Bowl* (179–83; 2005: 51); and the last poem is "Given" from the 1992 collection *Cowboys and Indians, Christmas Shopping* (62–63; 2005: 86). Some of the poems have a different typography in their original publication, but all references will be taken from *How the Songs Come Down*.

Maintaining traditions is an important aspect of Native American tribal cultures. Taiaiake Alfred, a leading Kanien'kehaka (Mohawk) scholar and activist, writes, "Native leaders must aspire to embody traditional values" (1999: xvi) as "the basis on which to build a better society" (1999: xviii). In the two poems "Aunt Jewell as Powwow Princess" and "An Eagle Nation," Aunt Jewell passes traditional values to the younger people, and Revard passes those values to the next generation in the poem "Given," thereby enacting what Alfred advocates: a demonstration of traditional values as a means by which to improve the group. The continuation of traditional values is an act of decolonization, an act of continuance and survival, an act of self-determination, or as Revard characterizes his poems, a way of "[building] a small community in which people can live a little more completely and joyously than solitude allows" (Revard 2001: xvi). Revard emphasizes the communal nature of tribal people, the need to be with others, and the sharing of language that enlarges the human experience in a positive way.

Revard portrays Aunt Jewell as someone who helps people live more fully. Lakota anthropologist Beatrice Medicine writes about the role of Native women in the transmission of culture:

> With such a diverse and varied range of living examples, one can . . . see a variety of ways of presenting the role of native women in caring for children and passing on cultural knowledge. The commonly held and frequently expressed belief that women are "the carriers of native culture" has reached slogan-like status at conferences and community gatherings. As appealing as this theme is, however, it poses some dilemmas for understanding women in both traditional and modern Indian societies. Many native women reject the call to political activism in the wider women's movement while praising the importance of women in the maintenance of traditional tribal life. Similarly, Indian women are prone to say that their preeminent concern is with community survival—treaty rights, the protection of native resources, and child welfare—rather than with making common cause with other women in the struggle for equality. (2005: n. p.)

Medicine succinctly discusses the difference between how mainstream feminist readers tend to view the image of strong Native women and how Native women see their roles. One can easily assess Aunt Jewell's role as that of an important Ponca woman who has raised children, including Revard, when his family spent time on the Ponca Reservation with Aunt Jewell, her great-aunt, and her mother, as described in his 1998 memoir *Family Matters, Tribal Affairs* (1998: 16). Aunt Jewell's important role in the tribe/family is also an example of gender complementarity, a tribal construct of gender relationships, typically women and men, in which they have their complementary roles within the group, each one being important and valuable to the well-being of the tribe.

"How the Songs Come Down"

Aunt Jewell also has contributed to the maintenance of traditional tribal life, for example, through songs, as Revard notes in the poem "How the Songs Come Down," originally from his 1980 collection *Ponca War Dancers*, and now in his new collection:

> the songs come down. That lullaby our Ponca aunt would sing,
>   the one we always asked for when
>   sleep could not get to us past
> the werewolves who howled
>   inside the radio, she would sing to us
> over and over, but she never told us, out there on
>   the cool dark porch under the full moon,
> what the Ponca words were saying: it was a song her blind
>   great-aunt had made up after the Poncas
> had been forced down from Nebraska onto
>   the Oklahoma reservation, and she made it there
> one night to sing to her brothers when the whisky
>   was almost drowning them: its words said,
>   *Why are you afraid?*
>   *No one can go around death.* (2005: 68)

In *Family Matters, Tribal Affairs*, Revard writes a prose account of composing "How the Songs Come Down" and how Aunt Jewell would sing a particular song to help them sleep:

> I have written . . . of the song we used to ask Aunt Jewell to sing us later, the Ponca song we could go to sleep unafraid with, and how it turned out that its Ponca words said, "What are you afraid of? No one can go around Death!" The aunt had made that song when, in Oklahoma, her brothers were so discouraged and the whiskey was getting the Poncas down so far, that she found this strongheart song, a warrior song to encourage them. (1998: 16)

Aunt Jewell's great-aunt is the composer of the song, but Aunt Jewell is the one who sings it for Revard, an example of the song crossing three generations. The song's lyrics and the poem describe the history of the family and tribe, of being forced to move to the reservation and of the ensuing alcoholism. Nevertheless, the song and poem also speak of encouragement in the face of forced relocation, a sign of strength, continuance, and survival. The question about fear implies that the people should not be afraid, that death is a natural occurrence, and the lack of fear suggests that death will not be the end of the people. The "strongheart song, a warrior song" becomes a lullaby for the children, so they will be comforted when falling asleep and have no fear of what the night and dreams might bring. Although the great-aunt who composes the song cannot see, she has the vision to see what her relatives need, and Aunt Jewell carries on that tradition by singing the song for the children.

The concluding lines of "How the Songs Come Down" show Aunt Jewell as an elder who reaches the point where she must share her songs with her children, the next generation:

> She tells her children lately now, Aunt Jewell, some of
>   those real old things,
>   now that the time has come
> to pass them on, and they are ready
>   to make new places for what she
>   would sing us in
> our moonlit darkness like
>   a bronze and lively bird. (2005: 69).

Although the juxtaposition of lifeless and animate images in the simile "like a bronze and lively bird" recalls the singing gold bird in William Butler Yeats' "Sailing to Byzantium," more potent is the image of a brown/"bronze" Native woman whose song speaks of mythic time, conflating details of the past with the present and a permanence that will move into the future, an image of survival. Revard also uses the symbol of the "bird" to speak about the continuance of the songs and dances in the dedication of *How the Songs Come Down*:

> *Dedication*
> *to*
>
> *the small birds only*
> *whose life continues on the gourd,*
> *whose life continues in our dance,*
> . . .
> *now they will sing and we*
> *are dancing with them, here.* (2005: n. p.)

The bird signifies continuance of the people's participation in the songs and dances. Clearly, Aunt Jewell, represented as a "bronze and lively bird," is a carrier of traditional Ponca culture, sharing the stories and traditional knowledge that must be continued, as Revard says, for a more joyous community.

"An Eagle Nation"

In the poem "An Eagle Nation," Aunt Jewell is the prominent character in the narrative and serves as a vehicle for meditating on how Revard's Ponca, Osage, Irish and Scotch-Irish ancestors converged over time in Oklahoma. Aunt Jewell's journey of traveling to the zoo, speaking to a caged bald eagle, and attending the Red Earth powwow to watch her grandson dance, offer an opportunity to reflect on how the family has survived despite "how it all has changed" (2005: 43). The poem opens with a memory of Aunt Jewell being physically flexible:

> You see, I remember this little Ponca woman
> who turned her back to the wall and placed her palms
> up over her shoulders flat on the wall
> and bent over backwards and walked her hands down the wall
> and placed them flat on the floor behind her back—that's
> how limber she was ... (2005: 40)

The characterization of Aunt Jewell as "little" applies only to her physical size because as the poem unfolds, her stature as a respected elder proves quite powerful. The image of her backbend conjures notions of flexibility, or adaptability, a necessary ingredient for survival, as she pushes against the "wall," an object of resistance mentioned three times. Aunt Jewell also seems rather remarkable, like an acrobat who amazes the audience with her tricks of bending in half like a rubber band, and the image of her flexibility impresses Revard as young boy.

In addition to Aunt Jewell's athletic ability, Revard also marvels at her speed. In her youth, Aunt Jewell was a sprinter: "And FAST! You wouldn't BELIEVE how she could sprint: / when an Osage couple married, they would ask Aunt Jewell / to run for the horses for them" (2005: 40). Historically, horses played a role in marriage for both the Osages and the Poncas. Garrick A. Bailey writes about the Osage bride in the marriage ceremony: "On the second day, the bride, dressed in special wedding clothes, mounted a horse and traveled to the home of the groom, followed by her relatives on foot" (2001: 485). Donald N. Brown and Lee Irwin write about the Ponca courtship in the late nineteenth century: "A young man gave horses and buffalo robes to the family of his prospective wife" (2001: 422). Revard includes information about Aunt Jewell that illustrates how historical marriage customs involving horses adapted and evolved. Her speed is a trait that does not diminish as she ages but only changes contexts:

> Now she's the eldest in her clan, but still the fastest
> to bring the right word, Ponca or English, sacred or
> profane, whatever's needed to survive she brings it, sometimes in
> a wheelchair, since her heart alarms
> the doctors now and then. (2005: 40)

Revard's admiration for Aunt Jewell's talents grows as her verbal dexterity in language replaces her physical flexibility and speed, a skill that benefits not only herself but also all those around her. The emphasis on Aunt Jewell's bilingual talents underscores the importance of the role of her native Ponca language and English in communicating with her people and those outsiders who do not speak the Ponca language. Aunt Jewell might be in a wheelchair, no longer sprinting, but her tongue is quick to say whatever needs to be said for survival.

In the poem, as the family prepares to travel to the Oke City Zoo for a picnic, Revard emphasizes the many grandchildren that Aunt Jewell has, so many, in fact, that they "stopped counting years ago" (2005: 40). Cherokee scholar Donna Hightower Langston writes about motherhood and aging for Native women: "Being a mother or grandmother increases one's status in Indian country. . . . Aging . . . in traditional Indian communities . . . is a sign of power and status, something women might look forward to. . . (2004: 130). The legacy of grandchildren indicates continuance of the people, one more element in Aunt Jewell's growing status, and provides a connection to a later part of the poem at the Red Earth powwow.

The different threads of "An Eagle Nation" continue to interweave, and Aunt Jewell's Ponca language reappears when she speaks to the caged bald eagle at the zoo. The sign on the cage reads like a metaphor for the Natives forced onto reservations:

> *This bald eagle was found wounded, and*
> *although its life was saved, it will never fly again,*
> *so it is given this cage to itself.*
> *Please do not feed him.* (2005: 41)

In contrast to a white couple who has tried unsuccessfully to catch the eagle's attention, Aunt Jewell speaks respectfully to him in Ponca, and the eagle responds by opening his eyes, turning his head, and making a "low shrill sound" (2005: 42). Overcome with emotion at the understanding between herself and the eagle, Aunt Jewell tears up. The connection between Aunt Jewell's native language and the eagle reaffirms the importance of the language in communicating with the world around her.

Instead of returning home after the visit to the zoo, Aunt Jewell wants to continue on to the Red Earth powwow to see her grandson Wesley dance. When the family arrives and learns that they have to pay admission, they are offended because they believe that a powwow should be free. Aunt Jewell says, "That's not our way" (2005: 42), indicating the changes that have evolved in these gatherings. When the family sees Wesley on the Arena floor, they also see Grampa Paul Roughface "gliding/with that eagle's calm he has" (2005: 42), another comparison to the grace and strength of the caged eagle at the zoo. The poem ends with Revard's eagle's eye view of all the previous images—family, eagles, land, dancing, drums, song, and the changes they have endured—all converging on the dance floor, but the prevailing theme is that despite "how it all has changed," the people are still here:

> the voices still
> are singing, the drum-heart
> still beating here, so whatever the placards on
> their iron cages may have to say, we the people,
> as Aunt Jewell and Sun Dancers say,
> are an EAGLE NATION, now. (2005: 43–44)

"We the people" echoes well-known language from the U.S. Constitution:

> We the People of the United States, in Order to form a more perfect Union, establish Justice, insure domestic Tranquility, provide for the common defense, promote the general Welfare, and secure the Blessings of Liberty to ourselves and our Posterity, do ordain and establish this Constitution for the United States of America. (National Archives 2005)

Although Revard uses familiar language from a U.S. federal charter of freedom, he does so to affirm the sovereignty of the Eagle Nation and the sovereign nation-to-sovereign nation relationship between the Eagle Nation and the United States. Regardless of any changes throughout history or signs on real or metaphorical cages, the people are still here. Following "we the people" is the placement of Aunt Jewell as an equal with the sacred Sun Dancers, which illustrates her high status, and jointly they claim their existence as a nation of people characterized by the unruffled power of the eagle. The final word of the poem, "now," emphasizes the survival of the people, that the singing and beating will continue.

"Aunt Jewell as Powwow Princess"

Aunt Jewell's status continues in the poem "Aunt Jewell as Powwow Princess." Revard explains the context of the poem, the 1995 Cahokia Powwow at which Aunt Jewell was named Powwow Princess because the organizers wanted to show how important the elders are to the survival of the people. Langston notes, "Many female elders find that their status as elders enhances their political participation and contributions to future generations" (2003: 130). Aunt Jewell once again passes on information to Revard. This poem repeats many of the images found in "An Eagle Nation"—such as powwow dancing, the Sun Dance, Revard's "Ponca family as / an Eagle Nation," (2005: 52) and the words to describe the caged bald eagle, "KAH-GEH, 'brother'" (2005: 53)—but most importantly, Aunt Jewell once again passes on lessons to Revard. When he sees Aunt Jewell's dead brother, Uncle Gus, dancing, she helps Revard to understand what he has seen, that sometimes the Old People "want / to come into the circle and dance" (2005: 52). Aunt Jewell's most important directive is to listen:

> Aunt Jewell said, LISTEN, and I said I heard
> them singing KAH-GEH, "brother," and I looked at her
> but she said firmly LISTEN to the WORDS,
> and finally I heard: SHON-GEH-SKAH,
> White Horse, Uncle Gus's name, they sang.
> So then I understood
> why she was telling me about the Sun Dance; it was because
> that afternoon she'd seen—without my saying anything—
> that I was worried . . . (2005: 53)

As in the last line of "An Eagle Nation," Aunt Jewell is once again associated with the sacred Sun Dance. Only a respected and honorable woman holds such high status, and her instructions to Revard are to listen because that is how he will learn and understand.

Honor and respect for the elders moves in the poem from Aunt Jewell to Uncle Gus to the five hundred Harley Davidson riders who bring bags of food for the American Indian Center of Mid-America food pantry (2005: 54–55). The bike riders show respect for the community, and in turn the singers sing an honor song for the riders. The poem ends with a "heavy rain," reinforcing the replenishing image of the food donations. Revard says, "his experiences growing up with [Aunt Jewell's] Ponca songs and powwows on the reservation, and later in life as a powwow organizer and gourd dancer, have shown him song and dance are vital to humanity: "The dances and the songs bring us together, and keep our histories alive, and help us survive" (Ziegler 2005: n. p.). The powwow provides the context for the Harley Davidson riders to join the community, for the Natives to benefit from their generous donations, for the ancestral spirits to visit their relatives, and for the cultural traditions to continue.

"Given"

"Given" is the last poem of the collection *Cowboys and Indians, Christmas Shopping* and continues the idea of giving and singing, but rather than humans giving and singing to one another, the narrator speaks about the world that is given to its inhabitants. The poem's dedication is "for the children," and I would argue that Revard passes on information to the younger generations just as Aunt Jewell did with him. In fact, in answering a question about "the role and responsibilities of non-Indian scholars who read, interpret, and comment on Indian fiction and poetry," Revard says, "They need to give respect, care, need to work hard to think and feel their way into the spoken or written stories, need to listen with great care to the people who understand better than they do or can and learn all they can from them. They should give credit to them as scholars are expected to give credit to those from whom they have learned" (2003: 141). He has learned the lessons of listening that Aunt Jewell taught him, and he has passed on that important information.

In "Given" he writes, "We see, we *learn* / to see and hear and feel" (2005: 86), as he describes the regenerative forces of nature in spring, the connections among earth, sky, animals, and humans, and the earth's singing that joins everything:

> we look up into
> those heavens of green and blue and white where the trees
> without moving are given the earth and
> the sun and the stars, and those who have wings now
> are singing and those who have climbed
> from sea to earth and air and live now on dew and the tree's
> plenty are singing where the moon brings back
> a softer light from the sun, where the stars bring us the great
> glittering darkness that has no end. (2005: 87)

Revard has written about the theory of birds developing from a particular group of dinosaurs: "I like to think of a robin as a tiny Tyrannosaurus who put on feathers and survived, who learned to sing and has human approval therefore, and who understands that when the stars dim and the sun brightens for us we move from the great mystery of infinity to the great mystery of here and now in a way only song can celebrate" (1998: 186, n. 4). Birds, for Revard, are the connections between the cosmos and people, between the unknown and known, and they carry the songs that connect everything.

Revard's poems are songs that connect everything. He explains why he writes poems: "I write poems because the world has music, and we need to sing along. I don't think music and singing are just for fun or for pleasure. I think music and song come down from way back in dinosaur time. And ever since the first hisses got tuned into whistling, the music has socialized the singers, has created communities" (Ziegler 2005: n. p.). In other words, the songs and music are important for conveying cultural information that is necessary for the health and well being of the group. Aunt Jewell has passed on the songs and music to her family and tribe, an example of the woman passing on culture that is important for the survival of the community. In the same way that Aunt Jewell has given this cultural gift to the next generation, Revard continues that tradition. His poems are for the larger community, not just for a "small community" (2001: xvi) as he modestly says is the purpose of his poetry, but for anyone who will listen because "the voices still / are singing" (2005: 43–44).

I end with Revard's appropriate words about teaching the works of Native American writers:

> Indian writers will always be a few voices in a babbling crowd, and to be heard at all they need to be strong clear voices. To be heard AND listened to, a voice must be saying something that makes a difference to the listener—and that necessarily means bringing laughter, or tears, or understanding, or a need for action and a way to act effectively. A teacher who finds poems, stories, commentaries that speak clearly and bring these results, will be a useful teacher, not just an academic but a part of a community and helping strengthen and lighten and hearten the community. (2003b:10)

Works Cited

Alfred, T. 1999. *Peace, Power, Righteousness: An Indigenous Manifesto*. Don Mills, Ontario: Oxford University Press.
Bailey, G. A. 2001. "Osage." *Handbook of North American Indians*. Vol. 13. Part 1. General Ed. W. C. Surtevant, Washington: Smithsonian Institution. 476–96.
Brown, D. N., and L. Irwin. 2001. "Ponca." *Handbook of North American Indians*. Vol. 13. Part 1. General Ed. W. C. Surtevant, Washington: Smithsonian Institution. 416–31.
Langston, D. H. 2003. "American Indian Women's Activism in the 1960s and 1970s." *Hypatia* 18.2: 114–32.
Medicine, B. 2005. "Women." *Encyclopedia of North American Indians*. Houghton Mifflin. 4 Apr. 2005. http://college.hmco.com/history/readerscomp/naind/html/na_043400_women.htm.
National Archives and Records Administration. 2005. *The National Archives Experience*. 29 June 2005. http://www.archives.gov/national_archives_experience/charters/constitution_transcript.html.
Revard, C. 1980. *Ponca War Dancers*. Norman, Oklahoma: Point Riders Press.
———. 1992. *Cowboys and Indians, Christmas Shopping*. Norman, Oklahoma: Point Riders Press.
———. 1993. *An Eagle Nation*. Tucson: University of Arizona Press.
———. 1998. *Family Matters, Tribal Affairs*. Tucson: University of Arizona Press.
———. 2001. *Winning the Dust Bowl*. Tucson: University of Arizona Press.

———. 2003a. "Crossing Cultures: An Online Interview with Carter Revard." *Studies in American Indian Literatures* 15.1: 139–141.
———. 2003b. "Some Notes on Native American Literature." *Studies in American Indian Literatures* 15.1: 1–15.
———. 2005. *How the Songs Come Down: New and Selected Poems.* Cambridge, U.K.: Salt Publishing.
Ziegler, E. 2005. "Indian Poet Sees Work as Way to Unite People in Peace." *The Pocatello Idaho State Journal.* 5 Apr. 2005. http://www.journalnet.com/articles/2005/04/05/news/local/news12.prt.

"Ponca War Dancers": Creating a Pan-Indian Circle

Robert M. Nelson

First published in the journal *River Styx*, "Ponca War Dancers" is also the title poem of Carter Revard's book of poems published by Point Riders Press in 1980. Like much of Revard's other work, "Ponca War Dancers" is a narrative poem featuring an informally exuberant and seemingly inexhaustible storytelling voice, weaving back and forth through time and space, coating its backbone of story with a rich accretion of family anecdote and diversional wordplay—qualities which appear at their most flamboyant in stanza 3.

    The title refers to the members of the *Helushka* Society, a Ponca warrior society roughly analogous to the legendary Cheyenne Dog Soldiers. In his 1989 essay "Songs of the Ponca: *Helushka*," Jim Charles, himself a *Helushka* dancer, notes that "*Helushka* is an ancient word, and its literal meaning is unknown to [present-day] Poncas" (3). Charles tells us that early anthropologists "erroneously" translated *helushka* as "war dance" but that "most members of the *Helushka* were warriors and war heroes" (3). Reflecting the history of many American Indian traditions, the *Helushka* was disbanded around 1920, during the terrible latter years of the period of coercive assimilation, but revived in 1958; today, according to Charles, "the term refers to the synthesis of songs and dance, beliefs and way of life of the *Helushka* Society" (3). In this synthesis, the Ponca war dance is just the visible part of *helushka*, the kinetic expression of whatever personal vision or accomplishment is being commemorated in the form of dance. The songs, and the stories *behind* those songs, are equally part of *helushka*, each one just a part of "the long story of the People."[1]

Stanza 1: Uncle Gus

Our first glimpse of the poem's protagonist, Uncle Gus, emphasizes his traditionalism, as well as the depth and breadth of the estrangement of his traditional Ponca ways from the lifeway of many a young adult Indian in the latter part of the twentieth century. Raised to the norms of conventional mainstream civility, his new niece-in-law violates traditional "Ponca ways" by speaking directly to him instead of properly either avoiding conversation with an in-law of the opposite sex altogether or addressing him only indirectly through conversation with others (both behaviors modeled by Uncle Gus, to no avail, in this stanza). Ethical estrangement becomes physical and geographical when "he quietly / left Kansas City" (1980: 53), presumably both to preserve what is left of traditional Ponca social behavior and at the same time to protect his new kinswoman's good name from the consequences of her inadvertent overfamiliarity.

Stanza 2: Circles of Vision

This disjunction between Uncle Gus and his urban Indian in-law is repeated in the narrator's own perspective as it informs the opening movements of the second stanza, allowing us to view Uncle Gus through the lens of the narrator's own ambivalence.

The very first line of the second stanza links Uncle Gus's quiet traditionalism, established in the first stanza, to his status as "the greatest of Ponca dancers" (53); the suggestion here is that knowing and living the traditions is a prerequisite to dancing well in the traditional way. Ponca dancers are widely acknowledged in Indian Country to be the best traditional dancers, typically taking top prizes in this category of dance at intertribal powwows, so being "the greatest of Ponca dancers" establishes Uncle Gus as a paragon of traditionalism. And Uncle Gus succeeds in making traditionalism visible even to the narrator, who until this moment never dreamed that this "heavy-bellied / quick-talking man / that kids swarmed around" (53) was capable of such motion. Formally,

---

[1] The quoted phrase is Leslie Silko's: see "I Always Called Her Aunt Susie" in *Storyteller* (1981: 7).

this image of Uncle Gus, in his role as a Ponca war dancer articulating "the Spirit's dance" (54), functions as the central point or hub of stanza 2, around which both emic and etic perspectives gather in much the same way Uncle Gus's motion with respect to the drum generates "Wakondah's circle" (54).[2] Farthest from the center on one side of this formal structure, in the early lines of stanza 2, are the uninitiated eyes of the narrator who sees Uncle Gus going "off to drink" with "some of my white uncles" and who "never understood" this kinsman until "when he was sixty-something / I saw him dance for the first time" (53); on the other side of this stanza, in its closing lines, we are given a glimpse of the peripheral, etic circle of "bleachers and tourists," those "white eyes watching" which see only "an old Indian slowing down / and between dances going / to have another slug of / hell, maybe Old Crow or even / Canadian Club, / good enough for the champion" (54).[3] Located between Uncle Gus and the etic circle of tourists is the circle of "grave, merry faces" of the emic audience: "Osage and Ponca" but also "Otoe and Delaware, / Quapaw and Omaha, Pawnee Comanche and Kaw," in short a pan-Indian circle of vision whose identity with Uncle Gus and the dance is confirmed by their shared ability to "[see] what he was doing / and how he did it well" (54). This circle of emic vision is mirrored formally on the other side of this stanza by the emic members of the audience, located between the narrator's uninitiated eyes and the image of Uncle Gus dancing, who "got quiet / except to whisper / 'the champion.'" Along with the narrator, they see Gus, "potbellied but quick-footed," caught up "light as a leaf in a whirlwind" (54), his motion articulating the otherwise invisible motion called Wahkondah in Ponca.[4]

2   Readers familiar with the Native American novel tradition may recall the emic/etic fluctuation of perspective that Archilde Leon, the protagonist of D'Arcy McNickle's 1936 *The Surrounded*, experiences while watching the blind old man Modeste perform traditional dance in chapter 24. In Revard's presentation, however, there is no fluctuation, but rather a steady "pan" of visual field that remains clearly centered on the image of "the greatest of Ponca war dancers."

3   There is wry irony in Revard's choice of names of whiskeys, "Old Crow" suggesting Indianness and "Canadian Club" suggesting the ethnicity of "that 'Gatsby' bunch" (Kennedys) that appears in the next stanza. The irony is further heightened by a grammatical ambiguity accentuated by the pause of the line break: the whiskey is a "slug of / hell" regardless of brand name, a far cry from that other "Spirit" ("Wahkondah") that enables Uncle Gus to dance as well as he does.

4   Charles' spelling is "Wakonda"; for an extended definition of the term (quoting from Fletcher and La Flesche's 1905 *The Omaha Tribe*), see "Songs of the Ponca" (1989: 12).

What they are seeing, as well, is the renewed and renewing identity that Gus creates between himself and the drum, the fusion of the motion of his spirit vision and the motion of sound in the motion of his dance.

Uncle Gus's own vision—the one he acquired "in a strange land where / he had gone and fasted" and which informs his performance in this stanza—is a traditional power vision, one that authorizes him to function as a role model and "to lead his people" (54). It is important to recognize here that Gus's vision also anticipates the need to resolve the distance separating emic from etic space: as the narrator puts it, there was "nowhere to lead them except / into white ways" (54). In a sense, then, we are invited to see Uncle Gus as modeling a positive strategy for coming to terms with the forces of cultural assimilation—the strategy of clearing a space in the white world for Native traditionalism, a space created by traditional vision and buffered from outside forces by a protective circle of knowing, appreciative audience. This circle of witness, in turn, functions in the role of traditional warriors—those who, like the Ponca *Helushka* society members, the Cheyenne Dog Soldiers, and the Kiowa *Kaitsenko*, commit their lives to preserving elders like Uncle Gus and the ways these elders embody.

Stanza 3: AIM and Wounded Knee

Several references to the American Indian Movement or "AIM," and especially to the AIM occupation of Wounded Knee, work to establish the role of that event and its participants in the coalescence of an emerging pan-Indian identity. The stanza opens by locating the narrative as taking place "a year after Wounded Knee" (55) rather than in the more familiar (to an etic audience) "year 1974," suggesting that the events of Wounded Knee mark a watershed, transformative moment in Indian history, a temporal site in terms of which history may be meaningfully located as "before" or "after" that event. Indeed, one of the first signifying attributes of the narrator's comrades in stanza 3 is that they are "all strong in AIM" (in the text this phrase is set off formally on its own separate line) but "none of them underground yet / from Wounded Knee" (55). In many ways analogous to the Black Panther movement on the West Coast, AIM originated as an ad-hoc urban Indian movement in the Twin Cities (Minneapolis-St. Paul, Minnesota) committed to community uplift work as well as to the defense of the community against local police violence and other forms of civil rights violation. By 1974, the time of the poem, the AIM movement had attracted national attention through a series of increasingly more coordinated and more militant activities, beginning with its involvement in the 1971 occupation of Alcatraz Island and running through its part in the 1972 "Trail of Broken Treaties Caravan," a transcontinental march on Washington, D.C., which culminated in the trashing of the BIA building, to the highly publicized occupation of Wounded Knee, a crossroads village on the Pine Ridge (Oglala Sioux) reservation, in the early months of 1973.[5] The Forty-Nine song the car's occupants are singing, which begins "*Let's all go up to Porcupine*," also identifies them as familiar with the Pine Ridge reservation, Porcupine being a village to the north of Wounded Knee where some of the activities most important to the traditional members of the Pine Ridge population take place. In this song, the town of Porcupine figures metonymically as the place where this new generation of Indians gathers to "*dance the Forty-Nine*" (56).[6]

Roughly speaking, the schism between "traditionals" and "progressives" on the Pine Ridge reservation (as elsewhere in Indian country at

---

5   Most readers will also recognize Wounded Knee as the name of the site where, in 1890, Big Foot's band of 350 Miniconjou Sioux refugees was massacred by the U.S. 7th Cavalry, an event which most students of frontier history take to be the last battle of the "Indian wars." For a comprehensive history of the AIM movement, see Paul Chaat Smith and Robert Warrior, *Like a Hurricane* (1996); for a credible account of the AIM's involvement in the events of Wounded Knee and the virtual civil war taking place at that time on the Pine Ridge reservation, see Peter Matthiessen, *In the Spirit of Crazy Horse* (1980: 58–83); see also *Lakota Woman* (1990), a book co-authored by Mary Crow Dog and Richard Erdoes, which presents itself as an autobiographical account of the 1973 events as witnessed by an insider and which is the basis for a 1994 movie bearing the same title. Revard's cousin Carter Camp, the "Carter" who appears in the poem, was the person in charge of security during the siege; Russell Means and Dennis Banks were the main spokesmen for the AIM participants.

6   For those unfamiliar with 20th century American Indian pop cultural phenomena, a "Forty-Nine" can be thought of as an ad-hoc, more or less clandestine gathering of members of the younger generation that takes place in the midnight hours, often following an "official" powwow. Several different (and sometimes hotly contested) accounts of the genesis of both the name and event exist; for one of the earliest, see Edward Curtis (1930: 215–6). Part songfest, part dance, and all party, the Forty-Nine is also a serious celebration of collective Indian identity: in the "Author's Note" to his play *49*, Hanay Geiogamah states that "[w]hile taking part in a 49, young Indians are in an extremely heightened state of awareness of their 'Indianness' and that "[t]hey achieve, with amazing rapidity and with a minimum of friction, a group conviviality that is intertribal" (1980: 86).

this time[7]) was, until Wounded Knee, a generation gap as well. Traditionals also tended to be elders, born and raised on the reservation and thus to some degree geographically inoculated against many of the forces of cultural assimilation. The progressives, including then-tribal council chairman Dick Wilson and his "goons" (self-proclaimed "Guardians of the Oglala Nation"), were by and large of a younger age, raised in the post-WWII era after two generations of coercive assimilation[8] had succeeded in creating the illusion, among the US white majority as well as throughout Indian Country, that "traditional Indian" and "twentieth century American" were mutually exclusive categories, with members of the former category either vanishing or vanished. Against this cultural backdrop, AIM represents an emerging new identity option, one especially inviting to the more than 50 per cent of culturally disadvantaged Native Americans who by 1960 had been born and raised in urban rather than reservation settings. At Wounded Knee, young AIM members from all over the country allied themselves with Oglala traditional elders and their families against their progressive coevals, turning the generation gap into a new variety of cultural gap: not progressive Oglalas vs. traditional Oglalas but rather Indian anti-traditionalists vs. Indians—of whatever tribe, and including Indians with no clear tribal community to be part of—working as a pan-Indian force to preserve and propagate a distinctive Indianness. What emerges is a new, third variety of Indian community, not reserved to any one tribe or geographically fixed setting, in which relatively young warriors function to defend and preserve their elders and children and in which the elders reciprocally teach the younger members of the community the intra-communal knowledge and beliefs which shape the collective identity. What unites them is the warrior spirit manifested in the social and political activism

---

7 This schism was far from restricted to the inhabitants of the Pine Ridge reservation: practically every reservation community has gone through a similar collective identity crisis at some time or another. Most of them have stopped short, however, of the virtual civil war that was in progress on the Pine Ridge reservation at the time of this poem. Two earlier well-known examples are the 1906 "Hopi Split," which was more or less resolved when Hopi progressives abandoned Old Oraibi and established the new communities at New Oraibi (also known as Kykotsmovi, where the Hopi Tribal Council offices are today) and Moenkopi, and a similar late-nineteenth century fallout at Laguna Pueblo, which resolved when conservatives relocated themselves and their ceremonies in 1881 to neighboring Isleta Pueblo.

8 The term is Edward Spicer's: see *The American Indians*, (1980: 183).

that networks these people together in the common project of preserving traditional Indian vision and values.

Stanza 3: The New Warriors

When read within this context, and recalling the structure of stanza 2, Stanza 3 becomes a portrait of the latest generation of Ponca warriors and also of the pan-Indian circle composed of these Ponca warriors and their non-Ponca allies. Compared to the image of Uncle Gus at the center of stanza 2, they are indeed a motley crew. Crammed into the narrator's old Dodge Dart, on the way to the Ponca City auditorium to attend the funeral feast for Uncle Gus, are at least ten young adults.[9] The first group, "Carter and Craig and Dwain [later called Buck] and Serena," consists of the narrator's (and also the author's) cousins, "sons and daughters of [Uncle Gus'] sister Jewell" (55), that is, all Poncas on their mother's side.[10] Following the pattern established in stanza 2, this quartet of young Ponca warriors is augmented by a second, but this time pan-Indian, group: "Stephanie from Third Mesa" (Hopi), "Mickey / from

---

9   That the automobile is a Dodge Dart is ironic on a number of registers. For one, the Dart was one of the first American compact cars, so that cramming ten bodies into one would be somewhat analogous to seeing how many college kids could be stuffed into a phone booth, a sport that enjoyed a brief rage in the late 1950s; thus, the image of the packed Dart suggests youthful exuberance, not to mention a degree of frivolity, to anyone old enough to be an AIM veteran in 1973. For another, the make of the car, "Dart," is particularly apt given the militancy of at least some of the car's occupants, about a close as one could come in the early '70s to an "arrow" or "tomahawk," two easy icons of Indian warfare. Finally, it is probably no coincidence that the Dart was the particular object of Ralph Nader's *Unsafe at Any Speed* (1965), the popular book that spearheaded his famous campaign against the negligence of the U.S. auto industry. The double irony, for an emic audience at any rate, is the play on the stereotype of the "rezmobile," as often an old truck as an old car, and the allusion to the notoriously high rate on reservations of deaths associated with auto "accidents." There is, too, the slightly less obvious irony attendant on the number of the Dart's occupants—a perhaps intentional play on the once-popular nursery song "Ten Little Indians."

10 The final page of the 1980 Point Riders edition of *Ponca War Dancers* contains a photograph titled "Buck Creek, 1934"; included among the thirteen kinspeople in the photo are Carter Camp, Dwain Camp, Woodrow Camp (who appears as the bootlegger "Uncle Woody" in the poem), Jewell McDonald Camp ("Aunt Jewell"), and Carter Revard and his twin sister Maxine. In the photo, Aunt Jewell's hands rest on the shoulders of young Carter Revard, who is standing in front of her.

Pine Ridge" (Sioux), "Geronimo" (Apache), "Big Jim Jump" (Osage), and "Mary Ann / teaching us Cherokee" (56).

The exuberance of the Indians in the car characterizes the formal structure of this part of the poem as well. Just as the narrator is having trouble singing and driving straight at the same time, the formal structure seems to wander peripatetically between the margins of the page, some lines even appearing to bump up against them and then, like a car sideswiping a guard rail, bouncing back into the poem's narrative space. Enhancing this sense of almost unbridled motion, the first sentence of the stanza runs for 63 lines, or a little over two pages, of text; like the rather difficult feat of packing ten not-so-little Indians into a Dodge Dart, the narrator crams images and information enough to cover some three decades of family history as well as provide a thumbnail history of the American Indian Movement and the subsequent anti-Indian bias of state and federal law enforcement agencies.[11]

The controlled chaos of the first three-quarters of stanza 3 changes pitch, however, when the crew arrives at the auditorium and the motion of the poem comes under the control of "the Osage drum / [brought] out of mourning to honor Uncle Gus" (57). In stanza 2, Ponca Uncle Gus is shown performing "at the Osage dances" (53); here in stanza 3, we see the honor being reciprocated by "the Osage War Dancers / [who] had come to dance for him" (57) in the Ponca City auditorium. These intimations of bicultural identity are reinforced when the narrator tells us that "all the Ponca and Osage women / had fixed the frybread" (57) for the funeral feast. This particular pairing of nations reflects Revard's own upbringing, born Osage on his father's side and raised in a Ponca kinsman's household.[12] This pairing is further reinforced by the similarity in

---

11 Such bias of course predates the AIM activity of the late '60s and early '70s; during this period, however, and given his association with AIM, however peripheral, the narrator would have been perfectly justified in being "scared shitless wondering / if we'd get shot / by [Oklahoma state] troopers or by [federal] FBI / or maybe by some 'skins that had been lied to or bought or blackmailed" (Revard 1980: 56). The third source of concern refers to "black ops" Cointel operations designed to foment distrust and uncertainty within the ranks of AIM and other militant and/or anti-war movements in the U.S.; for more on the Cointel project, see Ward Churchill and Jim Vander Wall, *The Cointelpro Papers* (1990).

12 The female head of this household was Jewell McDonald Camp, the "Aunt Jewell" of the poem who was also in fact the sister of Gus McDonald.

name of the Ponca and Osage dance societies called "war dancers."[13] At this time in history, the suggestion is, to be a model Ponca is to share a degree of identity with the Osage way, and vice-versa: the story of one speaks to, and with, the story of the other. Such a sharing is the seed crystal for the broader pan-Indian identity enacted and celebrated in the powwow gatherings (and in the post-powwow Forty-Nines) taking place all over Indian country by the '70s.

Pan-Indian or not, every powwow has its head male dancer. A few lines later, "toward the end of the dancing," the narrator finds himself out on the margin of the activity, behind the bleachers, watching the war-dancers in the company of "an old cowboy" (58). We are not told whether this figure is Indian or not, and perhaps the ambiguity is intentional, designed to test a reader's ability to see cowboy *and* Indian, rather than cowboy *or* Indian. But either way, the figure draws the narrator's attention and ours back to the head male dancer of this poem when he says, "offhand / 'They're good / but they won't ever be as good / as Gus McDonald'" (58). With this statement, the narrative quickly calms down and sobers up as Carter,[14] in four sentences within the space of four lines, speaks the words that identify him as the latest in a long line of Ponca warriors: "Mike, they'll nail me some time or other / for Wounded Knee. I know it, I'm prepared long since. / But I'm back with my people now" (58). Here, the mantle of the Ponca *helushka* spirit transfers from uncle to nephew as the image of Carter Camp, backlit by the evocation of Uncle Gus, emerges as the latest model of Ponca historical identity, evading for awhile (as every member of every generation of Poncas has evaded, for awhile) the threat of cultural termination and relocation. As though rehearsing the story of his father, Uncle Woody, hiding out from "the marshals in V-8 Fords" a generation earlier, Carter is on the run from "the helicopters [that will be] sweeping / the Okie hills once more" (55) in pursuit of AIM veterans of Wounded Knee and destined to be "nailed" and removed, not to a reservation but to a

---

13 The name of the homologous Osage society is *Il Lonsha*; Charles records the various ethnographic spellings of both terms in an endnote to his essay "Songs of the Ponca: *Helushka*" (1989: 15 n 2).

14 Here and throughout "Ponca War Dancers," "Carter" refers to Carter Camp; in the poem as in fact, Revard is called "Mike" by his Ponca relations, possibly to differentiate him from his older cousin Carter Camp.

federal penitentiary.[15] The formal mission of any penitentiary, of course, is to coerce inmates into repenting and repudiating their former, illegal ways; by this point in the poem, however, we understand that Carter, like his more famous forebears Standing Bear and White Eagle, will not lose his Ponca vision and spirit while in captivity. The dance goes 'round, but a Ponca war dancer is always coming home, always becoming "back with my people now."

Stanza 4: Winter-count

This point is made forcefully in the fourth and final stanza of the poem, where at last Gus McDonald's purely Ponca identity, Shongeh-Ska,[16] becomes the sign both literally and metonymically of the spirit of "the people / who shall not perish from the earth / not even if they have to use / such European words as these / to keep the Ponca ways together" (59). His niece Serena posts that sign on her "Indian Crafts shop" for all to see, exposing to public view what was always there to be seen but not before posted under its Ponca name. This is the same life force that informs the motion, or "dance," of all of the action in the poem—including the writing of it. Some "war dancers," be they Ponca *Helushka* or Osage *Il lonsha*, convert a brave deed into a dance or its accompanying song; some, like Uncle Gus before and now the narrator of the poem, convert a vision, specifically a vision of how the people must learn to move with the historical space they occupy, into the motion of a dance and the words of a song/poem. In stanza 4, "not being much of a warrior [him]self" (59), the narrator offers his word-dance, his contribution to the long story of the people, in the form of the poem he is writing. Something new is happening to the *Helushka* traditions when the narrator reinvents the enemy's language, "use[s] / such European words as these / to keep the Ponca ways together," using phonetic lettering to do

---

15 Some would say there isn't much difference. During occupation of Alcatraz Island during 1969–71, Indians from an assortment of tribes were quick to note the historical serendipity of being in a position finally to turn a federally-run prison back into an Indian-run reservation: see the "Proclamation: To the Great White Father and All His People" issued by the "Indians of All Tribes" (Matthiessen 1980: 37–38).

16 The approximate English translation of the name is White Horse; the -ska means "white, shining" and is part of most names in the McDonald family (Revard 6 March 2005: E-mail to author).

the cultural work of the older, more traditional hand-drawn "winter-count" (59)[17] image of an important moment in the history of the people.

Stanza 4 closes with a reprise of the Forty-Nine song being sung by the young veterans of the Wounded Knee occupation on the drive to Uncle Gus' funeral in stanza 2. The tune is the same, but the words are changed: Porcupine, the Pine Ridge reservation village that is the setting for the dance in the Forty-Nine song, is here replaced by White Eagle, the Ponca traditional dance grounds named after the head chief of the Poncas at the time of their forced removal to Oklahoma in 1877.[18] While the pan-Indian neotraditionalists express in dance and song the warrior spirit in places like Porcupine, South Dakota, the Ponca war dancers do likewise in White Eagle, Oklahoma; sometimes, as in the episode commemorated in this poem ("a kind / of memorial song" [59]), there is no boundary between the two but only a fusion, made visible in the concentric circles of motion (the dancer) and memory (his witnesses). The winter-count image for "the year after Wounded Knee," then, is the image of Gus McDonald transforming into Shongeh-Ska, "dancing still" as an inspiration to the new generation of warrior dancers but also returned to the world of the ancestors, "back with his people now" (59).

---

17 Tanis Thorne provides a very good definition (with illustrations) of the term "winter count" at http://eee.uci.edu/clients/tcthorne/wintercount/.

18 The 1980 Point Riders Press edition of *Ponca War Dancers* bears a photograph of White Eagle on its cover. A copy of White Eagle's account of the removal, recorded by Susette La Flesche in 1879, is available at the American Native Press Archives website, http://www.anpa.ualr.edu/digitallibrary/Ponca%20Account.htm.

Works Cited

Charles, J. 1989. "Songs of the Ponca: *Helushka*." *Wicaso Sa Review* 5.2: 2–15.
Churchill, W., and J. Vander Wall. 1990. *The Cointelpro Papers: Documents from the FBI's Secret Wars Against Dissent in the United States.* Cambridge, Massachusetts: South End Press. 2002.
Crow Dog, M., and R. Erdoes. 1990. *Lakota Woman.* New York: Grove Weidenfeld.
Curtis, E. 1930. "The 'Stomp' Dance and the Forty-nine Dance." *The North American Indian* v.19. Norwood, Massachusetts: Plimpton Press. 214–20.
Geiogamah, H., ed. 1980. *New Native American Drama.* Norman: University of Oklahoma Press.
La Flesche, S. 1879. "Ponca Account." American Native Press Archives and Sequoyah Research Center. http://www.anpa.ualr.edu/digital_library/Ponca%20Account.htm.
Matthiessen, P. 1980. *In The Spirit of Crazy Horse.* New York: Penguin.1992.
McNickle, D. 1936. *The Surrounded.* Albuquerque: University of New Mexico Press. 1978.
Nader, R. 1965. *Unsafe at Any Speed: The Designed-in Dangers of the American Automobile.* New York: Grossman.
Revard, C. 1980. *Ponca War Dancers.* Norman, Oklahoma: Point Riders Press.
——. 2005, 6 March. E-mail to R. Nelson.
Silko, L. M. 1981. *Storyteller.* New York: Seaver.
Smith, P. C., and R. Warrior. 1996. *Like a Hurricane.* New York: New Press.
Spicer, E. 1980. *The American Indians.* Cambridge, Massachusetts: Harvard University Press.
Thorne, T. "What is a Winter Count?" http://eee.uci.edu/clients/tcthorne/wintercount/.

"Reading That Part of the Past":
Accessing History in the Poetry of Carter Revard

Jerry Harp

In Carter Revard's poem "A Sun Dance Story" (1998b: 87–90), the speaker recalls an anecdote recounted by his Cousin Buck. In the story, Cousin Buck is hitchhiking to a Sun Dance when two men in a pickup truck stop to give him a ride; the driver is a white man, "but an Indian man / opened the door" (88). Cousin Buck describes how, because he has walked a long way in the "Kansas sun" (90), his forehead is almost blistered, and how the Indian in the truck offers him "a drink of the coolest water / I ever drank" (88). While the poem begins with a description of the "good and honored job" (87) of Water Boy at a powwow, and how the person fulfilling the role of Water Boy is usually someone young, "someone learning, being taught / by bringing water how we are"(87), the speaker recounting Cousin's Buck's tale goes on to explain that the reason Cousin Buck's story means so much is that "the man / who gave him water wasn't young" (87). The old Indian man gives Cousin Buck even further comfort by suggesting that the latter put some of the water on his forehead; "that cooled me off almost / like a block of ice" (88), recalls Cousin Buck. Feeling refreshed, like he has "just been swimming / or taken a cold shower" (88–89), the hitchhiker gets out at a crossroads, where a guy in a green van picks him up, and when Cousin Buck turns to wave to the two men in the pickup, they are nowhere to be seen. As a matter of fact, according to the man in the green van, there was never a pickup truck there at all; there was not even a crossroads.

The poem never makes a clear declaration of what Cousin Buck has experienced, or who the two men in the pickup are. Might they be representatives of a spirit world? Is the Indian in the truck, ambiguous because he appears to be an aged man playing a young man's role, a representative of an ancestral past? One might take a cue from the ambiguity of the old man's appearance and role, an ambiguity that suggests a kind of fluidity between what it means to play the role of an aged man and to fulfill the function of a young man. For whatever else Cousin Buck's story indicates, it recounts an experience of fluidity, a permeability between Cousin Buck's everyday world, where he is hitchhiking to get to a Sun Dance, and whatever world the two in the pickup truck have come from. As Robin Riley Fast emphasizes in her *The Heart as a Drum*, in much American Indian thought and literature, one encounters "a double perception [that] implies, in many instances, the mutability of boundaries, literal and other, and the fluidity of experience in the fields of tension and possibility that surround them" (1999: 5). Or as Janet McAdams puts it specifically in relation to Revard's work, one finds in Revard's poems "meetings of, encounters between, and juxtapositions of different worlds" (2003: 194). I take both of these statements to apply to the permeability among a variety of kinds of spaces, both literally and figuratively conceived: geographical, spiritual, historical, etc. What I am emphasizing about Carter Revard's poetry is the way that it articulates moments of fluidity in which one encounters parts of the past that otherwise remain inaccessible.

While these moments of encounter with the past occur as leaps of perception and understanding, these are also encounters that can occur only in the midst of intellectual and spiritual disciplines. In Revard's poems, leaps of understanding the past on intimate terms take place in connection with a preceding knowledge of the history, philosophy, theology, and stories of one's tradition, and in the context of an ongoing commitment to spiritual practices and disciplines—such knowledge and disciplines as are implied by Cousin Buck traveling "from Oklahoma to South Dakota" to participate in the Sun Dance. In other words, there is no facile mysticism here, such as may too easily—and finally condescendingly—be attributed to a given tradition by an outsider. If, as Sherman Alexie puts it, non-Indian writers writing about Indians "usually say 'Great Spirit,' 'Mother Earth,' 'Two-Legged,' 'Four-Legged,' and 'Winged'" (2001: 50), we non-Indians writing about Indians can also get a little slushy when talking about spirituality and accessing the past in Indian traditions. Thus, what I want to describe are some of the ways that Carter Revard accesses the past by leaps of poetic imagination in relationship to his rigorous discipline and his learning.

The leaps of poetic imagination that occur in Revard's poems are congruent with Gaston Bachelard's assertion that "the poetic act has no past, at least no recent past, in which its preparation and appearance could be followed" (1958: xi). Bachelard contrasts the poetic act with acts of philosophy and science, discourses in which new ideas become persuasive in part because of their deployment of a familiar discourse, or because they convincingly show a productive variation on a familiar discourse (xi-xiv). Even a revolutionary scientific theory must persuade by showing how it can solve a large number of the same problems as the older theory that it would replace, as well as solve problems that the old theory could not (see Kuhn 1957: 264; 1962:160–70; 2000: 28–32). In Bachelard's view, the act of poetry convinces largely by its startling newness and even its strangeness. Even if it should turn out that these differences of language among the discourses of science, philosophy, and poetry are differences only of degree, the differences are nevertheless worth acknowledging for the varying modes of knowing that they lead to. In relation to Bachelard's explorations, I am suggesting that the mode of language or discourse that one employs will open up its own distinctive modes of knowing parts of the web of connections that constitute the world. One such mode of language is to be found in Carter Revard's poetry. For while here is a poetry in which knowing history means approaching the past with a narrative, or as is usually the case an array of narratives, this is also a poetry in which knowing history means accessing moments of the past by leaps of imagination; further, knowing history also means relating to the earth and animal life by similar imaginative leaps. The work of imagination that I am stressing here is not the making of mere fictions or falsehoods, but rather the imagination that Coleridge describes as the "living Power and prime Agent of all human Perception" (1817: 304). This mode of imagination is the fundamental power by which humans shape the welter of sensory experiences into an understandable and meaningful world. Of course, from infancy into maturity much of this shaping occurs, under the influence of social forces, without explicit or thematic knowledge, but it is also the prerogative of the self-aware person consciously to construct, critique, deconstruct, and reconstruct models of cognition.

One may understand the endeavor of poetry as one of the intellectual disciplines by which humans engage in these self-aware cognitive processes. Certainly this is the case with Revard's poetry. One may well recall, in connection with this theme of the shaping power of the imagination, T. S. Eliot's famous description of the process of poetry in his essay on the Metaphysical poets:

> When a poet's mind is perfectly equipped for its work, it is constantly amalgamating disparate experience; the ordinary man's experience is chaotic, irregular, fragmentary. The latter falls in love, or reads Spinoza, and these two experiences have nothing to do with each other, or with the noise of the typewriter or the smell of cooking; in the mind of the poet these experiences are always forming new wholes. (1960: 247)

Eliot's theory of the dissociation of sensibility, along with his somewhat condescending remarks about "the ordinary man's experience" notwithstanding, the sense of the world that emerges in this passage is one in which everything is connected with everything else, forming a complex, and complicating, network of associations and relationships (see Ong 1981: 24–34). Interior states, philosophical texts, sounds, and smells, along with the conceptions of poets, are already part of the complex network of actuality. The implication that arises in many of Revard's poems is that the more one becomes acquainted with specific parts of this network of associations, and the more one's sensibilities become trained in receptiveness to this network, the more one is able to make leaps from knowing one part of the network to knowing more remote parts, in however inchoate or complete, nascent or explicit a way. According to the Osage "*Ne ke A Tun ka* (Great Words of the Ancient People)," "To touch the earth is to touch the past, the present, and the future" (Burns 2001: xii). Or as Bachelard, again, puts the matter in discussing the way that the poetic act can make a sudden leap into the past, "[T]hrough the brilliance of an image, the distant past resounds with echoes" (1958: xii). I take this line to mean that the remote past echoes into the present—echoes, that is, becomes present as sound, however brilliant the (visible) image. In other words, while this accessing of the past occurs in relation to visual imagery—such as that implied by the title of this present essay—and other sensory experiences, the experience is not primarily like gazing upon a visual scene; rather, this accessing of the past occurs more like the experience of listening for and to an evanescent, though no less real, fading presence of a sound. While all human knowing is a process that occurs in time, the kind of knowing that I am stressing here is one whose constant motion is most intense—thus the aptness of Bachelard's sonic metaphor. Because sound "only exists when it is going out of existence" (Ong 1982: 32), it is the "process sense par excellence" (Ong 1977: 136). The moment of hearing an echo of the past can function as a supplement to the more explicit modes of knowledge upon which the moment's leap into the past remains dependent.

Such are the profound echoes that one encounters again and again in Carter Revard's poems. Of course, any reader of Revard will know that he has long been a student of many histories, not only of Osage history and tradition, but also of English literary history and the history of the English language (Revard 1998: xii–xiii; McAdams 2003: 193–4). While Revard's poems, as a matter of course, rely on some explicit knowledge of such histories, these poems also open into moments of reading the past, of touching the past and hearing its echoes, in strikingly intimate terms. Part of what Revard's poems do is transcribe these moments of subtle perception into intelligible human language. In fact, as Revard points out in his poem "Earth and Diamonds" (2005: 73–6), integrating details into a narrative of one's own making is much the way that one arrives at truth: "FACT meant SOMETHING MADE, in Roman mouths, / then English let it take the place of TRUTH" (74). Revard here alludes to the etymology of the English word "fact," which is the Latin verb *facere*, meaning to make or to do. Despite Sergeant Joe Friday's insistence on "just the facts," facts never exist in isolation from the narratives and other interpretive frameworks that humans always use to make sense of experience and the world. True enough, "the truth is out there," but I can only know the truth that is *out there* by means of the work that I do *in here*, in my own consciousness. I can only make sense of what I perceive out there by integrating it into my interpretive frameworks, which must themselves remain sufficiently flexible to take in new inputs and to undergo revision when necessary. As Revard puts it in "A Giveaway Special," "Under the old names, new beings gather; within the new beings, old ways survive" (1993: xi). The relationship between sensory input and one's interpretive frameworks is thus dialectical, mutually influencing. It is in relation to this dialectical relationship of experience and interpretation that a "fact" is something made or something done.

Such facts can then enter into some very subtle moments of perception, as in Revard's "Outside in St. Louis" (2005: 62–3), whose speaker contrasts his own perceptions with those of pigeons:

>   Me,
> I hear the traffic, step
> with caution from the curb—

> they, inside the whisper of
> a soft St. Louis rain, may hear
> the ocean speaking: not just the long swells that lash
> Pacific shores, but those that boom
> on Hatteras, commune on their
> subhuman channels with pigeons' minds. (62)

While this speaker cannot finally know precisely what pigeon perception feels like, he can nevertheless learn something about how his own and others' perception works by allowing some disciplined free play into his meditation. By speculatively and self-consciously entering this meditation, he encounters the rain already infiltrated by the whisper of a voice that in turn becomes the ocean speaking. The perception of the voice in the rain is already supplied by the voice that speaks the lines, but then this projected voice becomes the voice of the other in the speaking of the ocean, which communicates by means of the whispering rain. The perception of the distant voice of the ocean works only if the listeners, the pigeons as projected by the speaker, are at once inside the rain and listening into the rain that they are inside—just as the phrase "inside the whisper of / a soft St. Louis rain" functions at once adjectivally (modifying the pronoun "they") and adverbially (modifying the verb "hear"); the speaker, along with the pigeons, exists inside the whisper of the rain that he hears. Just as one needs the voice of one's interpretive matrix, one also needs to be able to listen self-consciously beyond this matrix to perceive what is in the world. Thus sensitized and receptive to the subtle happenings of actuality, the poem's meditator becomes enraptured by the natural sophistication of the pigeon's way of traveling "by star-maps glittering in the / molecules of their genes." By the end of the meditation, he is prepared to perceive "from our here and now / into some other space and time" (63). He is prepared, in other words, for such moments of historical perception as the remainder of this essay will explore.

Revard's poem "Rock Shelters" (1993: 9–11) provides an instance of deepening one's knowledge of the past with a tactile sense of contact such as occurs when moving through the physical location where events have taken place. Recall again Louis F. Burns's reference to the "*Ne ke A Tun ka* (Great Words of the Ancient People)," to the effect that touching the earth means touching the past, present, and future. In accordance with this method of reading a place, the poem begins with attentiveness to the details of the place that the speaker is moving through:

> Up here, bluff-slabs of sandstone
> hang out from the rim,
> painted blue-gray with lichens, sheer
> over dusty level of a
> sheltered place: water sometimes
> down over places worn and knobby drips
> and darkens, softens earth to hold our
> lifeprints . . . (9)

As the water drips down the "bluff-slabs of sandstone," it "softens earth" in preparation for the inscription of "lifeprints" that the speaker observes. As this is a mode of writing that takes place over a period of centuries, if not millennia, the reading of these lifeprints requires an array of specialized skills, including how to move through the place, touching and knowing how to be in touch with its significance. As the speaker goes on to observe, "mostly here's / just humus" (9): thus, he must first differentiate the lifeprints from what is "just humus," and then go on to discern what the lifeprints are and what they mean. Carrying out this activity, he comes to announce a sense of connection to the place, a recognition that "we were / once here," but the significance of the points of contact is not immediately clear:

> . . . but in this damp earth just outside
> the overhang are mussel shells—
>   worn
> to flaky whiteness, rainbow of
> iridescence long since dead. Here's charcoal too,
> deep under the hanging slab. See,
>   we were
>   once here. (9)

On the way to the poem's end, as the details of place accrue, the speaker enters a scene of the past where differences in the very feel of time and distance are registered by the ways that they are measured. Distance was measured by the numbers of creeks that one must cross, and "Greenwich did not / keep time for us" (11). As Revard comments on the matter of experiencing time, for many American Indian peoples the experience of "ceremonial time" is of central importance, a sense of connection "not merely to what we did last year and what we're going to do next year but to what people have done time out of mind and to the beings who were here and from whom we come into the world" (in Bruchac 1987: 246–7). While the speaker of "Rock Shelters" may not be in the midst of a ritual in the strictest sense of the term, he is certainly, in his contact with the space signaled by the title, entering into a kind of ritual contact with the past.

In fact, by the end of the poem, the speaker experiences a merging of the past with the present and the latter's technological shifts. The speaker's attitude toward these technological changes is complex, as befits his complex sense of the world and his relation to it. If on the one hand certain technological innovations enable an exploitation of the planet, such as occurs in the trajectory of action in which galaxies "before long, may / be sold for profit," on the other hand technological innovation also enables a new feeling for the world. The poem registers a kind of awe-struck openness to the sheer givenness of existence in the brief thought experiment that begins "Think / of walking on blue / stars like this one . . . " (1993: 11). As is well known, it is the commonplace circulation of photographs of Earth taken from outer space that leads to the conceptualization of our planet—our "star" in the language world of the poem—as blue. Thus, the whole array of technological achievements connected with space travel leads to a new way of envisioning the earth and its meaning. At once majestic and vulnerable, this blue planet or "star" in the midst of vast space is the locus of the movements of vast trajectories of time and history; fittingly, the poem ends on a note of embracing the earth with regard for its past and looking ahead to possibilities of the future:

> Think
> of walking on blue
> stars like this one, new
> plants, new beings, all the rock
> shelters where we'll crouch and see
> new valleys from.
> Here is my
> mussel-shell. Here is the charcoal.
> We were here. (11)

While the speaker looks ahead to moments of further discovery of "new / plants, new beings, all the rock / shelters where we'll crouch and see / new valleys from," he also orients himself to the world in terms of Osage traditions: "Here is my / mussel-shell. Here is the charcoal. / We were here." These details of the mussel-shell and the charcoal, both of which are important in Osage life (see Chapman 1974: 66–7, 152, 222), call for further commentary.

According to John Joseph Mathews in his indispensable *The Osages: Children of the Middle Waters,* the fresh-water mussel functioned as part of a network of symbols giving material form to the mysteries of experience. The wrinkles on the mussel-shell serve as reminders that "to attain wrinkles one had to live through many dangers" (1961: 47). At one point in his telling of Osage stories, Mathews even formulates a speech by the mussel-shell: "I have passed successfully the seven bends of the river [River of Life], and in my travels the very gods themselves are unable to follow the trail, and your trails, Oh, Little Ones, will like mine be invisible" (47). In Osage thought there is even an obligation to attain old age (Mathews 1961: 51, 445), an obligation that the mussel-shell, given its associations, would no doubt help one to bear in mind. Certainly the Osage people bore the shells on their bodies, as they wore "gorgets made from the fresh-water mussel, symbolical of the sun" (Mathews 1961: 255; see also 737).

Like the mussel-shell, the charcoal carries multiple associations and meanings. Included among important Osage ceremonial items is "a small deerskin pouch in which powdered charcoal was carried by the warrior" (Burns 2004: 67). In Osage tradition charcoal is associated with the forces of destruction and transmutation that also become parts of the process of creation. As Mathews puts it, "[I]n order to make lodge coverings and bullboats and shields and utensils and robes, you had to destroy the buffalo; and to make charcoal, you had to destroy the redbud tree" (1961: 51–2). Charcoal also provides a ritual means of surviving among the often harsh elements and happenings of the world: "They sought the aid of all-devouring and devastating fire when they blackened their faces with his [fire's] charcoal" (64). In ending his poem "Rock Shelters" with the details of the mussel-shell and the charcoal, Revard has chosen items especially befitting the issues of longevity and transformation, the mussel-shell with its wrinkles of old age and the charcoal that brings its reminder of the "everlasting evidence of irresistible fire" (Mathews 1961: 50). Not only do these details put the speaker in touch with the long history and traditions of the Osage peoples, they also function as emblems of the perdurance of Osage life and culture. These emphases are important for one who would read the past in intimate terms. They are reminders that reading the past means reading it through the transformations of its perdurance.

The prose poem "A Cardinal, New Snow, and Some Firewood" (Revard 1993: 21–4) explores further intricacies of reading the past in the details of the present. Similar to "Rock Shelters," this poem begins with the speaker's physical interactions with a place, beginning with the gathering of firewood; as the interactions continue, moments of further understanding begin to emerge in the speaker's awareness:

> Once when I was getting firewood down by Buck Creek I had a long talk with a cardinal who was wintering there. Of course I don't understand the summer language of cardinals, the kind you hear when green things come back. That isn't meant for us but for themselves, and all I can make out is that it has to do with love and war. I've stood and listened, looking up through the white locust blossoms at the blue sky, in all that fragrance and new bright green, and a scarlet flash singing there, but it was just birdsong, it hid the meaning like a nest someplace away from where it sang. Finding it would probably kill it anyhow. (21)

With the delicacy of his strong movements, the motions of physical labor, the speaker reveals that he is intimate with country things. With a lightness of humorous touch, he states that it is specifically the summer language of cardinals he does not understand, implying that he can better understand cardinals' winter language. This lightness of touch is important here for the kind of tactility that it registers; it is the kind of touch, or "tact," that according to Gadamer (1975: 17), enables moments of understanding and judgment in particular circumstances, even though one might not be able to articulate one's reasons.

In the speaker's tactful recollection of the woods in summer, when he looks "up through the white locust blossoms at the blue sky, in all that fragrance and new bright green," he has to listen a long time before getting the idea that the cardinal has hidden "a meaning like a nest someplace away from where it sang." The difficulty of listening to and understanding the cardinal is underscored by the slipperiness of the pronoun "it." In the first verse paragraph's final sentence, "Finding it would probably kill it anyhow," it is not entirely clear if this pronoun refers to the bird, the birdsong, or the meaning that the cardinal has hidden. Reading the details requires a tactful skill in part because the bird, the birdsong, and the meaning are so integrated, so much a part of each other, that one cannot entirely separate them. Attending to one means that one must attend to all three. Attempting to separate them would constitute an act of murderous dissection. Thus, reading well means knowing when to let be, to stand and notice, allowing the bird, its song, and its meaning to reveal themselves; and reading well also means knowing when to press harder, search for further meaning, as the speaker later does when he engages in dialogue with the cardinal.

For the moment, however, he must remain still, knowing that there is in the cardinal's song a meaning about love and war—and thus it is a meaning of deep import—but it is also a meaning that will exist for him only as long as he allows it to emerge for him, without trying to pin it down. It is enough that he has labored to place himself in the moment of meaning; were he at this point to press for greater clarity or precision, the meaning would already be gone, like the cardinal fleeing from a pursuer.

But understanding the birdsong and its meaning in winter requires tact also, a tact sensitive to the need to refrain from marring the text to be read:

> But in winter, when there is new snow, and snow-lined branches in a blue sky, and the crimson flashes down to a bush for coral berries or a wild rose-hip, sometimes if you're sitting quietly near it will talk. And their winter language is like the new snow, I can read it for a while, until it gets tracked all over with human things that come out of me and walk around as if it was their back yard. (1993: 21)

The human things of which he speaks are not only the footprints that mark the snow, but also the mindprints that mark the text. There is of course no human reading of any text without an interpretive framework, which is a kind of mindprint marking any text that one reads. But a clumsy reading is one that imposes an interpretive framework so heavy-handedly as to enable the reading of pretty much only the framework itself, irrespective of the text that one would use the framework to negotiate. A subtle sense of tact is called for to use one's interpretive framework in such a way as to allow a text's meaning to emerge and even at times to alter how one uses the framework—even at times to alter the framework itself.

But human meanings are always partial. Thus, what one reads must always come in parts. If the speaker of the poem exercises sufficient tact in reading the present state of the snow-covered land, then he can begin to experience and understand moments and resonances of the past. After he brushes off a stump to sit down and has remained still for a time, he notices a weasel's tracks, which lead him to notice yet other tracks—inscriptions that he goes on to read: "The snow told me where it [the weasel] had lunged after a cottontail, and where the rabbit jumped and veered and got away . . . " (1993: 21). Having achieved a state of calm in this moment of reading that is both tactful and active, he experiences an opening of the cardinal's language:

It was while I was reading that part of the past that the cardinal sang.
"The weasel isn't there, he's down by the creek. He found a covey of bobwhites and killed two," the cardinal said. (21)

When the speaker's attempts at a reply are disrupted by something that seems like delirium, the cardinal lets him know that the problem is that he is speaking at all. The moment's delicacy demands that he continue in his stillness, reading without speaking, for any human statement immediately overstates: "'You don't have to talk,' the cardinal said. 'The snow is inside you and I can see what you say walking there. When you speak out, the sound tramples around and all the meanings that are friendly go into hiding and the others start sniffing for me'" (22). Because the surface that receives the inscriptions, the snow, exists both within and outside the poem's speaker, reading the markings outside of him requires that his inner writing surface remain in a state of calm. He need not speak aloud because the cardinal can sense what the writing inside him says by the way he walks: "I can see what you say walking there." In speaking, the cardinal voices the man's own meanings back to him, just as in writing the poem, the poet formulates the cardinal's voicings of the speaker's meaning.

In fact, a debate about precisely where the voices of the poem are coming from is written into the very text of the poem. The source of these voices is, of course, the poet, but Revard writes into the poem the complications of where the poet's voice comes from. It is a voice written by many other texts stretching back through millennia. The agency of textual production is multiple, though it is also an agency in which the poet certainly shares. The conclusion that the poem comes to articulate is one that emphasizes the interconnectedness of animal and human, waking and dreaming, past and present, reader and writer. All are part of the same complex text, and to access one part of this text means in some sense also to gain access to other parts of the text, for all are part of the web or weave of meaning. The English word "text" comes from the Latin word *texere*, meaning to weave or to intertwine. A text is thus a weave or intertwining of many things and their multiple meanings. "And someone made you up as well as me?" asks the cardinal. The man replies, "Of course. But not just one person. He, and all the people reading these words. They made me up, a lot of different me's according to their minds. They made me up, they're looking at me, hearing me. The snow is in their minds. These words are tracks in the snow" (1993: 23).

As part of the text to be read, one who would read must know something of his or her interwovenness in the text. The more sensitive, disciplined, and aware one becomes in one's listening and reading, the more of the text one can access and come to know. As the cardinal says,

> Have you any idea how many kinds of snow there are? The spread of white blossoms, say, in April and May, they remember. They record what bees are doing, and the trees remember it in August and you taste it as apricots, apples, plums. I can retrieve tiny variations in air pressure from June, and return them as song in December. You can retrieve from stone the consonants of Babylon. (1993: 23)

One can, like the cardinal, sense history, read a part of the past, by engaging with the world in multisensory acts of reading, as the man speaking the poem can taste the activities of bees in fruit, as the cardinal can register in its song variations of air pressure, as one can recover an ancient language from inscriptions on stone. By placing the human activity of making meaning by means of language in a litany including the work of bees pollinating trees and of the bird making song, Revard emphasizes the continuity of human language with the rest of nature. Human language is a part of the very nature that humans use language to understand, and like the work of the birds and the bees, language is endlessly fertile.

The end of the poem emphasizes further the continuity of human language with the rest of nature. It is not until here in the poem that the reader discovers what the "Firewood" in the title refers to. The speaker has gone out to the woods to pick up some cordwood that "we had stacked the week before" (1993: 23). Because this wood has grown as trees in the interweaving of earthly things, it has been recording parts of the world during the many years of its growth. By putting language to some of these records of the world, the poet extends the work of recording history by the language that is a part of the earthly text, and he invites the reader to continue the work by acts of reading that are also acts of writing in that they too create meaning:

> I was thinking how the cut wood remembers years of sunlight, then lets go in snapping, sighing light and warmth from the ashes. What the red coals say, I was thinking, I'll have to listen to. What the words release, I leave to those who read. Some of it lived there ten thousand years ago, some never was. Across the snowy pages dark words leap and sway. A red bird is singing in them. What year, what year? he sings. This one, this one, this one, they answer. Blossom, blossom, blossom, he sings. And they do. (23–24)

As noted earlier, fire is spoken of in Osage tradition as an irresistible force (Mathews 1961: 50). In the passage just quoted, it is precisely this irresistible force that renders accessible the meanings recorded in the wood. The man's listening leads to words that themselves carry long centuries of history, as Revard the scholar of Medieval literature and the history of the English language (Revard 1998: xii-xiii) well knows. As the wood releases meanings in its burning, so the words that the writer uses to describe the burning wood themselves carry more than he, or anyone, can access or know at any given moment. As Ong says of "subjects subsumed under the term 'humanities,'" they "always say more than they mean because they mean more than they can say" (1981: 34). While this statement may be true with conspicuous intensity of statements in the humanities, I submit that it is also true of all uses of language, uses that always carry multiple possibilities of meaning, such that a given text uncannily shifts in significance as it moves through history and across geography (see Ong 1995: 4–18). It is for this reason of language's constant motion of meaning that all interpretations are partial, and that the action of the reader is necessary to make a text meaningful. As the speaker of the poem points out concerning what is released in the act of reading, "Some of it lived there ten thousand years ago, some never was" (Revard 1998: 24). In the act of reading, the reader supplies something that was not exactly there before: the interpretation, or the sense that the reader makes of the text. Even the most valid of interpretations must be articulated in words, which will have their own implications and will call forth further interpretations, which will call forth further interpretations, etc. None of this is to say that language is nonreferential, but rather that language is multireferential, and that the work of interpretation is never finished.

On the other hand, it may be that the statement, "Some of it lived there ten thousand years ago, some never was," could also imply that while some of what the reader discerns really happened, some of it is fiction. But then I take it that in this poem the boundary separating history, or fact, from fiction is also permeable, like the boundaries separating animals from humans, waking from dreaming, past from present. After all, the telling of fictions can get at truths otherwise inaccessible, even when these truths remain intuited or otherwise deferred. The dark words on the page remain active. They are what blossom and burn at the end of the poem.

Revard's poem "What the Eagle Fan Says" (1993: 35–6) explores the past by means of a double trail of associations that demonstrate the complex weavings of the world's text. On the one hand, the Eagle Fan connects the poem to American Indian traditions. In one Osage story, an eagle gives an Osage chief "a downy feather from under his tail" (Mathews 1961: 60). Revard notes that the feathers that he is writing about were given to him on the occasion of his election to the Board of Directors of the American Indian Center of Mid-America, and they were beaded by a friend into a fan that Revard carries when he dances as a Gourd Dancer (Revard 2003: 191). On the other hand, the poem is written using the form of an Anglo-Saxon riddle: an alliterative, four-stress line with two stresses falling on either side of a caesura. As Craig Williamson says in his introduction to the Anglo-Saxon riddles, "each riddlic creature takes on the guise of another" (1982: 3). Revard himself emphasizes that the Eagle Fan speaks in the guise of a beadworker's needle "linking day and night colors as they are linked on a Gourd Dancer's blanket (half crimson, half blue), and as they are linked in the beading of the fan's handle" (Revard 1993: 35–6):

> I strung dazzling thrones   of thunder beings
> on a spiraling thread   of spinning flight,
> beading dawn's blood   and blue of noon
> to the gold and dark   of day's leaving . . . (35)

Here, then, is a poem of intricate connections, not only of Osage and Anglo-Saxon traditions, but also of the eagle's flight with the beadworker's needle, day colors with night colors, the sky with the earth. The linkings proliferate as the poem proceeds. The eagle fan, recalling the eagle's flight, affirms its connections to humans, as it

> heard human relatives   hunting below
> calling me down,   crying their need
> that I bring them closer   to Wakonda's ways,
> and I turned from heaven   to help them then. (35)

Thus, the eagle helps link humans to "Wakonda, the life force of the universe" (Din and Nasatir 1983: 3). Fletcher and La Flesche emphasize that Wakonda is a "mysterious life power" in Osage thought, but Mathews often speaks of Wakonda, which he spells "Wah'Kon-Tah," in terms that suggest a sense of the Divine as personal (See Mathews 1932: 23–5, 62–3, 200–209). For my purpose of reading "What the Eagle Fan Says" in the present context, the following recounting by Fletcher and La Flesche will prove helpful:

Old men have said: "Wakonda causes day to follow night without variation and summer to follow winter; we can depend on these regular changes and can order our lives by them. In this way Wakonda teaches us that our words and our acts must be truthful, so that we may live in peace and happiness with one another. Our fathers thought about these things and observed the acts of Wakonda and their words have come down to us." (598)

Being in touch with Wakonda's ways means also being in touch with the lifeworld and history of the Osage people, how one is to order one's life in accordance with the "words [that] have come down to us." The eagle feathers finally become the feathers of the Eagle Fan speaking of how

>   lightly I move now   in a man's left hand,
>   above dancing feet   follow the sun
>   around old songs   soaring toward heaven
>   on human breath,   and I help them rise. (1993: 35)

The poem appropriately ends with the historical present firmly linked to the historical past, the "old songs," from which the present arises. In its multiple linkings, the poem intricately articulates a sense of the world as an interwoven text that the poetic voice is deeply engaged in reading and rereading. Revard's poems function in part as invitations to engage in this work of endless interpretation, a celebration of meanings' proliferation.

Works Cited

Alexie, S. 2001. "The Unauthorized Autobiography of Me." *Pleiades* 21.2: 41–54.
Bachelard, G. 1958. *The Poetics of Space*. Trans. M. Jolas. Boston: Beacon Press, 1964.
Bruchac, J. 1987. "Something That Stays Alive: An Interview with Carter Revard." *Survival This Way: Interviews with American Indian Poets*. Ed. J. Bruchac. Tucson: University of Arizona Press.
Burns, L. F. 2004. *A History of the Osage People*. Tuscaloosa: University of Alabama Press.
Chapman, C. H. 1974. *The Origin of the Osage Indian Tribe*. New York: Garland Publishing.
Coleridge, S. T. 1817. Biographia Literaria: Or Biographical Sketches of My Literary Life and Opinions. Eds. J. Engell and W. J. Bate. *The Collected Works of Samuel Taylor Coleridge*. Vol. 7, part 1. Princeton: Princeton University Press, 1983.
Din, G. C., and A. P. Nasatir. 1983. *The Imperial Osages: Spanish-Indian Diplomacy in the Mississippi Valley*. Norman: University of Oklahoma Press.
Eliot, T. S. 1960. "The Metaphysical Poets." *Selected Essays*. New Edition. New York: Harcourt, Brace & World.
Fast, R. R. 1999. *The Heart as a Drum: Continuance and Resistance in American Indian Poetry*. Ann Arbor: University of Michigan Press.
Fletcher, A. C., and F. La Flesche. 1911. *Twenty-Seventh Annual Report of the Bureau of American Ethnology to the Secretary of the Smithsonian Institution, 1905–1906*. Washington: Government Printing Office.
Gadamer, H. 1975. *Truth and Method*. 2nd ed. Trans. J. Weinsheimer and D. G. Marshall. New York: Continuum, 1999.

Kuhn, T. 1957. *The Copernican Revolution: Planetary Astronomy in the Development of Western Thought.* Cambridge, Massachusetts: Harvard University Press.
——. 1962. *The Structure of Scientific Revolutions.* Chicago: University of Chicago Press, 1970.
——. 2000. *The Road Since Structure: Philosophical Essays, 1970–1993, with an Autobiographical Interview.* Ed. J. Conant and J. Haugeland. Chicago: University of Chicago Press.
McAdams, J. 2003. "Carter Revard's Angled Mirrors." *Speak to Me Words: Essays on Contemporary American Indian Poetry.* Eds. D. Rader and J. Gould. Tucson: University of Arizona Press. 193–206.
Mathews, J. J. 1932. *Wah'Kon-Tah: The Osage and the White Man's Road.* Norman: University of Oklahoma Press.
——. 1961. *The Osages: Children of the Middle Waters.* Norman: University of Oklahoma Press.
Ong, W. J. 1981. *Fighting for Life: Contest, Sexuality, and Consciousness.* Amherst: University of Massachusetts Press, 1989.
——. 1982. *Orality and Literacy: The Technologizing of the Word.* New York: Routledge. 2002.
——. 1995. "Hermeneutic Forever: Voice, Text, Digitization, and the 'I.'" *Oral Tradition* 10: 3–26.
Revard, C. 1993. *An Eagle Nation.* Tucson: University of Arizona Press.
——. 1998a. *Family Matters, Tribal Affairs.* Tucson: University of Arizona Press.
——. 1998b. "A Sun Dance Story." *The Iowa Review* 28:1: 87–90.
——. 2003. "Herbs of Healing: American Values in American Indian Literature." *Speak to Me Words: Essays on Contemporary American Indian Poetry.* Eds. D. Rader and J. Gould. Tucson: University of Arizona Press. 172–192.
——. 2005. *How the Songs Come Down.* Cambridge, U. K.: Salt Publishing.
Williamson, C. 1982. *A Feast of Creatures: Anglo-Saxon Riddle Songs.* Philadelphia: University of Pennsylvania Press.

To Make Their Bodies of Words

Robert Bensen

Carter Revard the poet came of age in the age of imagism and postmodernism and said, "Yes, thanks, but . . . ." To his native Great Plains he invited the plainspoken William Carlos Williams, doctor of the American tongue, to meet Will Rogers and his unfailing good humor, his satiric bite. Revard might have factored Walt Whitman's equation of land and line over the expanse of the prairie, but it was already fenced, dug, drilled, and sold to entrepreneurs. He took the Rhodes Scholarship road to England, then worked his way back to the tribal roots of Old English to make poems to help his tribe. For this one of the Children of the Middle Waters (*Ni-U-Ko'n-Ska*), descendant of the Sky People (*Tzi-Sho*) who made their bodies of the things of this earth, and of the Water People (*Wah-Sha-She*), this one had a way with words.

He took this way through the literatures of Europe and through the oral libraries and ethnographies of Osage and Ponca story and song. His poetry came in the way that his mentor John Joseph Mathews described that the *Ni-U-Ko'n-Ska* made the "prayer-song," to get the gifts that *Wah'Kon-Tah* had given to creatures, making them "part of their own bodies and spirit, even charging them with their dreams and their fears and their urges, so that the symbols might give back to them that with which they had been charged" (1961: 7). What Mathews described as a motive for the prayer-song seems to me fitting for Revard's practice of poetry, charging his words with the mysteries and understandings that give rise to them.

One

Carter Revard's early poem from his first book *Ponca War Dancers*, "Looking Before and After," is central to Revard's ideas of the poem as source and site of visionary experience, cultural growth, and ceremonial event (1980: 29). The poem recounts the ordinary, simple act of gazing in a clear, shallow, trickle-fed pond. Images from above and below join to form a new composition. The poet follows the process, mesmerized and open to the transforming power of what the rational mind may call an optical illusion, but which leads to a more encompassing, richer vision both of the images in the poem and the poet's ongoing purpose in his work.

The poem is a single sentence arrayed across 32 lines, which recreates the "dazzle" and disorientation of motion above and below:

>   ... there is
>   footdeep water so clear that over
>   its brown silt bottom haloes dazzle round the
>   shadows trailed by water-striders in
>   their spindly-crooked dimpling across its
>   springy surface so
>   each bright-edged darkness glides up to
>   and over brown crawdads bulldozing through
>   the mud-dust ... (1980: 29)

The lines do not break at breath-places, but inside the long, breathless phrases, each break a charged hitch in the verbal stride. But those breaks aptly sharpen our angle on this sharply drawn succession of images, out of which emerges a "shadow-cluster" that assumes the form of a skull that

>   ... wanders,
>   lunges, glides,
>   spins upside down and turns
>   to butterfly! that stops precisely ... (29)

under a larkspur flower. The sequence of dance-verbs (wander, lunge, glide, spin, turn) turns at the verse's turn (on "turn") from dance to metamorphosis, reflecting the poem's larger movement from the physical to the non-physical, or rather from the way the senses open to what lies beyond sense.

This movement enters Revard's poems through his understanding of Osage and Ponca cultural identity, which is elaborated in many later poems, especially in the landmark Aunt Jewell poems (if I may so name them), which include "An Eagle Nation" (2001: 31–34), "Aunt Jewell as Powwow Princess" (2001: 179–83), and "How the Songs Come Down" (2005: 65), in which his aunt serves as the poet's guide and teacher in coming to terms with the mysteries that the poems present.

The shifty visual footing in the poem disorients the poet first, who with the reader learns to see in a new way and to trust this new vision. Anything can appear as what it is not. The correctives of reason or familiarity or precedent need not apply. The mirroring surface creates illusions that the poem follows in the sequence of images, the easy tumble of language down the playfully enjambed ledges of lines, until the shape-shifting settles into the "butterfly of shadows." The phrase in the poem's title "before and after" operates in space, as well as in extensions of time, opening the poem to what has become of what has been, as it passes through the dramatic moment.

In the prose setting he later wrote for "Looking Before and After" in *Winning the Dust Bowl*, Revard says that "looking into the pool of water" showed him "how to write a poem that would begin this set of family pieces" (2001: 198), the elegies in "Home Movies" for his recently departed relatives (1980: 29–39). "But," he writes, "I saw that only after I put the pool and its beings into words" (2001: 198). When the water-strider's shadow made a skull that, inverted, became a butterfly of shadows that stopped on a larkspur's reflection "to taste a flower" (198), he could not see *before* him what he would see *after*, that his poem would figure forth "how the skull could become a butterfly, the surface sky and flowers live peaceably with the creatures beneath, how the shadow beings could taste again some sweetness, *in words at least*" (emphasis mine; 2001: 198).

This prose after-image of the poem discloses a compositional process—how the initiating vision, given form in language, answers a need in life that does not depend upon the poem-maker to realize. That robing of event *in words, at least*, leads beyond invention, beyond intention, into the gift of vision. The poem may not *in words, at least*, concern the death of his grandfather, three uncles and twin sister, but in its surface can be read the working out of absence and grief—in the surface that mirrors the boundary between the sunlit present and the presence of what is beyond.

Two

"Looking Before and After" is a microcosmic rehearsal for a poetic practice that will take on more profoundly cosmic matters in a great many poems to come, notably the three Aunt Jewell poems. These poems honor his beloved aunt who passed into the spirit world in 1999. In them she serves as guide and teacher in his passionate pursuit of understanding the inherited Native world, especially what that world *before* will mean to those who come *after*, and how the work he does now will accompany the people who came from the stars into the space age, using the stellar illumination of the Creation story to light this world as well. The poems begin their pursuit when the apparition or appearance of something—spirit-beings, songs—from another world disrupts the poems' stable, apparently settled present.

While his scholarship and translations from Anglo-Saxon and early French tribal literatures are his academic profession, his poetry's intellectual and literary lineage includes the Osage traditions of Frances La Flesche and John Joseph Mathews. Drawing upon La Flesche's studies of ceremony, Mathews resolves the theory of evolution with the origin story of the people who came from the stars, upstreaming toward a plausible explanation of Osage belief and identity (1961). After his naming ceremony, Revard wrote "Traditional Osage Naming Ceremonies: Entering the Circle of Being," which places the individual in relation to the cosmos, to the people, and to the self (1987: 446–66). That relation is certain but not static. For the individual it promises a lifelong construction of identity. For the poet it provides the idea of a poem that is the site of testing, revelation and renewal of tradition, which is the tradition of renewal.

Informing that process is the Osage creation story, which reiterates the way the people "before time" came together among the stars and decided "to descend to this world," but were in need both of substance from which to make their bodies, and of names to make themselves "persons" (1987: 452–5). That they made their bodies of substances proper to this earth only makes more urgent the mystery of who they are:

> The leader ... turned to his followers and said to them: "Here stands *Wah-Sha-She*, whose body is the waters of the earth." The river spoke to the Water People through its embodiment, *Wah-Sha-She*, and said in the liquid tones of the cowbird: "Oh, Little Ones, if you make your body of me it will be difficult for death to overtake you, and you will make clean and purify

all that comes to you. When you come from your home in the sky to make the flowers grow, Grandfather will paint your face with many colors ... and smile upon the Little Ones."

The leader talked with the others and they henceforth called themselves *Wah-Sha-She,* Name Givers. The River embodiment, *Wah-Sha-She,* had named the Water People with his name, *Wah-Sha-She,* and they could symbolize all the waters of the earth. (Mathews 1961: 12)

They are and are not the substance of their bodies; they are and are not the personhood of their names. They are properly both, from their creation (or coming to earth), for each individual member, according to Mathews, has "a home both in *Tzi Sho,* the Sky Lodge, and *Hunkah,* the Sacred One [Mother Earth]" (15). In that mystery is a creative act that permits being on earth, but also extends being from elsewhere that is in part obscured by the here and now.

Revard rehearsed Mathews's version of Osage history in an early poem from *Ponca War Dancers,* "People from the Stars" (1980: 45), and more fully aligned with it his writing of family and tribal stories in the essay, "Walking Among the Stars": "I am naming, as I go, as I approach the House of Mystery, those who have cast themselves into our stars and are walking with us here. I am Carter Revard, Nompehwahthe, at Buck Creek, Oklahoma, June 21, 1984" (1998: 26) Revard's poetics are founded, as I read him, in that approach to Mystery, that naming, that making the poem's body of words. The poem inside the words is and is not the words, but must be known through them, if it is to be known at all. The poet is implicated in the mystery as well; he comes to know what has to come through him and takes from him the embodiment of words.

All those who enter the poem "Aunt Jewell as Powwow Princess" (2001: 179–83) feed the poet's understanding of the transpiring event and the recognitions that follow. Knowledge comes in Revard's poems often from some intuitive leap or connection that the poems invite with their abrupt, sideways or some-other-ways dis-/re-/connections. The poem can be a site for the entry of some past or otherness, a meeting ground, a reflection pool, a mediation between the Seen and the Unseen. In "Looking Before and After," images from above and below collect in the vision of the water's surface. In "Aunt Jewell as Powwow Princess," the powwow is lit by both the daylight and spirit-light, which reveals the presence, the co-incidence, of both worlds. He first sees Uncle Gus, a spirit-being, in full daylight, but "under the half-moon in the daylight skies / there at Cahokia," (2001: 181) and he says that later he "did not see Uncle Gus again that evening, as the moon / was being covered by new clouds" (183). Such extraordinary moments depend upon the coincidence or confluence of the Seen and the Unseen that seems to have happened for the poet's benefit. The water that fills the pond trickles in from some unknown underground source, as in "Coyote Tells Why He Sings" the "little rill of water, near the den, / That showed a trickle" helps teach Coyote song, but only after a pelting storm changes its tune, and only after the Thunder has awakened him (2001: 3). Revard's idea of the poem and his understanding of his place in the Wazhazhe cosmos grow together. Revard recounts in the poem's prose setting that Joseph Bruchac asked if he had written the poem mindful of when he'd been brought into the Thunder clan in his naming ceremony. "I told him I did not consciously mean to make that connection, but realized soon after that I had done so. So Coyote came and gave me my voice, and maybe the Thunder had come to give him his, and now we try to make from all the sounds of the world a music worth singing to the moon" (2001: 7).

Three

Sometimes poets choose their subjects and sometimes the subject chooses the poet, but the best poems often come when the poet's lifetime preoccupations ready him (in this case) to hear the moment beckoning. Revard must have written "Aunt Jewell as Powwow Princess" with a sense of election to bear equal burdens of opportunity and obligation, which he does in lines as deft and light as dance. He must have had a sense of occasion for the powwow held at the site of the oldest, largest metropolis of Ancient America, Cahokia. For his beloved Aunt Jewell MacDonald's being chosen as Powwow Princess at age 84. For the chance to sit by her and to participate in the Gourd Dance. For the apparition of his long-departed uncle among the dancers, and for the apparent coincidence of his uncle's song being called to honor his sister. For his aunt's oblique lesson in recounting the story of the Rosebud Sun Dance a few years previously. For the riding-in and gifts brought by the hundreds of bikers on Harley Davidsons in the venerable manner of warriors. For the blessing of rain at the end of a day that was both September 1995 and some much earlier time at the same time.

If the Wazhazhe who came to make their bodies to live on this earth continue to create life here, then the events and efforts of one's life, including history, including the making of poems, is a continuation of that story, and one reads experience as a new version of a very ancient pattern. That idea seems confirmed by Revard's own insightful comments on the poem, given in an e-mail message:

> I hoped to connect the arrival of the bikers with the 'taking care' of the spirit dancers. We have to encourage the spirits to stay in 'their' world, so to speak, and one way to help them is to take care of those still with us in 'this' world. For the poem's purposes, the bikers come in as a living version of the spirit dancers (that's a pretty crude formulation of it of course) . . . The bikers did not put on warpaint or turkey feathers, but they came in as the hunters and warriors would, enter with food and clothing. In fact of course, Evelyne Voelker had worked out this event with the bikers after their officers phoned the Indian Center and said they wanted to donate to us because their previous donations had been misused. Evelyne had the imagination and moxie to arrange for this to be done at the upcoming Cahokia Powwow. As you probably know, there are a lot of bodies buried in the Cahokia mounds and grounds, a good many apparently sacrificed. The sense of that should be part of reading the poem. We (the Indian Community people here) hesitated a long time before deciding we could dance at Cahokia. It took a lot of ceremonies and prayers before we could do it. I guess a note to this effect would be of some use to readers. (13 February 1996: E-mail to author)

We do not *see* the spirit-being he sees, nor those that Aunt Jewell recounts from the Sun Dance, but only the effect of their being seen on her and on the speaker. What we see is the speaker perplexed and disturbed by the presence of his uncle in broad daylight. This sight renders him, in his term, "AGHAST"—a word that signified in its original Anglo-Saxon tribal usage that "something was walking in their SOUL" (2001: 179). The spirit-being that is Uncle Gus creates in the poet a corresponding presence in his soul, as it were, that baffles him, awakening some knowledge he cannot yet articulate. That Aunt Jewell is chosen to be Powwow Princess is an honor, but the place of honor that Revard accords her is in the title and in teaching and helping the poet understand this apparition and the state of being aghast.

Revard said in an email message that he changed the title of "A Powwow Story" when another poem came to him that he wanted to call "A Sun Dance Story" (16 Sept. 2005). In the newer poem, Revard's cousin Dwain was given a ride when he was hitchhiking to a Sun Dance. Details in the poem suggest that the help that arrived for Dwain was not of this world. One of the two men in the pickup gave him a drink of water "that seemed to have extraordinary coolness and restorative strength," and the men vanished, as did the truck and the road itself when Dwain got off at a crossroad (see Jerry Harp's essay in this volume for his explication of the poem). The change in the powwow poem's title gave Revard the opportunity to change the entire focus of the poem from the story to the role his Aunt Jewell played in it.

Revard wrote that he wanted to "bring her into the title" (16 Sept. 2005: E-mail to author). The phrase suggests the same deliberate act of bringing the bikers back at the end of the powwow and in the poem to honor them for coming with gifts like warriors. It suggests the way a song is brought into a drum and looked after, and the way the grandfathers with red faces are brought into a cleansing lodge, carefully. Bringing her forward to the place of honor rebalances the poem, placing her *before* the poet as the teller of a story which illuminates his story that comes *after*, which then reenacts his own aghast-ness and the restaging of his own learning.

To write of his aunt's brother, twenty years departed, who appeared at the dance must have required the caution similar to that which permitted the ceremonies to take place at Cahokia Mounds, in the presence of the many Old People buried there. This poem, for Revard, partakes of the event it remembers and completes in the telling. Writing the poem the very evening of the September 1995 powwow at Cahokia is the powwow's closing ceremony.

Four

The poem eventually known as "Aunt Jewell as Powwow Princess" was among those Revard read at the Newberry Library for the Modern Language Association convention in Chicago in December, 1995. He graciously sent a paper copy of the poem at my request on January 16, 1996, and we exchanged several email messages in February concerning the poem, then entitled "A Powwow Story." I must have questioned the singular form because the poem contained several stories, but I failed to see how they cohered in the single story of the powwow. "Your query about how many stories," Revard wrote, "has set me thinking on whether to clarify it a bit for listeners . . . If the printed version is still unclear, let me know and I'll make a serious run at fixing it" (16 January 1996: E-mail to author).

The final version published in *Winning the Dust Bowl* (2001) and *How the Songs Come Down* (2005) is longer than the 1996 version by the addition of lines in the opening exposition following the initial line of astonishment, in which he explicates his own use of the archaic word "aghast" (in italics in 1996, in emphatically bold capitals in 2001). The associations between *aghast* and ghost, Ghost Dance, the dances among the ghosts of Cahokia, and his departed uncle dancing at the powwow, Revard wanted readers to be prepared to see, possibly in a way he was not prepared to see at the time, but which Aunt Jewell's obliquely offered teaching helped him to do.

The opening lines of the 1996 version state what will become the operating premise and promise of the poem's vision:

> I was *aghast* at what I saw.
>   It's like those quarks—
> you know how each thing, deep inside,
> is something else? inside the word 'aghast' there is
>   a 'ghost' . . . (16 January 1996: Letter to author)

The discourse on "ghost" in the 2001 version is prepared for by the addition of fifteen lines that enrich the playful x-ray vision into the penetrable stuff of the self, of the daylit present that is a permeable moment:

> I was AGHAST at what I saw,
>   I've got no way of seeing things like that.
>   Felt kind of like I was sitting on a rock
>   and suddenly I saw a label on it
>   that said, URANIUM.
> Sometimes it's super-real, you see into things,
>   I mean you see
>   what isn't there, but yet it makes
> the things you CAN see have a different meaning.
>   I think for some Indian people just
>   like for physicists who figure how
>   to look inside some distant star, it's possible
>   to see how each thing, deep inside,
> is something else, all made of crazy things
>   they may give crazy names,
>   quarks or whatever they may choose.
>   Well hell, for instance right
> here in that word 'aghast' which I just used, there lives
>   a 'ghost' . . . (2001: 179)

Revard added (among other things) the admission that "I've got no way of seeing things like that." The syntax permits two readings, that he has no way of seeing "like that"—the visionary mode that takes in both this world and the spirit world—and of seeing "things like that"—things from that world which astounded him that day.

In the earlier opening, the speaker immediately begins to explain, by a simile, his statement, directing the discourse into the analogue between the nuclear molecule and words. The revision deepens the moment of amazement by reflecting on the problem of vision, sketching a cartoon-like, satirical self-portrait of sitting on a rock of uranium and having his powers of sight irradiated, and being thus empowered with x-ray vision. The problem of sight in the poem resembles that in the earlier poem, "Looking Before and After," though here the problem is played out between what he had seen that Aunt Jewell saw that he had seen, and what Aunt Jewell tells him about the Sun Dance at Rosebud. There she was warned that the Old People would be coming to dance in the spirit-light:

>   And then she heard their cries and saw
>   among the shadowy dancers spinning there
>   so many others just outside the arbor crowding in
>   long lines from where
>   the moon had risen—but they WERE
>   all right, she could see, without exactly
>   SEEING—
>   . . . So then I understood
>   why she was telling about the Sun dance, it was because
>   that afternoon she'd seen—without my saying anything—
>   that I was worried because I had just seen,
>   myself, under the half-moon in the daylight skies
>   there at Cahokia where the great city
>   of Indian people once had been,
>   her brother dancing, Uncle Gus,
>   who left us twenty years before,
>   and I don't see such things, but I saw him there
>   twice, dancing . . . (2001: 180–81)

He had said before that he has "no way of seeing things like that" (2001: 179). The problem of creating a new vision in "Looking Before and After," is writ larger and more baffling in this poem. Aunt Jewell saw the Old Ones "without exactly / SEEING," while the poet, who claims not to see such things, saw Uncle Gus dancing not once, but twice. Somehow, it was not just a matter of understanding that this world and the Spirit world are mutually permeable, and that beings can be called or come without calling, but not understanding that in 1996 any better than now, I wrote Revard with my concerns. He replied:

I certainly meant the Ghost/gast/soul stuff to be directly relevant to the poem's work with spirit dancers and Old People staying with us, reminding us, bringing us back to the responsibility of feeding the spirit and the body. I thought a key phrase was the one about everything deep inside being something else, and I hoped this would be picked up for its relevance not only to Indians as "different" but as "different within likeness"—the way an atom is not less an atom for being, inside, quarks and such, or a person is not less a person for being, inside, Osage or Ponca or Irish or whatever; and then too this "inside" and "outside" is a pretty dodgy metaphor once we start trying to ask just where the "Osage" is located, in and out of the person, and vice versa, those looking for "redskins" wanting Osage to be outside and the person inside, those looking for "Osage" looking at things both inside and outside. But once I had laid down this trail of English words which smell of the old ghost/soul meaning, I moved on to the story into which this trail was leading, a story which illustrated the point made at the beginning. The Ghost Dance was supposed to "dance back" the Indian world after a fashion. Our dances do that, but we have to be careful: the point is to take care of each other, to keep each other fed and clothed and aware of being Indian people, not to try and join the ancestors in some apocalyptic way. We are careful to include, in our giving of the food and the ways, the elder people who have moved on ahead. But we don't want to be taken back with them, or to lose our 1995–6 reality where we have to understand ourselves and others. The dances both include the elders and keep us here in the present. When I began "I was aghast" it was a comment on how stunned I was to go see Uncle Gus there with us; and behind the phrase is the sense that this WAS a kind of "Ghost Dance," it HAD "brought back" things and persons in some way-but it was like our English words, which contain within themselves the "soul" or "ghost" or former senses and meaning so when I SAY I was "aghast," and comment a little on the way older realities and meanings are still alive in words, and the way "alien" realities are alive in "ordinary" phenomena, it is one path into the poem's view of what I saw, and how Aunt Jewell connected that with the Sun dance and the way our people have found of "taking care of" that deep reality coming up like volcanoes or diamonds into the present. I say: "I was aghast at what I saw—you know how everything contains some deeper alien real version of itself, and that reality becomes apparent only now and then—well, anyway, we were over Cahokia and something happened there . . ."

Something like that was the narrative line. I meant for the reader to have to go back and re-view the first lines to understand just what they do introduce. Could be I will want to make things more explicit instead of hoping readers will know what the Ghost Dancing was and what the Sun dance "spirit dancers" and Uncle Gus's appearing in the Cahokia circle have to do with each other. (12 February 1996: E-Mail to author)

This message anticipates the prose setting he wrote for the poem in *Winning the Dust Bowl* (2001: 175–9). That setting sets forth in measured and detailed ways the contexts of the poem for Aunt Jewell's being selected Powwow Princess and the significance of the Cahokia Mounds. It particularly details the sequence of events at the powwow that delineates what the poem has folded within the powwow story told by poet-speaker's anxious, astonished self. The email is explicit about that state of mind, which Revard's prose setting does not mention, but which he is subject to in the poem's drama. In the email explanation of his using *aghast*, Revard paraphrases the first version of the poem's opening, where he interjects into the narrative the claim that "—you know how everything contains some deeper alien real version of itself, and that reality becomes apparent only now and then— . . ." His paraphrase elaborates slightly the first version, which is a question: "you know how each thing, deep inside, / is something else?" The "something else" in the email becomes "some alien real version of itself . . . that . . . becomes apparent only now and then." These lines in the published version attribute to "some Indian people" the ability "to see how each thing, deep inside, / is something else, all made of crazy things / they may give crazy names." These three versions define what Revard says he hopes readers will "re-view" to "understand just what they do introduce" (12 February 1996: E-mail to author), which I take to be the crisis in vision that has grown from the early, relatively easy resolution in "Looking Before and After" to the day of the Cahokia Mounds powwow and the problem of seeing an uncle dance who died twenty years previously, a problem that multiplies, given the shared, public nature of the vision.

The revisions reveal Revard's struggle to define what he calls "the mystery"—a mystery that the poems are written to incorporate in words, and to conduct the reader toward (2005: 65). The poet's defining the process by which the "mystery" of how we are shown these things is necessarily incomplete and unsettled, but points the way we need to look. The poet in "How the Songs Come Down" poses yet another arrangement for considering how we come to know what we need:

> you have to know before sense makes sense, before
>   their cobweb clues conduct you to the heart
> or exit of the mystery; then the selves
>   walking in public streets or prone in their private houses let
> their facts spill through although they always hold
>   surprises back-like
>   beaverdams, a tangle of
> memories in the molecules retain a part of

> what passes only, and the long-dead
> words touches smells keep time as
> lovers hold each other in the tangle of
> their private selves. (2005: 65)

This poem is predicated on the puzzle that is apparent only at the end, which was how the song his Aunt Jewell used to sing to him and his sister and cousins "came down" as a lullaby, and how they understood it before they understood its origin in the forced Ponca relocation from Nebraska to Oklahoma. The songs came down through some agency that Revard can ponder and present through a series of tableaux and mediations linked by intuitive leaps that the reader will find cohere only in the end with the lullaby and its child-sized version of the problem that is not a problem, but a gift.

The song that Aunt Jewell sang spoke to them as children, perhaps much as Aunt Jewell in her wheelchair spoke to the eagle in his cage—two wounded captives—in "An Eagle Nation" (2001: 31–34). She called the eagle "Kahgay," and the bird answered with a crouch and stare and a "low, shrill sound" (2001: 33). The poet had been growing uneasy over the zoo captivity of the eagle, which is a figure for the captivity of Indian peoples, present company included, who with the bird were subjected to the inane white man clapping and clicking his tongue and whistling and squeaking at the bird (2001: 32). Revard's ultimate claim that "we ... are an EAGLE NATION" risks succumbing to the confinements and injuries of history, even as it sheds them as he and his aunt and their family members climb the stands for an eagle's-eye view of the dancers at the Red Earth powwow. Their rising lifts the verse as well, makes it to rise and soar with the very memory of that history, which included some of the life story of his Aunt Jewell, and thinking as he watches the dancers:

> ...how all the circles
> had brought us into this Oklahoma time and what
> had passed between cage and wheelchair before
> we mounted up to view on this huge alien floor the long-ago drum
> in its swirling rainbow of feathers and
> bells and moccasins lifting up here
> the songs and prayers from long before cars or wagons,
> and how it all has changed and the ways are strange but
> the voices still
> are singing, the dream-heart
> still beating here, whatever the placards on
> their iron cages may have to say, we the people,
> as Aunt Jewell and Sun Dancers say,
> are an EAGLE NATION, now. (2001: 34)

The poem makes its body of words move from the Declaration of Independence ("we the people") to the trochaic finish of a powwow drumbeat: "áre an éa-gle ná-tion" [my emphasis]. The moment of vision afforded as they "mounted up" for the highest vantage over the voices that reach them from the dance floor, and the "dream-heart" beating inside the drum, belie the placard that tells the history of captivity and helps perpetuate it. For the poet, the enactment *in words, at least*, of the drum speaking the dream at its heart, lets the drum-beat in that final line resound in the resounding beat inside "now," the beat on which everyone's feet come down, come down to earth once again.

Works Cited

Mathews, J. J. 1961. *The Osages, Children of the Middle Waters*. Norman, Oklahoma: University of Oklahoma Press.
Revard, C. 1980. *Ponca War Dancers*. Norman, Oklahoma: Point Riders Press.
———. 1987. "Traditional Osage Naming Ceremonies: Entering the Circle of Being." B. Swann and A. Krupat, eds. *Recovering the Word*. Berkeley: University of California Press. 446–66.
———. 1991. *An Eagle Nation*. Tucson: University of Arizona Press.
———. 1996, 16 January. Letter to R. Bensen.
———. 1996, 12 February. "Re: Hartwick reading/lecture." E-mail to R. Bensen.
———. 1996, 13 February. "Re: Hartwick reading/lecture." E-mail to R. Bensen.
———. 1998, 24 March. "Re: [NL] Erdrich and Kerouac (was: Beats and Comparison)." E-mail to R. Bensen.
———. 1998. *Family Matters, Tribal Affairs*. Tucson: University of Arizona Press.
———. 2001. *Winning the Dust Bowl*. Tucson: University of Arizona Press.
———. 2005, 16 September. "Re: Permissions needed (?)." E-mail to R. Bensen.
———. 2005. *How the Songs Come Down*. Cambridge, UK: Salt Publishing.

Carter Revard's Angled Mirrors

Janet McAdams

Osage poet Carter Revard has said that his poems should be read, not in a chronological fashion, but rather like "angled mirrors, so that full-face, profile and rearview versions of their subjects may be seen together" (2001: xiii). These "angled mirrors" are present throughout Revard's work, in strategic juxtapositions of not only seemingly divergent poems, but certain sets of binaries, such as Western literary traditions and Native ones, technology and the earth, and local and global—even cosmic—cultures. Revard's central poetic task is the destabilizing of these binaries, often by transforming one into its *other*. In this essay, I assess what Joysa M. Winter has called the "amazing paradoxes" (1995: 14) of Revard's life and career, and I use these "amazing paradoxes" to theorize more broadly about contemporary Native poetics, drawing upon certain key theoretical tropes from the field of postcolonial studies to argue that Revard's poems constitute what Mary Louise Pratt has described as "contact zones" and to demonstrate how, through the juxtaposition of these textual "angled mirrors" a new space is mapped. "Contact zone" is Mary Louise Pratt's term for "social spaces where cultures meet, clash, and grapple with each other, often in contexts of highly asymmetrical relations of power, such as colonialism, slavery, or their aftermaths as they are lived out in many parts of the world today" (1993: 444). I look closely at three of Revard's poems, "Coyote Tells Why He Sings," "What the TV Said," and "Homework at Oxford," whose strikingly different elements generate the contact zones where the different traditions that inform Revard's work encounter each other, interact, conflict, come together.

Born in Pawhuska, Oklahoma, in 1931, Revard is the author of three collections of poetry: *Ponca War Dancers* (1980), *Cowboys and Indians, Christmas Shopping* (1992), and *An Eagle Nation* (1993), as well as a collection of essays, *Family Matters, Tribal Affairs*, and a memoir, *Winning the Dust Bowl* (2001). The focus of this essay will be on three of Revard's poems, "What the Coyote Says" from his early *Ponca War Dancers*, and two more recent poems, "Homework at Oxford," from *An Eagle Nation* and "What the TV Said," which first appeared in *Cowboys and Indians, Christmas Shopping* as "Something Indoors" and was reprinted in *Family Matters, Tribal Affairs*. However, because Revard's three volumes of poetry overlap, with each containing poems from previous books, it is difficult—and perhaps not especially useful-to characterize Revard's body of work in a linear fashion. Rather, his poems as a group form a matrix, in which they connect and interweave and reverberate off each other. These juxtapositions of different poems and different voices—and their engagement with different traditions—generate an infinite number of representations and reflections. While I discuss only these three poems, they are significant ones for their attention to certain key issues in the poet's work: communally-constructed identity, politics and personal experience, and—as will be my focus here—the meetings of, encounters between, and juxtapositions of different worlds.

In the works of Revard these juxtapositions constitute poetic maps that comprise, transform, and rewrite seemingly distinct "Old World" and "New World" formulations. These revisionary cartographies depend upon and make possible the plurality of voices that speak in Revard's poems. In this essay, I am especially not arguing that Revard and other contemporary Native poets who draw upon nonnative traditions of writing are somehow caught or trapped in the in-between, that is, my concern is not with the by now overworked critical trope of mixed-identity. My interest here is the new space the text itself maps out, a performed site, always dynamic. Perhaps because I am both a poet and a critic, I remain tied to certain notions of authorial agency. Native poets, I believe, in making use of Western forms, no more lose their "authenticity" than they do by writing on computers. My focus, thus, is on the textually staged encounters in Revard's work among different elements, since he characteristically introduces a third element (and sometimes a fourth or fifth one) into these received binaries that destabilizes their binarism, setting things in motion, and generating the shifting, conversant dynamics that characterize many of his poems.

These disruptions are in part effected by the complex manner in which voice is constructed in Revard's poems. The voicings in his poems continually interrogate the singular "I" through ironic displacements and a questioning of who is reading and who is being read. These different manifestations of voice can be closely tied to the poet's lived experiences in Oklahoma and Oxford, England, just as the two most evident literary traditions informing his work—Native American and the literature of Old and Middle English—arise from these locales. The tension between these two traditions[1] has produced some of Revard's most significant work.

The Different Voices

I am naming as I go, as I approach the House of Mystery, those who have cast themselves into our star and are walking with us here. I am Carter Revard (Nompehwathe), at Buck Creek, Oklahoma.

In "Seeing with Another 'I': Our Search for Other Worlds," Eugene C. Eoyang writes:

> In the major intellectual movements in this century ... a recurrent theme runs throughout the various discoveries and insights in different fields, from relativity theory to quantum mechanics to the Heisenberg principle to phenomenology to semiotics to deconstructionism to chaos theory. Different as these paradigms are, they all highlight the relationship between the object and subject, between the knower and what is known. In each of these mind-sets, the traditional opposition of bipolar thinking is undermined, and a dialectic model of knowledge has been posited. (1994: 93)

Eoyang goes on to suggest that in order to uncover "what we take for granted" we should "examine some of our most familiar reference points" (93). Revard's poems undermine "bipolar thinking" by forcing us to examine the limits and boundaries we take for granted. Transformations are of crucial importance in Revard's work; often, these transformations occur in the contact zones between binaries, when one familiar polarity is re-visioned as its opposite and vice versa.

---

1 I do not intend, with this phrase, to suggest a monolithic Indian tradition of writing (or an Osage one), but rather to suggest the many different cultural traditions from which a writer such as Professor Revard might draw.

These binaries are articulated and disrupted through seemingly different voices; however, "voice" is a complex trope when subjectivity is constituted relationally, within a matrix or web of relationships. With Revard, as with many, if not all, Native writers, communally constructed identities influence and inform the speaking voice in the literature. Revard's own desire to speak to and for his extended family and larger community is evident from the prevalence with which these family anecdotes and stories appear in his poetry, from the many dedications to family members, and even from the author photo that appears on *Ponca War Dancers*, which defies convention by depicting the Revard/Camp/Jump family and not a solo image of the author himself. Revard writes, "Poetry is not just what is unique to an author, an 'I,' it is mostly about what is shared, what is common to authors and readers" (2001: xvi).

In his essay, "History, Myth, and Identity among Osages and Other Peoples," Revard writes about Geronimo:

> Something strange appears when we look at some autobiographies of Indian people: the notion of identity, of how the individual is related to his world, his people, his self, is not quite what is found in an "Ameropean" autobiography....
>
> Only after [a] Genesis-like history of his world's creation, his people's creation and deliverance, of their land's creation, of why they are called Apaches, of what it means to be taken from the land created for the people, does Geronimo speak of himself... (1998: 88–89)

According to Revard, the essential facts of Geronimo's autobiography range "from the cosmic through the geologic to tribal, subtribal, family, and then only, last and in full context, to the 'individual' self that was Geronimo" (126–27). I quote at length from Revard's essay not only to underscore the importance of rethinking the "I" in his work and that of other Native American poets, but because these particular elements—geologic, tribal, cosmic, familial—are omnipresent touchstones of identity-making throughout his work. This relational constitution of identity is especially Native American, as has been well documented (see Weaver 1997: Introduction and *passim*). Yet, it is also important to bear in mind that so-called individual identity, despite its high visibility in contemporary U.S. society, is anomalous, for, as Eugene Eoyang writes, "... the concept of the individual self, as a separate, privileged entity set apart from the community, is a fairly recent development, even in the West. Its pervasiveness blinds us to other notions of existence which stress the contiguity of humanity rather than the atomistic autonomy of each individual" (1994: 98).

In an interview with Joseph Bruchac, Revard mentions the "different voices" that have arisen from his "amazing and paradoxical life," as an Oklahoman from a mixed Osage, Ponca, and white family, and as a Rhodes Scholar and Professor of medieval English literature (Bruchac 1007: 242). Born in 1931, Revard and his twin sister Maxine attended a one-room school, working part-time as school janitors, and graduating valedictorian and salutatorion. One of his high school teachers encouraged him to enter a radio quiz show called *Going to College*, which resulted in a scholarship to the University of Tulsa. As a Rhodes Scholar at Oxford, he studied English literature, and eventually went on to Yale for a Ph.D. in Medieval English literature. Revard became a professor at Washington University in St. Louis where he taught medieval literature and Native American literature until his retirement in 1998.

Because these different voices constructed in Revard's poems can be tied closely to his biography, it is crucial not to collapse "voice" and identity into a single category of literary investigation. Revard juxtaposes and sets into the play the different voices available to him, voices he traces as emerging directly from his experiences growing up in Oklahoma and as an Oklahoman transplanted to Oxford. Revard's earliest experiments with poetry were written within the parameters of traditional English verse. "Once I got in college," he explains, "I got stuck with the idea that I would write in traditional form" (Bruchac 1987: 240). The intersection of two experiences from either side of the paradox helped Revard discover a different voice:

> I was then teaching at Amherst, after getting through the Yale graduate school. I discovered one morning, up in the Emily Dickinson house, that I could talk about something ... I was in the top half of the house and it was raining, and I woke up in the morning about 6:00; it was starting to get dawn. I heard that dripping sound ... Then I remembered when I was about fourteen, hiking up Buck Creek Valley ... We were up there and a thunderstorm came up, so we got under the rocks. Under there were things we took to be coyote sign. (Winter 1995: 14)

Revard's realization that coyotes take in sounds and bring them back out as "song" prompted him to take "the coyote's voice," resulting in his breakthrough poem, the sonnet "Coyote Tells Why He Sings."[2] Thus, two

---

2 "Coyote Tells Why He Sings" appeared in *Ponca War Dancers* as "The Coyote" (1980: 11).

events occurred through the conception and writing of the poem, the ability to move beyond the limitations of traditional English verse, while still drawing upon it, and a reclaiming of his Oklahoma voice, which, he explains, he lost his second year at Oxford. "Then when I needed the Oklahoma voice the coyote gave it to me" (Bruchac 1987: 242). "Coyote Tells Why He Sings" is one of Revard's most frequently anthologized and quoted poems. It is a terse illustration of the paradoxes he lives and writes:

Coyote Tells Why He Sings

There was a little rill of water, near the den,
That showed a trickle, all the dry summer
When I was born. One night in late August it rained;
The thunder waked us. Drops came crashing down
In dust, on stiff blackjack leaves, on lichened rocks.
And the rain came in a pelting rush down over the hill,
The wind blew wet into the cave; I heard the sounds
Of leaf-drip, wet rustle of soggy branches in gusts of wind.

And then the rill's tune changed; I heard a rock drop
And set new ripples gurgling in a lower key.
Where the new ripples were, I drank, next morning,
Fresh muddy water that set my teeth on edge.
I thought how delicate the rock's poise was:
The storm made music, when it changed my world. (2001: 3)

The poem is a significant one in Revard's oeuvre not only for its liberating effect on its author. In its fourteen lines are many of the concerns that characterize his work: the recognition of "voice" constructed outside the dominant mode of individualized subjectivity; the intersection of Native American subject matter and a traditional English verse form; and transformation, in particular, transformation on a world scale. The title is key to the first of these concerns, since the story being told is that of the coyote's, who gives the poet his voice, so that the "I" is both coyote and poet. Revard has said:

> ... I was thinking what it would be like to be a coyote pup, and it hadn't rained all day, and the puppy gets up and all of a sudden this thunderstorm comes along. I'm thinking of what it would hear.
> When water starts rising, the streamlet makes little sounds. Then when it rises a couple of inches in a half hour, it goes down a pitch. The

storm made music. When the coyotes are singing at night, they hear all kinds of things like this. Maybe that's one of the ways they learn how to sing. So I put that in the poem. When it changed, there was pitch. It's like when the drum changes or the singer changes. The coyote learned how to sing, and all of a sudden there was music. The coyote had given me my voice. (Winter 1995: 14)

This "voice" that the poet has been given is that of the coyote, but the coyote is imitating the sound of water, translating it into his own language. The poet, in turn, takes the coyote's voice into his own, translating these sounds into his language. However, all these voices, these sounds, originate in the storm's music, the sound of the rain and wind, and, most important, the thunder. Revard's family clan is the Thunder, which suggests less that this voice is a borrowing but rather an inevitable transition from thunder, the source of his clan's power, through water to the coyote through the poet. It would not be accurate to say that the poem yokes the poet's inner and outer landscapes or that it brings together voices from inside and outside him, even though that might seem apparent at first glance. Such characterizations presuppose the existence of these as separate entities. Rather, what occurs in the poem is the revelation of the continuous and intertwined nature of the landscape, the coyote, and the poet, as another being, as an Osage person and member of the Thunder Clan.

The second of these concerns, the intersecting of Native American and traditional English writing, is one instance of a supposed binary being deconstructed and its polarities transformed. "Coyote Tells Why He Sings" is a sonnet, divided into the octave and sestet of the Italian or Petrarchan sonnet; however, the poem's form is not a rigid container into which a conflicting subject matter is poured. The poem's content cannot be clearly divided from its form: the voice of coyote, which is the voice of the water and becomes the voice of the poet, disrupts the metrical pattern of the sonnet. Revard's intention in this poem was to write a sonnet not in iambic or dactylic meter but with "six beats, a variable number of syllables" and no rhyme, so that it would sound like "talk" (Bruchac 1987: 242–43). The resulting poem, though, continually makes stylistic reference to the sonnet. It does not, in fact, rhyme, except for slant rhymes such as "den," "rained," "sounds," and "wind." Interestingly, even these slight rhymes occur only in the octave, disappearing as the poem makes its traditional turn at the opening of the sestet. Thus, while the poem may not follow the exact specifics of the Italian sonnet with its hendecasyllables and traditional rhyme scheme (abba abba, etc.), the sonnet form is organically present throughout.

The poem's closer adherence to the traditional form in the octave is significant. The division of the Petrarchan sonnet into octave and sestet is not just a line count but signals as well a division in thought, with a shift at the opening of the sestet. This is the poem through which Revard found his voice, the Oklahoma voice he reclaimed, and began to write past the limits of traditional English verse. Structurally, as well as in terms of content, the poem documents this shift, as the language in the octave rhymes slightly and is more literary— "stiff blackjack leaves, on lichened rocks" and "Of leaf-drip, wet rustle of soggy branches in gusts of wind," and the octave is the part of the poem just prior to the poet discovering his voice, the Oklahoma voice that sounds like talk. At the opening of the sestet, the poet hears the rock drop into the pool of water and the language becomes plainer: "I drank, next morning / Fresh muddy water that set my teeth on edge." The poem not only explains this transformation of voices but enacts them through language.

Revard has said that the last line "is a line I didn't get until the end of the day. I had thirteen lines, and I realized if I had another it would be a sonnet. And that last line turned out to be the theme of the whole thing, it summed it up" (Bruchac 1987: 243). With this, Revard's "play" with the sonnet form takes on another dimension, since it is traditionally the English sonnet—Shakespearian or Spenserian—that ends with a summarizing couplet. Thus, Revard's Petrarchan sonnet with its two distinct waves of thought ends with the "English" couplet: "I thought how delicate the rock's poise was: / *The storm made music, when it changed my world.*" The transformation of the poet's voice is, clearly, a transformation of the poet himself. As well, his world has changed profoundly, which is most evident if we compare the opening line of the poem with its delicate "little rill of water" to the closing line's forceful "*The storm made music.*"

Yet it is not so simple. I have noted earlier that Revard keeps these binaries in play by introducing additional elements, and thus sets up a dynamic field where categories cannot remain static. The sonnet form has been disrupted by the many revisions Revard makes, but there is no easy transformation from sonnet to plain style or "English" to "Oklahoman." For the last two lines, the summarizing couplet of the poem, in which this profound transformation is most clearly delineated, are the most traditional lines in the poem. The penultimate line is one stress away from exact iambic pentameter, which emphasizes the last line's strongly accented, perfect iambic pentameter. The added comma before the dependent clause creates a slight caesura that makes the following word, "when," more emphatic. The emphasized words in the resulting line then are "storm," "music," "when," "changed," "world." Thus, even as the transformation from one voice to another occurs and the poet's world changes from England back to Oklahoma, the poem circles back on itself and keeps these different traditions-and worlds-in play. And this, of course, is the third pursuit: the linking and transformation of different worlds.

Like the hybridized sonnet, "Coyote Tells Why He Sings," Revard's reworkings of Anglo Saxon riddle poems pair contemporary subject matter with traditional English verse forms, in order, he writes, "to use the 'classical' forms of English poetry to 'say things' about this world, now, and yet (I hope) be readable" (1998: 20). In these poems, Revard has maintained the alliterative metrics that characterize them: a four-beat line with a strong, central caesura. In the riddle poem, "whatever creature the poet taps must tell the listener/reader in enigmatic ways its lifestory" (21). Interestingly, these riddle poems are grouped in *Cowboys and Indians, Christmas Shopping*, but dispersed throughout the later *An Eagle Nation*, suggesting a fuller merging of different writing styles in the poet's work.

"What the TV Said" (1998: 179–81) is one of these contemporary Anglo-Saxon riddle poems. It employs a number of traditional tropes, a four-beat, caesured line and many kennings, such as "azure eyeball," "monstrous mushroom," and "iron horse":

> On this azure eyeball   where hell twice raised
> its monstrous mushrooms,   my mind's eye opened
> as the holster hardened   for its hot ghost-gun
> from barrels of black   dinosaur-blood; shortly . . .

Through these kennings, the complexity of this encounter is apparent, as each renames objects of the technological age, lacing these descriptions with irony and horror. The "azure eyeball" is the earth viewed twice through the lens of technology: the space ship which photographs it and the television that mirrors the earth back to itself. The "monstrous mushroom" tells the horrific ineffability of nuclear destruction. The "barrels of black dinosaur-blood" is oil, modern-day fuel; the dinosaurs are ostensibly extinct, but in fact survived by becoming birds.

"Iron horse" seems a play on so-called Tonto-speak[3] for the train. Revard's use of this phrase to describe a present-day automobile is both accurate and ironic, as it invokes earlier encounters, earlier namings.[4]

"Homework at Oxford" (1993: 75–83), also juxtaposes the poet's different worlds of Oklahoma and England. "Homework at Oxford" is a long meditative poem in which the speaker, displaced from his native Oklahoma while a student in England, is prompted by a long night of studying to remember his home. The poem opens in the speaker's rooms at Merton College: "Crouched and shivering, here on the soft blue-velvet sofa, / So mangy with wear it sags . . . " (75). It is not only the sofa that is worn, but the world itself. Ancient, the old world is rife with treasures but tainted with weariness. Furthermore, as Revard points out:

> It is not just "Oxford" and "Home" that are set up in opposition to each other in the poem; rather, it narrates one search for a good natural/supernatural overlook from which to view the world and myself in it, and it begins by posing a contrast between the Via Negativa of the medieval friar-mystic Meister Eckhart, whose "black book" I have been reading all through the dark night, and Breughel's painting of the Epiphany (which means the Making Apparent of Deity, the Showing to the Three Kings) of that very God for whom Eckhart is looking in deepest darkness. Eckhart preaches that one must leave behind every worldly sensory perception to find Deity; but Breughel pictures the Three Kings who, having followed a Star through the dark Night, arrive to find an ordinary "everyday" scene, a stable-and-animals scene, with an ordinary family and baby in it. (14 May 2001: E-mail to author)

The room's objects lead the speaker into further meditation, the Breughel painting on the wall, in which everything in the landscape is accorded equal weight: "so many things alive as Christ, / Pigeons,

---

3   In *When Nickels Were Indians*, Patricia Penn Hilden describes the "scholarly and ideological roots of a simple, childlike, and above all practical Indian, who expressed himself or herself in 'Tonto-speak.' Although the middle of the twentieth century continued to idealize key Native orators—especially those long dead in the Indian wars—it was generally believed that most Indians, good or bad, 'renegade' or 'hang-around-the-fort,' talked in an instantly recognizable combination of the first person singular subject (in the objective case: 'me'), simple, present-tense verbs ('want'), single syllable nouns ('meat'), and a variety of hand signals" (1995: 55).

4   While I don't wish to overdetermine this particular kenning, the train was especially unkind to Indian people, rapidly accelerating the "settling" of the West and the Indian diaspora. As well, the train proved a useful tool in decimating the great buffalo herds on which the Plains Indians so depended.

rooster, ramshackle thatch of the roof" (75). The speaker leaves the closed space of the room and ventures out into the garden where he sees cattle, which precipitates his "homework," his imaginative journey back to Oklahoma and childhood memory. He leaves his chilly sitting room and walks out into "the darkness of Merton Meadows" where he hears "the sighs of cattle bedded in the lush grass" (75). This familiar presence precipitates the speaker's remembrances of Oklahoma:

> ... I know
> The muffled drooling grind of teeth, long swallowing throbs.
> I hold my face to the herd, testing for warmth on eyes
> And forehead: only the smell of hot grass, bodies, manure,
> The ghost of milk; it might be morning darkness in Oklahoma. (76)

There are two kinds of "home *work*" being performed in the poem, the "fifty lines of Beowulf" the speaker is studying and the detailed remembering of "home" that takes place in the long, italicized, middle strophe of the poem. The speaker, who has "read all night," is prompted by "this black book / Of Meister Eckhart's" to journey, as the book describes, "deep in the soul's darkness / To the sweet fountains of life . . ." (75). These static representations of nature in the book and painting contrast sharply with the rich, full landscape of Oklahoma in which the speaker encounters crawdads, persimmons, blackbirds, geese, cattails, and herons. The heron wings on the classroom wall are linked to the Breughel painting. Each leads the speaker somewhere—in Oxford, out of the chilly and dark building, in Oklahoma into another sequence of memories.

"Oxford" and "Home" are set up in opposition to each other in this poem, and the italicizing of the Oklahoma section emphasizes the opposition. In this way, the poem is atypical of Revard's work. Old and New World juxtapositions rarely remain as stable as they do in "Homework at Oxford." About the poem, Revard notes: "I had not thought of the poem as showing homesickness, but rather, to use a fairly awkward term, homehealthiness. After all, here in Oxford the light brings a version of Oklahoma back, and nothing Oklahoman is alien here. The two places work together—this is symbiosis, not death of a transplanted memory" (14 May 2002: E-mail to author).

In "Homework at Oxford" the shift and play between places is further signified by stylistic changes. The Oxford portions of the poem are smooth and melodious, meditative, emphasizing the quiet of the speaker's solitude (and aloneness), while the home portions are noisier, and crowded with other people, with animals, with constant motion. The enjambment in the Oxford section slows down the lines, as does the frequent assonance and long vowels. They are stylistically a different point on a continuum rather than a radical shift. The lines are end-stopped almost throughout and the major changes have to do with diction, the use of words such as "yank," "wobbled," "scrabbled," "shriek," and "jerked" in the Oklahoma section. The Oxford section is in present tense; the Oklahoma part is in conditional/past imperfect implying events that take/took place on a regular basis, and is signaled by the conditional sentence: "... it might be morning darkness in Oklahoma." The memory that follows, we come to understand, is one typical yet memorable morning. The speaker's homesickness is evident almost throughout the poem. In his essay on Geronimo, Revard writes:

> He knew who he was and where he came from, and he was sure that to be removed from their *homeland* meant, for him and the Apaches, the loss not just of a "way of life" or a "home," but a change in, perhaps a loss of, their *beings*, or as we might say, their *identities*. In his account, the notions of cosmos, country, self, and home are inseparable. (1998: 86)

While Revard's essay focuses on Geronimo and the Chiricahua Apaches, he theorizes from them to include Native people in general (acknowledging, of course, that such generalizations are ultimately impossible). In this sense, then, "homesickness" is also a sickness for one's self. Because the self is constituted through others, to long for home is to long for them. In this poem, the speaker is away from himself, because he is away from the landscape of Oklahoma and from the people who populate the italicized section of the poem.

To complicate things further, the poem is fully nostalgic. One senses the speaker's longing for both these worlds, even though the poem's strategy is for a displaced speaker to describe his longing for the warm and fertile Oklahoma that is home as he writes from a cold and dark room in England. For this is the England of the conquest. The Europe that conquered the author's nation and killed his people. It is the Europe he claims for the Osage Nation in "Report to the Nation: Claiming Europe," a satirical essay from Revard's collection, *Family Matters, Tribal Affairs*. His feeling for Oxford is not so much contradictory as it is doubled, multiple, complex.

Yet it is too easy to cast Oxford as "bad," Oklahoma as "good" in this poem. It is more complicated, for after all, education—clearly located at

Oxford—is a "dazzling window," and certain subtle links between Oxford and Oklahoma are suggested. His grandfather is a hero in the poem just as Beowulf is a hero in a story in the poem. The poem ends mentioning "warriors who voyaged on foam-throated / Seabird over the waves to this wan shore" (85) reminding us that the poet, too, has ventured across the waves. Still, the poem may make subtle connections between the two, but it does not equate them. England is "wan" in comparison with the rich and fertile Oklahoma, and *Beowulf* is finally just a story in comparison with the poet's genuinely heroic grandfather who is struggling to feed his family during hard times.

These deepest meanings are revealed in Revard's poems through challenges to categories that appear both "obvious" and inevitable. Thus, these meanings are not effected through closure but rather the full articulation of questions about what, to use Eoyang's phrase, "we take for granted." The not obvious history revealed in "Homework at Oxford" is the heroism depicted in the domestic scenes from Oklahoma. While the binary opposition between Oxford and Oklahoma is a strong one and one the poet keeps reminding us of, this poem, as with all Revard's work, disrupts and infiltrates this opposition.

When voices, traditions, experiences sit at angles to each other, representations are never fixed; they are always changing, transforming, being made. The poems do not imitate a separate reality but "re-present" it, revising and shaping it continually. In this sense, their use of language is performative; they make a world even as they describe one. As such, they forge connections to the oral culture which informs them, because language, meaning, and texts tend to exist in full context within oral cultures, as opposed to literate ones where texts and language circulate widely and often out of context. We as readers receive Revard's poems as written text; however, because the poems strategize, map, and construct a world, their use of language is as much performative as it is statement.

This new world made manifest in Revard's poems is a dynamic one, existing in the charged relationships and movements between and among the supposed polarities he engages. Thus, Revard delineates borders even as he crosses and erases them; his poems constitute "contact zones" where heterogeneous and dissimilar forces encounter each other.

Poetry seems an especially powerful medium in which to document and construct these contact zones. As Elaine Jahner has written, "Poetry's metaphoric impetus is toward limits of all kinds in order to reach beyond them; but as it reveals the limits of culture, it also emphasizes the originary energy channeled through these limits . . ." (1994: 180). Revard's poems not only emphasize this "originary energy" but unleash it. Thus these poems, these zones, do not—and do not attempt to—reconcile difference. Instead, they map a new space, which exists dynamically, that is to say, which is always performed and never static.

I have noted that certain binaries are disrupted by being juxtaposed and shown to be linked and interrelated rather than in full opposition. Another gesture the poet uses to belie oppositional thinking is to introduce an additional element (or elements) into the binary. The juxtaposition of Old and New Worlds, for example, is complicated and undermined in "Homework at Oxford" by subtle links between these worlds. In other poems, the horizontal binary of Old World/New World—mapped out on either side of the ocean—is disrupted by the poet's introduction of worlds above, beneath, and within. In this way, the "cosmic" and "geologic" aspects that constitute identity, place, and, hence, the world itself, are articulated.

Conclusion

So like the mockingbird I have more than one song, but they are all our songs.

For Native peoples, Michelle Cliff insists, "Everything is contiguous. Everything is connected in time, space. Therefore, there are no boundaries. The petroglyph and what it signifies exists with the mobile home and what it signifies" (1995: 33). The world is always being written into being, and the voices that emerge from it, because they exist and speak relationally, necessarily do not speak from *a priori* static and discrete locations, but are always being generated and articulated. The voice of Coyote is a voice full of irony, the voice of the trickster. It is a voice that keeps us guessing, one which we can never fully fix or pin down, so that it is always changing and shifting. The collective nature of this voice arises from the very motion of these shifts.

Like many Native American writers, Revard emphasizes the importance of telling stories in his work. "Stories" do not seem exclusively Indian even as the poet emphasizes their importance in his own heritage and individual experiences. His poems do not collapse the distinctions between these traditions and cultures. Instead, they draw on a rich plurality. In Revard's poetry, no action is apart from the world in which it is performed; no being is separate. Instead, the world itself is a room of angled mirrors where every act is reflected and multiplied, where everyone's reflection is captured numerous times, in looking glasses filled with others.

Works Cited

Bruchac, J. 1987. *Survival This Way: Interviews with American Indian Poets.* Sun Tracks 15. Ed. L. Evers. Tucson: University of Arizona Press.

Cliff, M. 1995. "Poetry is a Way of Reaching Out to What is Reaching for You." *American Poetry Review* 24.4: 29–35.

Eoyang, E. 1994. "Seeing with Another 'I': Our Search for Other Worlds." *An Other Tongue: Nation and Ethnicity in the Linguistic Borderlands.* Durham, North Carolina: Duke University Press. 93–112.

Hilden, P. P. *When Nickels Were Indians: An Urban Mixed-blood Story.* Washington, D.C.: Smithsonian Institution Press, 1995.

Jahner, E. A. 1994. "Knowing All the Way Down to Fire." *Feminist Measures: Soundings in Poetry and Theory.* Eds. L. Keller and C. Miller. Ann Arbor: University of Michigan Press.

Pratt, M. L. 1993. "Arts of the Contact Zone." *Ways of Reading: An Anthology for Writers.* 3rd ed. Ed. D. Bartholomae and A. Petrosky. Boston: St. Martin's Press. 442–62.

Revard, C. 1980. *Ponca War Dancers.* Norman, Oklahoma: Point Riders Press.

———. 1987. "Something that Stays Alive: An Interview with Carter Revard." *Survival This Way: Interviews with American Indian Poets.* Ed. J. Bruchac. Sun Tracks Series 15. Ed. L. Evers. Tucson: University of Arizona Press. 231–48

———. 1992. *Cowboys and Indians, Christmas Shopping.* Norman, Oklahoma: Point Riders Press.

———. 1993. *An Eagle Nation.* Tucson: University of Arizona Press.

———. 1998. *Family Matters, Tribal Affairs.* Tucson: University of Arizona Press.

———. 2001, 14 May. No subject. E-mail to J. McAdams.
———. 2001. *Winning the Dust Bowl*. Tucson: University of Arizona Press.
Weaver, J. 1997. *That the People May Live*. Oxford University Press.
Winter, J. M. 1995, 14 January. "The Voice of the Coyote." *The Osage Nation News*.

From *Speak to Me Words: Essays on Contemporary American Indian Poetry* by Dean Rader and Janice Gould, eds. (c) 2003 The Arizona Board of Regents. Reprinted by permission of the University of Arizona Press.

"Present Myth": Old Stories and New Sciences in the Poetry of Carter Revard

Ellen L. Arnold

Moral philosopher Mary Midgley, in *Science and Poetry*, argues eloquently for the role of poetry and the arts in "putting life back together" (2001: 170)—healing the individual, social, and environmental fragmentation brought about by the "impersonal, reductive, atomistic methods" and "imperialistic, isolating" ideologies associated with Western science (1). Cutting science off from the rest of human intellectual life, Midgley observes, prevents us not only "from approaching the large problems about ourselves" but also "from appreciating the real importance of science itself" (9–10). One of several American Indian writers (including Leslie Marmon Silko, Linda Hogan, Gerald Vizenor, and others) whose work draws on resonances between traditional indigenous thought-worlds and the worldview emerging from the post-modern sciences of quantum mechanics and complexity theory, Carter Revard has long employed images and concepts from science and technology in his poetry as part of a complex mediation of Native and EuroAmerican traditions, values, and epistemologies. As Revard says about his poem "Dancing with Dinosaurs," "I have tried to turn the old stories, and new sciences, into present myth" (1998: 25). By weaving indigenous spiritual traditions together with metaphors and insights from contemporary science, Revard creates a mythology of interconnection and process that offers new ways of knowing and being in the world that participate with what he calls the "continuous procreating of the universe" (1998: 138).

Carter Revard's poems are filled with descriptions of a specific and intimately detailed natural world—bluestem grass, blackjack trees, meadowlarks, chiggers, geodes—in conversation with images from science and technology—quarks, black holes, computer chips, electrodes pulsing in neon tubes. Many of his poems critique the destructive effects of materialism and greed enabled by modern technologies, as when he mourns "the dead rapids and waterfalls / drowned in Glen Canyon and Lake Mead" to power "Las Vegas light flashing in crimson green / gold and violet" in the poem "Close Encounters" (1993: 27, 28). Yet he never loses sight of the miraculous beauty of science's insights into the fabric of the universe or the wonders of its inventiveness. For Revard, the songs of rain and birds, of humans and their instruments, the roar of planes through space, the humming of electrons through wires and computer chips, all contribute to the interwoven music of the universe. By "refiguring" the English language—by restoring the power of words to make visible the connections that interlink all of creation—Revard translates across apparently oppositional categories such as "natural" and "technological," "living" and "inanimate," "material" and "spiritual." Like the traditional Osage naming ceremony that carefully links individual identity to family, clan, tribe, place, and cosmos, Revard's poems are ceremonies of naming that resacralize the practices and products of science, as well as language itself, restoring them to the spiritual universe within a new/old cosmology of wholeness.

Cross-Pollinations: Science, Poetry, and Creativity

Ethnobotanist and poet Gary Nabhan, in his recent book *Cross-Pollinations: The Marriage of Science and Poetry* (2004), uses cross-pollination as a metaphor for the ways that the shifts in perceptions required by moving back and forth across disciplinary boundaries between science and poetry can seed creativity and new growth in both disciplines. "[C]ross-pollination is not some perk or frill," Nabhan suggests; like plants, "Artists and scientists also need cross-fertilization or else their isolated endeavors will atrophy, wither, or fall short of their aspirations" (13). During the period between 1940 and 1970, when Nabhan observes that the "the rift between those engaged in scientific and literary pursuits reached its widest dimensions" (39), Carter Revard was already actively bridging the gap between the arts and the sciences, weaving them together in his personal quest for truth and beauty in the world.

In an e-mail conversation with an online Native Literature discussion group about his early poem "ESP," Revard describes his fascination with science as a teenager in the 1940s:

> In high school I had loved the General Science course in the ninth grade, whose teacher (H. Earl Shamberger) had us subscribe to a little journal called Science Digest, modeled on Readers' Digest I guess. This got me into the science stuff, and on days when I did not have to go to work straight from classes, I might walk down to the Bartlesville Public Library, a mile or so from the school, and go back to the Science section, and try to puzzle through the physics textbooks and such ... (18 May 2001: E-mail to Nativelit-L@raven.cc.ku.edu)

In preparation for the radio quiz show in which he won his scholarship to the University of Tulsa, Revard "learned all the physics [he] could" from his Uncle Kenneth's Notre Dame textbooks (1998: 72). "There was an excellent chemistry course my senior year in high school," he reports, "and in my freshman college year I also took two semesters of first rate chemistry (Qual and Quant) and got a little better understanding" (18 May 2001: E-mail to Nativelit-L@raven.cc.ku.edu).

In college, Revard's interests in the interconnections between science and literature blossomed:

> When I was a freshman at the University of Tulsa in 1948–9 we had to do a second-semester research paper for the English Composition course taught by Professor Franklin Eikenberry, and the title of mine was RADIOACTIVITY: SEARCHLIGHT INTO THE ATOM. It turned out about fifty-some pages, and in researching it I saw lots of accounts of the history of how physicists had discovered radioactivity, how it forced them first to revise the entire intellectual framework of their notions of matter and energy, how it showed them that the atom was not "unbreakable" as its Greek name proclaims it to be (going back to Greek and Roman thinkers determined to reduce the universe to its elementary particles; another book I liked as result of the Eng Comp course was Lucretius, whose account of the way the universe happened depends on the theory of invisible elementary particles which at one point take a "swerve" and produce the universe, something like a Big Bang: Professor Eikenberry, at the end of the year, gave me a copy of the long poem by Lucretius, in translation of course since I had no Latin). And of course how Bohr developed the "planetary" model for atoms, and Einstein came along to work out the math equations linking energy and matter as transformational versions of each other, and Planck got quantum theory started and all that. (18 May 2001: E-mail to Nativelit-L@raven.cc.ku.edu)

In the process of arguing for "an alliance rather than a war between science and poetry" on this same discussion list, Revard elaborated:

> I much prefer reading SCIENTIFIC AMERICAN to almost any poetry or literary journal. When I was an undergraduate at Oxford, 1952–54, the British began publishing more popular scientific journals and I used to buy those regularly. I was trying to use the particle-physics stuff . . . in things I WANTED to be poems. I was fascinated by muons, and at that time the whole can of worms, or quarks, was just opening up—the term quark was still confined to Joyce's FINNEGANS WAKE in those days. When Crick and Watson untwisted the molecules of DNA and RNA, when the geologists suddenly began to accept and build on the former heresy of continental drift and plate tectonics, when the great radio telescopes at Jodrell Bank and elsewhere began bringing in news from far galaxies, when the song of the hydrogen molecules began to be heard, when quasars first swam into the astronomers' ken, . . . when dinosaurs sprouted feathers, so far as I could see the world was no less mysterious and satisfying to human perceptions than the prairie to a Pawnee in 1700 or so. (12 February 2000: E-mail to Nativelit-L@raven.cc.ku.edu)

For Revard, positivist science can yield momentous revelations, but its vision is always partial:

> Science is an avalanche and nobody should think it makes comfortable skiing. It buries people, it changes mental landscapes. . . I think of scientists as mostly just going back and forth along hillsides grazing away like cattle or sheep, and presently we see they have made paths that are amazingly neat-patterned terrace-like ways, and realize that gravity and consciousness and appetite together with some fine grass have shaped a hillside temporarily. The next thunderstorm of surprising information may completely reshape it. (12 February 2000: E-mail to Nativelit-L@raven.cc.ku.edu)

In "ESP," published in Kenneth Rosen's important early anthology of Native American poetry *Voices of the Rainbow* (1975), Revard uses an example of one such scientific "thunderstorm" to address the relationship between "matter" and "mind" and the individual's quest for meaning in the vastness of the cosmos:

> In 1895, for instance, Roentgen
>   quite accidentally saw that a screen
> was fluorescing when his cathode-ray
>   machine was on;
>   the concept *matter* had to be revised—
> and still more radically when, next year,
>   Becquerel found his halides fogged
>   by some invisible emanation
>   out of uranium ore, not sent by man. (Rosen 1975: 87)

These observations on the discovery of X-rays follow the classic scientific and philosophical question, posed in the first person, that opens the poem: "I know that mind / is only matter— / but will someone please explain / what matter is?" (86), and introduce its central concern, how the individual human mind perceives the invisible forces of the universe and makes meaning of them:

> The problem is that down in 1972
> I've got no phosphor screens,
> no silver halides,
> to let me know of such great accidents
> when things from outer space sweep through the mind . . . (87)

What the poet does have to make these "accidents" visible is the poem itself: ". . . and language helps, its metaphors transpose / invisible joy to visible love—see, / like stones in ultraviolet darkness, / faces of lovers luminesce . . ." (87). However, unlike the scientist's cloud chamber (a container of supercharged water vapor that reveals the trails of subatomic particles shooting out from a fissioning nucleus), ". . . most cloud-chambers of language / are obsolete, they catch / only what's looked for," and the "unimagined" (87) remains inexpressible. If the perspective of science is partial, language too is limited by its own frame of reference.

If poetry offers aesthetic and ethical dimensions to science, as Nabhan suggests, science offers poetry a precision of language with which to shape new metaphors and insights. In "ESP," Revard makes use of the language of science to concretize and illuminate the more nebulous human endeavor to comprehend the individual's place in the workings of the universe:

> But lately I have thought of just
> the right sensitive receiver:
> it is a wilderness big enough
> to find a vision in
> while quite alone. (Rosen 1975: 87)

This indirect reference to a vision quest—a cross-tribal practice involving a solitary journey into wilderness to seek spirit guidance, contextualized within a web of story and ceremony—at the center of the poem, expressed in simpler language and markedly slowed rhythm, creates a kind of mythic hinge between science's vision of subatomic mysteries and the individual's visionary connection to spirit and universe. By linking the vision quest to the cloud chamber's ability to make the invisible visible, Revard suggests that what is comprehended by the individual mind may be just as "material" as the radioactive particles we now take for granted as "real." Thus he extends the capacity of language to see and say beyond the limitations of what is "looked for," to experience and express the tracings of interconnections to which we are usually blind.

The poem turns next to the focused dailiness of individual experience, as the poet allows a fall leaf tossed into the air by his toddler, birds flying "dark / against the snow" and "snowflakes ... sailing into focus / against my windshield" (Rosen 1975: 88) to register their tracks in the cloud chamber of his mind, and then returns to the more concrete language of science to describe the potential for new understanding:

> And maybe later
> when my SELF has cooled
> near absolute zero
> it will grow super conductive
> like a helium-crystal laser, impossible but
> so sensitive
> that touched by the *gegenschein* it would
> flash out a Lazarus-light
> on memory's moiré,
> and there would float into view
> the hologram of all my scattered days
> their storms contained as a brilliant play of things
> that meadows could understand as rain,
> and stars as a zodiac of lightnings. (88)

At the end of life, the poet speculates, the "self" might become like a super-cooled conductor that can receive the faintest *gegenschein*—a backscatter of sunlight against solar dust—and, in the moment of passage into the next life, flash it bright against the fabric of memory to create a hologram, an integrated image of the individual's life experience. Holograms (first produced in 1947) are three-dimensional images of light wave interference patterns produced by intersecting beams of laser light, each small part of which contains (from its particular perspective) a view of the entire image. Revard's imagined hologram, created in the intersections of sunlight reflected off solar dust and the "Lazarus-light" of an individual's passage from earthly life to the next life, holds in its parts the whole of the universe. A visual metaphor that blends science with references to indigenous vision quests and biblical stories of resurrection and rebirth, the hologram relates individual experience to the universe in an image legible not only to readers but to meadows and stars, making meaning for earth and universe as well.

In the final passage, the poem contracts once more—focusing in on the struggle to perceive beyond the limitations of sensory perception, as the poet comments on how his progressive hearing loss (a reference to Revard's inherited otosclerosis [Revard 1998: 53]) heightens the sensitivity of his bones to the "vibrations" of the "spheres"—and circles back to memories of putting his head "against a telephone pole" to "hear the wires humming,"

> ... never needing
> to tap their tightstrung copper to be in
>   on what was said across those miles
>   of empty blowing prairie
>   on the coldest winter day. (90)

"ESP" encompasses scientific revelations into the structure of atoms and light within a wider human history of intellectual and spiritual quest, moving back and forth across borders between matter and mind, mind and universe, science and spirituality, indigenous and Western worldviews. By interlinking the tracings of particle paths and light waves with those of human memory and language, Revard demonstrates the common quest of science and poetry to make meaning visible, to express the ineffable. By allowing these multiple perspectives to intersect and complement each other, Revard's poems themselves often become dynamic holograms that also include other-than-human subjectivities in the making of meaning. As Midgley points out, the pitfall of science has been to claim "omnicompetence" (2001: 21) as the only valid source of knowledge about the world, thus creating false antitheses between reason and feeling, intellect and imagination, mind and spirit, and "distorting the whole picture of life" (2001: 55). As Midgley observes, the atomistic science of the Renaissance, which conceived the "world as a machine" to be "taken to pieces ... and reassembled more satisfactorily" (25) and fostered a parallel "social atomism," still operates to divide human beings against themselves and others (2). "ESP," like much of Revard's work, reweaves the fragments of life not by rejecting science, but rather by using its language to inscribe tangible figures of wholeness in which multiple subjects and forms of knowledge, mediated by mythic imagination, can open onto each other in interdependent ways.

"Earth and Diamonds," one of two poems by Revard selected for inclusion in Kurt Brown's 1998 anthology *Verse and Universe: Poems about Science and Mathematics*, addresses overtly this complementary and evolving relationship between science and myth. Like "ESP," "Earth and Diamonds" opens with a philosophical question: "How far from truth to beauty, say, / in diamonds?" (Brown 1998: 140). Observing that at one time it was a "scientific fact" that diamonds were made by the "heavenly / 'influence'" of stars, "but now it is a fact of science that earth / composes diamonds of itself," the poet uses another "fact of science"—that "the earth itself was made / in superstars"— to encompass these opposing statements within a larger, resonating wholeness, "so that the house which stars once built / still crystallizes in the shape of stars, / still shines like them" (140). As Janet McAdams observes in her study of Revard's "angled mirrors," "Revard's central poetic task is the destabilizing of . . . binaries" (2004: 193); in the "contact zone between binaries," McAdams states, transformations occur and "a new world is mapped" (195, 193). In "Earth and Diamonds," "facts" and "myths" mirror each other, reflecting and transforming to create a kind of dynamic hologram, which the poem then re-enters from multiple angles to explore its image of wholeness and interconnection from a variety of perspectives. Diamonds are made by earth *and* by stars, and now by people, who make them "from coal . . . just as volcanoes did" (Brown 1998: 142). Earth cannot be said to shine, but from space the astronauts "have seen our muddy planet shine / a blue star up in heaven" (140). The female bowerbird deserts the male's elaborately constructed and blue-painted bower as soon as she is mated, and the male "takes no interest . . . in / *those rising generations*," yet he still "paints just what he sees, he makes / his gemlike house / of blue lights," mirroring both earth's shine from space and the starlike gems earth makes within (143). And, if birds are dinosaurs "who put on feathers and survived," then we can no longer believe "that dinosaurs became extinct, just as we can / no longer hold that earth, not stars, / composes diamonds" (143). "Facts," no longer "pure," are shown to be matters of perspective, "facets" that "crack light and spill / its rainbows over earth" (140).

Similarly, myth is deconstructed to show its inherent "facts":

> So flights of angels, passing through our bodies
> may see a neutron shine
> gemlike with facets, all the points of
> inner structure netting
> the radiant waves and fishing out
> their rainbow messages of peace
> from the God of Storms.

> That, you'll say, is not
> a fact—but if we just remove
> the angels and insert
> a physicist, you may allow
> it is a fact . . . (141)

And facts are unfolded outward to become, seamlessly, myth again:

> it is a fact
> that neutrons have a structure
> and perhaps that each is like
> a crystal, certainly
> neutrons are being probed by beams of
> some other particles,
> and in the spectrum which comes back to us
> from deep inside these specks of space
> are messages concerning Universal
> Creation and Apocalypse. (141)

If, however, "we keep exploding facts / into old myths, and then compressing myths / into new facts" (143), this process is not a static exchange, but an evolution. New facts, like the understanding that birds evolved from dinosaurs, unfold into new myths that can encompass them, and now, when we look at birds, we see "DYNA-SOARS" (143), the living presence of a past we once considered gone. This new myth allows us to experience the past alive in the present, the unity of space/time—that abstract Einsteinian concept—as a material "fact" "singing at the windowsill" (Revard 2001: 25) and "dancing" with the Osage people, who have similarly "put on their feathers and survived" in the poem "Dancing with Dinosaurs" (25). Revard's new myths "word humans back into the world," to paraphrase his introduction to "Dancing with Dinosaurs" in *Winning the Dust Bowl* (2001: 25), allowing us to see anew our own inherence in universal systems, our own potential to join with the ongoing processes of creation or to sever ourselves from them.

"ESP" and "Earth and Diamonds" look both "out far" and "in deep," as Revard's poem, "Columbus Looks Out Far, In Deep" (2005: 155–56) asks Columbus to do: "What I don't see, after five hundred years, / is what the coral sees / or abalone" (155). Using the first person, the poet invites the reader to step into Columbus's shoes, and from there into the awareness of other creatures, to see the effects of our individualistic, mechanistic, imperialistic worldview on the web of interconnections of which we are part: "the whitening of coral skeletons," "the driftnets strangling dolphins / great ghostly sharks wavering past impoisoned /

seals with cancerous growths" (155). Looking outward through the perspective of theoretical science, "through worm holes / into the future," we can see with the sea creatures "what's waiting for us killers—/ plutonium tank-shells" and "the fading out / of human awareness" on earth (156). However, by following similar trajectories, looking simultaneously inward and outward, we may also see new possibilities for healing, like the May butterflies in the poem "Chiggers" (1992: 54), who meet flowers "as equals," "like / equations that have found / their Einstein and can sip the nectar / of hyperspace at will" (54). From a chigger's point of view, the poet imagines that humans become angels when they "lie down / in green pastures and get up / as Providence" to carry chiggers "into eternity" and time like "a chigger-bite . . . back to heaven" (54). "Maybe," the poet speculates, "souls / can't change until they've tapped into / red lasers pulsing under / the bright skin of stars" (54).

Transfigurations: World into Words

As Revard words humans back into the world, his poems also remake words themselves, restoring human language to the processes of creation. Complementing poems like "ESP" that link human language to the tracings of subatomic particles in cloud chambers and birds and leaves across the sky, "This Is Your Geode Talking," the second of Revard's poems included in *Verse and Universe* (Brown 1998: 138–39), re-embeds human language within the spoken and written languages of earth. Here, the poet speaks/writes through the perspective of a geode, one of those lovely layered, crystalled "stones" created over eons of time by the infiltration of water and minerals into a hollow sphere (here created by an oyster shell):

> I still remember ocean, how
> she came in with all I wanted, how we opened
> the hard shell we had made
> of what she gave me and painted into
> that lodge's white walls the shifting
> rainbows of wave-spray . . . (Brown 1998: 138)

Echoing the image of the bowerbird's blue nest, which attracts a mate and mirrors acts of creation within and beyond earth, the "marriage" of sea-creature and ocean is painted/written onto the walls of their shared abode. The story continues across eons as ocean recedes and the geode finds itself on land, where "sweet water chuckled and trickled, siliceated through / my crevices as once the salty ocean had, and I felt / purple quartz-crystals blossom," forming "new selves of banded agate" (139). At last, a "soft hand" comes down from the geode's dreams of the future and gives the geode "to diamond / saws that sliced me in two, to diamond dust that polished" the two halves to be made into bookends:

> I let them separate and shelve them heavy
> on either side of a word-hoard whose light leaves
> held heavy thoughts between
> the heavier, wiser, older lines of all
> my mirrored selves, the wave-marks left,
> by snowflake-feathery amethyst
> ways of being
>   —by all those words,
>   by the Word, made slowly,
>   slowly, in-
>   to Stone. (139)

Again, the use of the first person asks readers to step out of our individualistic limitations, to recognize the living history embodied in the geode and the generosity with which it allows itself to be opened and displayed for the expansion of human awareness. Framed by the geode, the written words of humans, the heavy but ephemeral thoughts recorded on "light leaves," are encompassed within the larger history and future of creation. The scientific understanding of how geodes are made and the technology that opens the geode to be "read" by human eyes enable a new vision of humanity's reciprocal relationship with/in cosmic evolution: recorded human history is dwarfed and contained by universal processes occurring on a vaster scale, and at the same time the written word is restored to those processes, reinvested with the power of the original Word to speak creation into being.

 "This Is Your Geode Talking" appears as "Geode" in *An Eagle Nation* (1993: 91–92) and *How the Songs Come Down* (2005: 4–5); the renaming of the poem for the 1998 *Verse and Universe* anthology heightens the sense of the poem as a "wake-up call" from the universe, a warning message transmitted via one of earth's non-human subjectivities about the need for humans to reconsider the anthropocentric, objectifying vision that characterizes their sciences and histories. The final three lines of the poem as it appears in *An Eagle Nation*, "by all those words, / by the Word,/ made slowly into Stone" (1993: 92), are altered in the 1998 version; the repetition of "slowly" and the repositioning of the words to "drip" slowly down the page into solidity, emphasize the implied challenge of the poem—will humans allow our hoarded words to harden into isolated, objectifying stasis, or will we open our vision to see our interconnectedness with the life all around us and restore our words, spoken and written, to the living processes of creation? While "This Is Your Geode Talking" makes no direct reference to Native traditions, it is suffused throughout with a definitively indigenous understanding of the potential of language to both create and destroy. The fact that Revard places "Geode" second in *How the Songs Come Down: New and Selected Poems*, following "Coyote Tells Why He Sings," the poem that describes how he found his Oklahoma/Indian voice (see Revard 2001: 3-7), in a section titled "Indian Territory," suggests that "Geode" expresses ideas central to Revard's poetic task.

In fact, Revard's entire body of writing takes up the challenge of "Geode," bringing words to life and allowing their interactions to make life visible everywhere. For example, in the poem "Communing Before Supermarkets," which appears in a chapter titled "Transubstantiating" in *Winning the Dust Bowl* (2001), the poet poses the "scientific" question, "how does the seed know to make / a watermelon and not an apricot?" (77), and in response, reflects on childhood memories of eating watermelons:

> *now the melon is turning into me, and my sisters and brothers,*
> *my mother and father and uncles and aunts and into the*
> *ants feasting there on the melon-rinds,*
> *and into the grass and the trees growing there, and into the dirt—*
> *and Sand Creek is turning, this day is turning to night, so now*
> *when we go home I'll remember and it will be turned*
> *into words, and maybe sometime*
> *it would all grow again a long way off, a long way into*
> *the future, and that's what a few pennies and dimes can do*
> *if you have them, a few seeds, a little rain where creekwaters rise,*
> *and the whole world turns into food for all*
> *the different beings in their times.* (ital. in orig.; 77-78)

The seed not only knows to grow into a melon (the "how" of which science has yet to fathom), but how to become as well bodies, grass, trees, memories, and words, which recreate the melon and provide the "seed" to encourage new plantings. The words on the page are shown to be fully contiguous with life's processes of growth, consumption, and rebirth, and they in turn transubstantiate the earth, bringing the melon back to life in some distant place or time. The words of the poem itself become holy sacrament, restoring the ordinary labors of planting, harvesting, eating, remembering, and writing to the miraculous and timeless cycles that connect us to "all / the different beings in their times."

On the other hand, Revard reminds us, technologies have lives of their own, and the constructions of human minds and hands are as much a part of the fabric of life and creation as seeds and melon-eaters. The riddle poem "The Poet's Cottage" (2003: 6–7), Revard says in "Some Notes on Native American Literature," the essay that contains the poem, gives a house "its chance to speak its being" (2003: 7):

> At your finger's touch   my turquoise flower
> of fossil sunlight   flashes, you call
> from mountain springs   bright spurts of water
> that dancing boil   on its blue petals
> crushed seeds, their life's   loss repaid
> with offered words. (6)

The gas stove addresses the person who ignites its "turquoise flower" flame, speaking its true nature as an intersection in a living, interconnected web of exchange across expanses of time among sunlight, earth, water, plants, and human consumers. Similarly,

>   Watchful electrons
> in copper wall-snakes   await your cue
> to dance like Talking God   down from heaven
> and bring Mozart's   melodies back,
> pixel this world's   woes and wonder, but
> through the wind's eye you see   the sun rising
> as creatures of earth   from heaven's darkness
> open iris-nets to   the harsh light
> of human mysteries,   your here and now,
> needle points   where numberless
> angels are dancing   always and everywhere. (6–7)

Radio and television and the electrons that power them conduct to humans heavenly music, news of "woes and wonder" from distant places, messages from the world of the spirits. The "wind's eye" offers humans a window on the sunrise and the waking of earth's creatures, but the world is also looking in on the mysteries of human life contained within. Revard explains, "To these creatures, the light reveals mysterious humans and the very great mysteries which we dismiss by calling them here and now"; the closing lines of the poem, he says, are "to remind us that these mysteries are small and sharp-pointed as that needle-point upon which the medieval scholars used to try and count the angels dancing" (8). Technology is renamed, re-figured in terms of the natural and the spiritual; humans, who often consider themselves the center of the universe, are shown to be, like the stove or television they can bring to life with touch or words, nodes in a vast wholeness. Yet, the spoken and written word, the human prayers of thanks acknowledging the loss of life required to feed humans, are central to this poem, integral to the system of exchange the poem makes visible and necessary to its continuation.

In the Preface to *Family Matters, Tribal Affairs*, Revard states that his writing makes "a community of words on Indian ground" (1998: xi); that living community of words "reclaim[s] what's worthwhile in Europe for our people" (24), actively unmaking and remaking the forms of EuroAmerican culture into more indigenous ones, reconnecting them to the circle of being that also includes the perspective of the universe. In Revard's work, the specifics of history—personal, family, clan, community, national, and international—are always suffused with the mythic history of creation. For example, the poem "Close Encounters" (1993: 25–28), like the Osage Naming Ceremony it references, opens with the Creation Story:

> We of the Osage Nation have come,
> as the Naming Ceremony says,
> down from the stars.
> We sent ahead
> our messengers to learn
> how to make our bodies,
> to make ourselves a nation,
> find power to live, to go on,
> to move as the sun rises and never fails
> to cross the sky into the west,
> and go down in beauty into the night,
> joining the stars once more
> to move serenely across the skies
> and rise again at dawn ... (25)

This pattern of descent and ascent is repeated later in the poem as "a myth of another color" when the poet arrives by plane "astonished, / and all but stellified / on wings of flame" (26) to give a paper at a conference in Las Vegas's Stardust Inn. Revard keeps always in the forefront of consciousness the fact that human and non-human beings are embodied intersections of time and space, creation and destruction—walking star matter. To borrow his neologism from "Close Encounters," his poems "stellify" (25) the planet; his words take the world apart to reveal the star matter that composes it and then put it back together, weaving the stars back into the patterns of time and space that make bodies, places, and histories in their intersections. Revard keeps the stories of the evolution of life from interstellar dust told by scientists and the Osage people always in conversation, creating a new naming ceremony that restores English language itself to earth, sky, and cosmos.

In his essay "History, Myth, and Identity Among Osages and Other Peoples," Revard explains how in traditional societies, "naming and language reflect and shape a sense of identity within the world, both outside and part of an Indian self" (1998: 131–32); before the "civilizing" of Indians, figurative naming—naming that is descriptive, based in close personal observation and experience—linked "personal identity to . . . tribal identity and relationship to the world of other-than-human 'natural' beings" (132). The Osage Naming Ceremony embodies the orderly movements of the cosmos and situates the named within family, clan, and tribal histories, as well as within the circle of being that includes all his people, the land, the animals and plants, earth and sky, the stars, and the stories of origin. In contrast, Revard observes in his essay "Making a Name," much of the English language has eroded into "sound-blobs" (1998: 109); names are arbitrary referents, "memory tag[s]" that have been "dis-figured" and "demythicized" (110). In the poem "Nonymosity," the poet observes that, like land, which "is / always some rectangle now because / circles or ovals can't be packed together,"

> Names have to pack together. They have moved
> halfway from poetry to numbers
> and numbers now are what we have to be
> to fit into computers . . . (1992: 18)

Addressing the reader, the poet asks:

> . . . What is your real name,
> the one that tells you what you are, the one
> that links you to your people's past
> that tells the others what you've done
> and what the powers have shown you,
> that is the lightning's path into your life?
> I name you here, DOPED SILICON, and you,
> MAGNETIC BUBBLE. Your children shall become
> COMPUTER CHIPS. We are in the clan of
> SOLAR CELLS, a sapphire conduit from the stars
> into our souls. . . . (18–19)

Even as the poet renames readers in terms of computer parts, he renames the inner workings of the computer in a ceremony that re-figures them, reconnecting them to their origins in the stars. The binary operations of computer chips—names gone all the way to numbers—are restored to a place in the cosmic order and transfigured across the boundaries between science and myth, between arbitrary representation and connectedness.

Revard's writing sometimes mimics the processes of mechanistic science, taking the world apart to look deeper and deeper within its layers of "parts." However, like quantum mechanics, which arrived at the realization that matter is ultimately intersecting fields of energy, Revard's poetic deconstructions and reconstructions demonstrate that parts—chiggers, geodes, humans, electrons, computer chips—however concrete and discrete they may seem to be, are at their core expressions of mysterious forces of great beauty and power. Even what is perceived to be not-alive, not-natural, is remade in terms of the natural, re-embedded within the processes of universal creation, making visible—re-figuring—the interconnections that weave the universe into a whole. The opening paragraph of Revard's introduction to *An Eagle Nation* epitomizes this process: "How time dawned on mind and was beaded into language amazes me the way an orb spider's web or computer chip does, or the dance of time and space and energy that patterned selves into my parents, who did not have me in mind, and into the four children and seven grandchildren who've so far surprised us" (1993: xi). Revard traces the timeless and infinite—the universal—in the specific and individual, keeping always at the surface of awareness the translation of universal forces by individual perception into individual consciousness and embodied being, and from there into spoken and written expression. The remainder of the passage reverses this process:

> Amazing that a brief quivering of air can re-present such wonders, that little coded curves of ink on paper might set the same vibrations pulsing from a human mouth in Buck Creek, Oklahoma, and from others in Singapore or some future meadow or unbuilt spaceship—from mouths now neatly packed into genes that have not even begun to express themselves as human parts, within their unripe sperm and ova. The creation of language, of writing, is less astounding than the invention of water, but not much less, and we each re-create, as we go, all that has been given us. (xi)

Speech and writing stitch space/time into history, translate the creative forces of the universe into minds and bodies, and simultaneously the universe is re-created with each spoken or written word.

This pattern of deconstruction and reconstruction characterizes much of Revard's poetry, notably his recent epic poem-in-progress, "Transfigurations" (2003: 16–21). This long poem in four sections, framed by references to William Blake's "London" and written after Ronald Reagan addressed the Oxford Union and Margaret Thatcher had "honored her Emperor," in Revard's words, "concerns the dreadful paradox of Empire, always founded on death and degradation" (24 October 2000: E-mail to author). In the second section, the poet is studying expensive silk ties to distract himself from "thinking how the rich men rule" (2003: 17); emperors die and empires collapse, but "rotten tyrants" (17) recycle, and the poet's thoughts keep circling back to the terrible costs of Empire and the beauty it makes possible:

> ... if only
> death WERE the mother of beauty—
> famished caterpillars eating
> poison-packed leaves and turning them into
> waving angelic wings, Monarch
> and Luna Moth and Tiger Swallowtail.
> But those are free, while fat silk-moths must not
> come forth, must never rasp
> and ruin the one long thread they spin into a shroud, never
> visit moonshadowed flowers, like deity must die
> to robe us in raw silk, then the chemists
> conjure from coal angelic glories, tweak
> oil film from fossil seas and set it
> dancing in rainbow swirls upon
> a dandy's ties—
> called up from time
> by Chinese women, German chemists, by
> old Englishwomen winding, unwinding—those "silkwives"
> of fifteenth century London—careful as Urania with
> that Phoenix egg from the rainbow-winged first
> universe when from her great
> brooding song this universe
> exploded as brilliant quarks
> that cooled into space and time and stars within each
> infinite pupa—
> flashing, turning to otherness, digesting
> self to blossom where
> in the Emperor's Masque his minions dance
> mirrored in silken brilliance,
> crimson pajamas, black satin sheets of bordello,
> a fop's foulard, Q.C.'s robes,
> thread turning and turning,

> spinning, weaving, O dark
> Mother of Bright Wings—genies slide
> with silken gravity of water down
> the turbine-wheel, becoming
> current alive with
> ghost voices; sand dunes melt into
> silicon sapphires, rare earth wakens as
> germanium touching golden wires
> to music as of Apollonian lyres—
> and see the Psalms of David
> melting with Christian alchemy into stained glass
> of Placebo and Dirige, much as Jerubbabel
> once channeled Babylon
> into Jerusalem, bright faces passing over
> the glass of Siloa's brook that flows
> fast by the Oracle of God, reappearing on
> the Thames, the Hudson, Amazon, Volga, Yangtze— (2003: 17-18)

The single long sentence that begins, "But those are free . . ." winds and unwinds like the silkworms' thread unwound by silkwives to reweave into fabrics for kings and fops, weaving the histories of Empires together with the processes of universal creation in intertwining patterns of murder and art, destruction and creation. Positioning himself and his words in the center of these histories, the poet demonstrates his recent concerns, to borrow Maureen Konkle's words, to "[put] Indians back into time" (2000:154), to foreground Indians as active political subjects in global contexts. But Revard also restores time to universal processes that are beyond time, weaving personal and local histories *through* national and international ones, and into the larger fabric of universal affairs in which time—history—is a pattern beaded into mind. Time and words become tracings of the beautiful and often violent processes of deconstruction and re-creation that time and minds must stop (like the severed geode) in order to make them visible.

The trope of the black hole—a celestial body created by the collapse of a massive star, which has a gravitational field so powerful not even light can escape it and is theorized to provide a bridge to other universes—appears often in Revard's work and provides an apt metaphor for the technology of transfiguration, the meta-work of his writing. In *Family Matters, Tribal Affairs*, Revard observes, "When I wrote 'How the Songs Came Down,' I was thinking of all the places I had been, and of how each person is so like a black hole out of which no light could ever emerge to another" (1998: 16). In the short story "How the FBI Man Nearly Found God," a black hole is compared to "solitary confinement"

(1984: 60); yet when the Osage physics student in the story yokes two black holes together, aligning them carefully with "all the solar system and galactic forces" (52), he creates a kind of perpetual motion machine that powers his magic motorcycle into other dimensions. The motorcycle's headlamp casts a beam that "like the Ghost Dance . . . brings the old worlds up again in any part of matter" (58), projecting the mythic space/time of the old stories against the Osage foothills. As Revard puts it in the poem "Postcolonial Hyperbaggage," "We need these / neat reversible black holes for crossing / Borders" (2003: 2). In "Transfigurations" the black hole serves as a trope for the poetic process, which unmakes the sense and thought world of the writer and compresses it into the traces of spoken words on the page. The second section concludes:

>. . . and far off, see the glittering Stars
> and Galaxies rain down into
> that huge Black Hole, as dead leaves go
> into a bonfire and come forth
> as flame, ashes, smoke and light and heat,
> but then become
> the next year's flowers—trees—grapes and
> wine, cider and brandy—world into words,
> speech into writing, Songs into Drum—
> wrenched down personal
> Black Holes into an insurrection
> of Dark Matter as a Quasar dies—
> till from decaying Space and Time arise
> and fly away new Bubble Worlds, brief rainbow minds upon
> their film of bursting time.
> O see
> the great and vibrant world become
> a tiny set of words upon
> a baby's tongue
> and how it grows, how all that old debris
> from superstars becomes this mass of
> proteins with sense and memory, foetus that
> coheres to selfhood, "crying for the light,
> and with no language but a cry." (2003: 18–19)

Like a black hole, written words emit no light until a reader engages them and the collapsed world emerges anew in interaction with the embodied consciousness of each reader. The poem itself oscillates like a doubled black hole between deconstruction and construction, murder and rebirth. It pulls the reader into its gravity field, collapsing the reading eye and mind into participation with the perpetual unmaking and remaking of objects and perceptions, world and universe, pushing out new "bubble worlds" and new minds that can hold paradoxes and contradictions, death and beauty, history and timelessness, spoken words and written histories in simultaneity. Words on the page, living stories collapsed into tracings on paper and respun in the isolated, individual act of reading, are, like individuals, like the events of history—nation states in conflict, the subjugation of earth and its peoples to the manufacture of Empire—black holes as well, sites of dismantling and remaking, locations in space/time that make visible the inherence of parts in wholes, the tracings of wholes in parts, the ongoing processes of unmaking and making that weave the universe whole.

Living by the Light of Myth

For Carter Revard, science and myth are complementary ways of knowing the world. As Revard points out in *Family Matters, Tribal Affairs*, we know from science that the Osage descent from the stars is "factually accurate," since humans are made of earth that comes from the stars, from the explosions of supernovas that "produced all the heavier elements in our human bodies," making it also "factually accurate" that we "*do* come 'from the stars,' just as we *do* come 'from the earth'" (ital. in orig.; 1998: 153). "Thinking about the 'old myths' can perhaps have its humbling uses," he says; "It may well be that myths are like the stars: we see by their light, even though they may have 'died' centuries ago" (152). Science and myth are two perspectives on the universe that open onto each other like doubled black holes. Yoked, they can power us across the borders of ordinary perception into mythic dimensions where we can see and experience the wholeness of creation.

As Revard observes in "Making a Name," the "dis-figuring" of language makes it opaque, "darkens knowledge," and creates a priestly elite of scientists and scholars who "hold custody of our understanding, our speech, our culture" (1998: 111). Revard's poetry returns words to ordinary people by returning them to story—to the creation stories told by both science and myth that tell us how things came to be and how they are related to each other. Re-figured, words are made "transparent" again, their power to make the workings of creation visible restored. As in traditional societies, names become "revelations" that "sing [and] soar from thought to sense and back" (110). Similarly, science and technology are taken from the priests and given to the people in a ceremony of renaming that weaves them back into the history of earth and stars that is also the history of humans, making them relatives in a system of intimate interconnection and mutual responsibility.

As Revard suggests in his essay, "How Columbus Fell from the Sky and Lighted Up Two Continents," myth helps us understand not only where we come from but also where we are headed. In the Navajo creation story, he tells us, when the Monster-Slaying twins are called on to rid the earth of the deadly monsters born of a quarrel between First Man and First Woman, their father the Sun explains to them that the monsters are Sun's children too, implying that whatever must be destroyed is also part of them. As they slay each monster, the twins "see to it that *something is made of its corpse*" so that evil is turned into good (ital. in orig.; 1998: 159). If we are to tame the monsters that lay waste to our current world—poverty, inequality, injustice, environmental degradation, toxic pollution—offspring of the imperialistic, mechanistic worldview Columbus brought with him from Europe, we must first recognize how "*we are related to the evils we must destroy*" so that "*they can be turned to good things* "(ital. in orig, 159). Bringing science to myth enables us to see and experience the material and sacred ways we are connected in a circle of being, and can light the way to healing and transformation.

Works Cited

Brown, K., ed. 1998. *Verse and Universe: Poems about Science and Mathematics*. Minneapolis, Minnesota: Milkweed.
Konkle, M. 2000. "Treaties, History, and the 'Full-Blood' in Indian Territory Native Writing," *Western American Literature* 35.2: 143–61.
McAdams, J. 2004. "Carter Revard's Angled Mirrors." *Speak To Me Words: Contemporary American Indian Poetry*. Eds. D. Rader and J. Gould. Tucson: University of Arizona Press.
Midgley, M. 2001. *Science and Poetry*. London and New York: Routledge.
Nabhan, G. P. 2004. *Cross-Pollinations: The Marriage of Science and Poetry*. Minneapolis, Minnesota: Milkweed.
Revard, C. 1975. "ESP." *Voices of the Rainbow: Contemporary Poetry by Native Americans*. Ed. K. Rosen. New York: Arcade. 1993.
——. 1980. *Ponca War Dancers*. Norman, Oklahoma: Point Riders Press.
——. 1984. "How the FBI Man Nearly Found God." *Greenfield Review* (Winter/Spring): 46–60.
——. 1992. *Cowboys and Indians, Christmas Shopping*. Norman, Oklahoma: Point Riders Press.
——. 1993. *An Eagle Nation*. Tucson: University of Arizona Press.
——. 1998. *Family Matters, Tribal Affairs*. Tucson: University of Arizona Press.
——. 2000, 12 February. "The Aquarian Distinction." E-mail to Nativelit-L@raven.cc.ku.edu.
——. 2000, 24 October. "WAL conference this week." E-mail to E. Arnold.
——. 2001, 18 May. "Cloud Chamber." E-mail to Nativelit-L@raven.cc.ku.edu.

——. 2003. "Some Notes on Native American Literature." *Studies in American Indian Literatures* 15.1: 1–15.
——. 2003. "Transfigurations." *Studies in American Indian Literatures* 15.1: 16–21.
——. 2005. *How the Songs Come Down: New and Selected Poems.* Cambridge, U. K.: Salt.

Translating Carter Revard:
An Adventure among Mixed and Fertile Words

Márgara Averbach

E-mail Magic

I am grateful for e-mail. I met Carter Revard through the Internet some years ago. It could never have happened any other way: how else could I, an American Literature teacher in Argentina, talk, debate and communicate with an Osage poet from North America? The adventure that would finish with my translation of Carter's poems into Spanish started in that new, different space some people call "cyber." Carter and I discussed everything through e-mail: from the war in the Middle East to politics in my country, Argentina; the place of women in the world; discrimination, hunger and injustice in general; Mark Twain; and of course, poetry and Native American situations and creations. The poems themselves came through e-mail first, in books sent by the old post service afterwards. And then, I discovered Carter Revard and wanted to translate him.

I had been translating Native American authors' short stories and poems for a time when this happened. I teach American Literature to students in the University of Buenos Aires. Literature students here can read either in the original language (English) or in translation (Spanish) if they cannot read English, because in Argentina, formation as literature scholars is essentially panoramic. Specialization comes later: as students are asked to read and study literatures written in many different languages, they cannot be obliged to learn all those languages, and many times they read in translations. That is why, when I teach Native American literatures, I translate short texts I have admired and loved for my students. Except for Louise Erdrich's first three novels, there are no translations of Native American authors readily available in Latin American countries.

Translation Problems

I have translated novels and taught literary translation for more than fifteen years. There are certain basic problems in translation that should be discussed briefly before talking about any specific work. The literary translator's task is very problematic. Literature's specificity does not depend on the message, but on the use of the linguistic code. In "El grado cero de la escritura," Roland Barthes compares the text with a window through which we can see something, a tree, for instance. He says that a perfectly transparent language would be one in which the window pane cannot be seen and only the tree is visible. He calls that kind of language "Zero Degree of Writing," and he states that it does not really exist; it is only a postulate. An example of something similar to the Zero Degree is the language of math or chemistry, for instance, $3 \times 3 = 9$ or H_2O. From Zero Degree onwards, the window pane begins to be more and more visible, and when we get to literary texts, the tree is no longer the center of the text. What is important is the texture of the window pane, the way the glass transforms the tree and expresses it as no other glass could. Taking this into account, it is logical to hear some theorists say that literary translation is impossible: if the key to the text is in the window pane and the translation is going to change the glass, can the result be something similar or even related to the original text (Barthes 1975)?

My opinion is that translating literature *is* possible—that is why I do it and teach my students how to do it—but I have to admit that copying the texture of one of these panes into a different one is an enormously difficult task. To achieve a decent imitation of the original text, the translator will have to pay attention not only to the meaning of the text, but also to the language of the original and devise ways to reproduce or re-codify the use of the original in the other language so that it can transmit to the reader of the translation as much of the original as possible. The translator will also have to build a bridge between cultures. An author generally writes for his or her own audience, people who share one or more of his or her cultures. A simple example: if someone translated a novel by an Argentine author into English and the novel made references to one of our National Holidays, let us say, the 25th of May, the translator should explain this to a non-Argentine reader, who probably does not know what the date means to the characters in the book and to all Argentine people.

In the case of poetry, there are hard and often bitter debates among translators. I will state my position here so my translations can be judged accordingly. There are people who believe that when you translate poetry, the only important thing to translate is the content, and that you should translate it line for line, and disregard phonetic effects like rhyme. The idea behind this approach is that phonetic effects cannot be translated, and therefore the reader of the translation should know that he or she is not reading poetry, but a kind of "retelling" of the poem.

I believe that if a poem in the original uses rhyme and rhythm, the translator should try to reproduce both without changing the general meaning (though he or she will have to change certain details to achieve this). It goes without saying that what the translator will achieve is not a mirror image of the original but a kind of adaptation or imitation, because the ways different languages manage rhythm and rhyme—among other poetic effects—can be completely different. For instance: rhyme in Spanish is much more complex and varied than English rhyme, and the Spanish rhythm has nothing to do with feet (spondee, iamb, etc) because our language distinguishes only between stressed and unstressed syllables and there are many unstressed syllables betweeen each stress, and vowels all have the same length in Spanish. Therefore, the difficulties are great, and there is always a better way to solve the problems than the one each translator has chosen. A poem is never fully translated, and no translation is the final translation of a text; one can be always sure that if one devoted another year to it, it would definitely get better. I submit my translations of Carter Revard's poems here as works in progress, and I do know I will go on changing them with time.

Translation can be used in a number of ways. In general, it is a way to make an author's work available to people who do not read the original language in which the author wrote, that is to say, a way to make the work available to another public. But that first, essential use of translation is not the only one. When a person translates or even explains the choices of translation to others, the original work can be understood in a different, deeper way. At our university, there are workshops and research teams where translation is used as a tool not to transmit the poems but to *understand* them.

In translation, we are forced to separate the language of the text from the "things" the text talks about. To use Michel Foucault's ideas, when translating, what he calls the "gap" between "the words and the things" becomes evident because there are at least two "words" (in different languages) which will mean more or less the same "thing" (Foucault 1985). So it becomes obvious that the idea of bread is *not* the word "bread." But there is more: when translating, in the process of choosing a word from the paradigm of the target language (that is to say the language one is translating to), the subtlety and variety of meanings in the original become evident to the translator. Therefore, translation can be used also as a way to get a deeper *understanding*, and that happens in the process of translation and it happens even if a final version is never reached.

Carter Explains His Songs

Carter Revard's poetry was surprising to me from the beginning. It is marked by a mixture of a pleasure in and understanding of Nature on the one side, and a deep knowledge of the sources of many cultures, including European ones, on the other. The fact that it is a poetry based especially on rhythm (not on rhyme) makes it more, not less, difficult to translate (as I explained before, English rhythm is very far away from Spanish rhythm in origin and method, farther than rhyme). When I had cultural questions (caused by my lack of knowledge of Osage culture), I turned to Carter for advice and explanation, and this is again e-mail magic. I felt Carter Revard's generous explanations, interpretations, data and concepts have changed my translations and make them better. He has explained with enormous patience things that were obvious for him and criticized my readings when necessary. I think his explanations and ideas show him as he is: a person dedicated to teaching, in the best of meanings related to that word.

"The Coyote"

Carter sent me a poem he had called "Coyote Tells Why He Sings." Afterwards, I received *Ponca War Dancers*, and there it was called "The

Coyote."¹ When I tried to translate it, I could not find a reference to the word "blackjack" (as a tree). When a translator does not find a word, translation is in danger. I was very uncomfortable with the idea of asking Carter—I still did not know him well enough at that stage—but I finally did. This was his answer: "A blackjack is a kind of oak tree that grows on the Osage Hills where I was born. It is a small, untidy and indomitable tree. Its leaves are thick and glossy dark green, not quite as crisp and glossy as holly-leaves and when there is a rainstorm, the big drops sound very loud on these leaves" (6 June 1997: E-mail to author).

This description of the blackjack is poetry in itself. Now, I believe that I should have translated it too and add it as a footnote. Carter cannot write without writing poetry. But apart from the pleasure of reading the description, it helped me solve the problem caused by the fact that I could not find a word for "blackjack" in Spanish. In cases in which there is no translation, there are some who prefer to keep the word in English.² I believe that type of decision does not help the reader understand the poem (or prose text); it only tells him or her that Carter Revard is talking about a tree (or a plant; it would not be clear with just "blackjack" as noun) that does not exist in his or her country. Not even the color would be clear for a non English speaking reader. The author's description of the tree did not solve the problem of translation directly: it did not give me a word for the tree itself but it did suggest that I had to keep the color when translating. It helped get to the idea of translating the line, "In dust, on stiff blackjack leaves, on lichened rocks," as "en el polvo, sobre las hojas tiesas, negras de los árboles, sobre líquenes y rocas," where I decided to state that the leaves belonged to trees ("árboles") and add "black" ("negras") to leaves so as to transmit part of the image of the specific tree to the reader of the translation.

Collaboration of this type can also help with more specific culture details. I had understood the verb "made" applied to music was used to express something solid, a making of a concrete object of beauty, such as a sculpture. But I did not know the cultural details, and Carter Revard, as Coyote, told me. (To help explain the first comment by Carter,

---

1 "The Coyote" appears in *Ponca War Dancers* (1980). The poem is reprinted as "Coyote Tells Why He Sings" in *Winning the Dust Bowl* (2001), with slight changes from the earlier version. The version that appears here is the same as the one that appears in *Ponca War Dancers*, though Revard gave it the second title.

2 For example, Silviana Ocampo has kept the word "bobolink" in her translations of Emily Dickinson's poems.

I want to explain that I had been looking for the poem in Carter's books to review the translation, and I could not find it with that title, because in *Ponca War Dancers* it was called only "The Coyote" [Revard 1980: 11].) Carter said:

> I'm glad Coyote stepped forward and let you find him. As you see, he was given his voice by Thunder, who waked him; and music was given to him by the Thunder-storm, and by the rain-water it brought, moving the stones in such a way that they changed the musical key of what he heard the water saying, so that Sound became Music. Or, as the last line of the sonnet says: "The storm MADE music, when it changed my world." Coyote had heard only sounds; and then, when the sound of the water changed its key, transposing to a deeper note in such a way that he realized: this is more than sound, this is Music. And then of course he absolutely had to sing. I realized, after having earlier titled the poem simply "The Coyote," that readers might not understand that what the coyote is saying DOES tell why he sings. And someone who has listened to coyotes under a bright moon will know that they are not just "howling," they are SINGING, and they sing because they have learned to hear the MUSIC of the world, not just its SOUNDS.
>
> My Osage name shows that I am of the Thunder clan. Nompehwahtheh means "fear-inspiring" or "Makes Afraid," and this refers to the fear that the Thunder being creates . . . When Osages decided to come from the stars to this world, we sent ahead our messengers to "scout" or reconnoitre this world we were going to live in. They met the beings who had learned to live successfully in this world: the Black Bear, Mountain Lion, Cedar Tree, and so on, and each time they met one of these beings, that being would say: "If you will make your bodies of me (i.e. incarnate me, incorporate me), then you will live to see old age, and live into the blessed days." Thereupon this being would tell them they could use certain names whose reference would be to this being and his or her attributes. So Thunder gave them, as one of the names they could use, the name Nompehwahtheh, which means "Makes Afraid." as the Thunder makes people afraid . . . I do not refer to all this directly in the poem, but when the Coyote, who is speaking in the poem, says, "The Thunder waked me," this will be understood as part of the poem's context and meanings. (7 October 2002: E-mail to author)

I had understood part of this from my own culture, but as a translator, I think, this type of complex explanation should be translated too and added to the poem as a footnote. If the author is alive and can help bridge cultures like this, his or her suggestions should be part of the poem, as they are in fact for the primary audience of the poem, the Osage people. The translation itself was not transformed by this explanation, but in an early version, I had chosen the verb "hacer" for "made" and after this comment, I thought it would be better to use a verb which could express even more than "hacer" the solidness of the idea, especially because "hacer" is the verb generally used for "music" in Spanish, so it would not express much to a Spanish reader. That is why I finally chose "fabricar." I have not added the footnotes with Carter's explanations but I would certainly do so if the translations were to be published.

The Coyote (Coyote Tells Why He Sings)	El Coyote (Coyote explica por qué canta)
There was a little rill of water, near the den, That showed a trickle, all the dry summer When I was born. One night in late August it rained, The thunder waked us. Drops came crashing down In dust, on stiff blackjack leaves, on lichened rocks, And the rain came in a pelting rush down over the hill, The wind blew wet into the cave; I heard the sounds Of leaf-drip, wet rustle of soggy branches in gusts of wind.	Había un arroyuelo, un sendero de agua, cerca del cubil, y tenía un hilito todo el verano seco, cuando nací. Una noche, a fines de agosto, llovió... el Trueno nos despertó. Las gotas rompieron como olas en el polvo, sobre las hojas tiesas, negras de los árboles, sobre líquenes y rocas. Y la lluvia vino a la carrera, a cántaros, hacia la colina, el viento sopló húmedo en la cueva y yo oí los sonidos de las hojas y las gotas de agua, el crujido del viento en ramas empapadas.
And then the rill's tune changed: I heard a rock drop And set new ripples gurgling in a lower key Where the new ripples were, I drank, next morning, Fresh muddy water that set my teeth on edge, I thought how delicate that rock's poise was, The storm made music, when it changed my world.	Y después, la canción del arroyuelo cambió, oí caer una piedra que hizo ondas nuevas, borboteó otra vez en un tono más bajo. Donde estaban las ondas nuevas bebí, a la mañana siguiente, agua fresca, embarrada, y me temblaron los dientes. Y pensé en la delicadeza, la elegancia de la piedra y en cómo la tormenta fabricaba música cuando cambiaba mi mundo.

"To the Muse, in Oklahoma"

The author's explanations gave me this type of enhanced understanding again when we were discussing (through e-mail) the metaphor of the "allomorph" in "To the Muse, in Oklahoma":[3]

> "[A]llomorph" is a word I picked up in high-school chemistry classes. So in the poem I compared "truth" to these other elements or compounds—the "truth" about something depends on the circumstances and temperature prevailing. Thus when I say in the poem "We walked upon the water," that could easily be taken for a lie, but if you remember that I am talking about the winter time, then you see that statement is perfectly truthful. We walked upon the water when it was in its solid form. Truth has a summer allomorph (watery) in which one cannot walk upon it, but also a winter allomorph (icy) in which it is natural, normal and usual to be able to walk upon. You have to know the version of truth you are dealing with. And muses—especially in the form of milk-cows—need to have both the allomorphs." (6 June 1997: E-mail to author)

In this explanation, Carter Revard does two things: first, he mixes weather, chemistry, social interests and the relationship between human beings and nature in one complex, wonderfully hybrid metaphor; and second, he is describing tolerance, the capacity of understanding the Other. To me, the allomorph metaphor is a perfect description of Otherness as necessary, as indispensable, as *visible*. As a translator, I would have chosen "alomorfo" as a good translation without the explanation, and yet, it was important for me to understand the choice of words in the original here and the explanation gave me a different reason for my own decision.

To the Muse, in Oklahoma	A la Musa, en Oklahoma
That *Aganippe Well* was nice, it hit the spot— sure, this bluestem meadow is hardly Helicon, we had to gouge a pond, the mules	Ese Pozo Aganippe era lindo, era lo justo... sí, esta pradera de tallos azules no es el Helicón, ya sé, teníamos que abrir

3 Again, this poem was received through e-mail. This version is identical to the one that appears in *Winning the Dust Bowl* (2001: 9–10): [o]an earlier version appeared as "To The Muse In Oklahoma" in *Cowboys and Indians, Christmas Shopping* (1992: 7), and yet another, slightly different version, "To the Muses, in Oklahoma," was reprinted in *Family Matters, Tribal Affairs* (1998: 84–86).

dragged a rusty slip scraping down through dusty topsoil into dark ooze and muck, grating open sandstone eggs; but then the thunder sent living waters down, they filled the rawness with blue trembling where white clouds sailed in summer and we walked upon the water every winter (truth's a zero allomorph of time), although it was more fun sliding. We'd go and chop down through six-inch ice by the pond's edge, pry the ice-slab out onto the pond from its hole where the dark water welled up cold to the milk-cows sucking nois- ily, snorting their relish—and when they'd drunk, we shoved the ice- slab over to where the bank sloped gently, took a running chute and leaped atop the slab real easy and slid, just glided clear over the pond, riding on ice. Or we stretched prone on the black windowy ice, looked down on darkness where fish drifted, untouchable, below our fingers. Ice makes a whole new surface within things, keeps killer whales from seals just long enough to let new seals be born before they go down to feed or be fed upon. —Come sliding now, and later we'll go swimming, dive in with the muskrats, black bass, water moccasins, under this willow let the prairie wind drink from our bare skin: good water fits every mouth.	un estanque, las mulas se daban resbalones oxidados cuando rascaban a través de la tierra polvorienta hacia el lodo oscuro, el estiércol, y hacían un ruido agudo al abrir huevos de arenisca; pero después, el trueno enviaba abajo aguas de vida, y ellas llenaban la crudeza con azul tembloroso en el lugar en el que las nubes blancas navegaban en verano y nosotros caminábamos sobre el agua cada invierno (la verdad es un alomorfo cero del tiempo), aunque era más divertido deslizarse. Y partíamos el hielo de metro y medio junto al estanque, levántabamos un poco el pedazo de hielo hacia el estanque, lo apartábamos del agujero de donde surgía el agua negra, fría, hacia las vacas lecheras que la chupaban con ruido, bufando de delicia . . . y cuando ellas terminaban, volvíamos a empujar el pedazo de hielo al lugar en que la ribera se inclinaba, suave, subíamos para tomar carrera y saltábamos sobre el pedazo con facilidad y nos deslizábamos, nos deslizábamos sobre el estanque, cabalgando sobre hielo. O nos estirábamos boca abajo en el hielo negro con ventana, mirábamos abajo a la oscuridad donde pasaban los peces, intocables, bajo nuestros dedos. El hielo hace una superficie totalmente nueva

	dentro de las cosas, mantiene a las ballenas
	asesinas lejos de las focas lo suficiente para que
	nazcan nuevas focas antes de que bajen a alimentarse o ser alimento de otros.
	... Bajábamos deslizándonos y después, íbamos a
	nadar, nos zambullíamos con las
	ratas almizcleras, las lubinas negras, las serpientes de agua, bajo
	este sauce dejábamos que el viento de la pradera
	bebiera de nuestra piel desnuda, abierta; el agua buena
	es buena para todas las bocas.

"Driving in Oklahoma"

Some time later, I translated "Driving in Oklahoma," from *Ponca War Dancers* (1980: 25). It was a somewhat different experience. First, I did not get to this poem by myself: I did not choose it. I was writing a paper on technology as seen by Native American authors (Averbach 2001), and when I asked Carter whether he remembered having written something on the subject, he mentioned the poem. These are some of the explanations he gave me about it:

> The deeper contrast is between the natural music and the technological. The bird makes the earth its home by song, and in some ways so do human beings, but we may forget that the technology is not the real source of the song, only a kind of medium, and that our fast motion, always going somewhere, may at times "cross" with the real singing which is not confined to "roads" and "machines." I was making a word-play also on "country music" in the poem, since the main genre of recorded music played along US Route #66 is COUNTRY MUSIC. So in the poem I am contrasting this radio-broadcast "Country Music" with the music of the (natural) country, the roadside music, the songs in the air from the birds. One kind of music is blasting out the windows of the speeding car, from its radio, and comes from time-capsuled "records" made maybe decades earlier, played a hundred miles away in some closed and windowless room by a bored "disc-jockey," and turned into electrons zapping through space way up to the ionosphere and bounced back into the metal "aerial" of my car radio's receiving apparatus, and transmogrified through its electrical apparatus into sound and music again. So the basic comparison in the poem is between the technological music

and power of its "country-music songs" on the one hand, and on the other hand the natural music and power of the bird's wild-country music. And the contrast strikes home to me as writer when, in the comfort and isolation of a speeding car, with the radio music blasting out my windows, I suddenly see and hear a meadowlark fly across the highway just in front of me, singing as it flies . . . They have very bright yellow breasts, a great black bib or vest curving down into and up out of it at their throats, and a beautifully intricate speckling and interweaving of browns and tans and other winter-grass colors on their backs. Where I was driving, US #75, when this meadowlark crossed in front of my car, the road is a straight north-south ribbon of concrete through rolling tall-grass prairie, and I was driving during the courting season when the males are all displaying and singing and competing for mates, so there were lots of birds fluttering and sailing and singing on both sides of the road, perching briefly on fenceposts or small plum or chokecherry trees along the roadside in the fields.

In the first part of the poem I referred to how "free" of heavy burdens I was feeling, and compare this feeling to that physical feeling an astronaut must have, when on the way to the moon, at that point where the GRAVITY of earth gives way to the GRAVITY of the moon. There is an exhilaration in being "weightless," a feeling you and I would know from what it is like in one of those children's swings when you reach the top of the swing and start back down—a kind of inner sweetness near the heart, at the "pit of the stomach" . . . When we are on a trip like the one I was on, . . . being "between home and away" as I phrase it in the poem, is like being between Earth and Moon gravities. In that capsule, it seems to be Technology which sets us free. But in the poem I describe how, speeding along, I saw and heard the meadowlark cross just in front of me, singing as it flew. So I pulled over to the road-shoulder, found an envelope and pen, and wrote the first draft of the poem. It is about being reminded of a simple fact: the Country is "defined wholly by song," this Oklahoma country is Meadowlark Country before and after it is Country and Western Music country. And the bird's song made me want to move again through that natural country, and try to "see" how that bird, even while it sang, was moving "so easy while it flies." (14 October 1998: E-mail to author)

The explanations confirmed some of the details of my own reading: the oppositions country music-lark music; technology-nature; the incredible cuts in the graphics of the poem were elements I had already seen. I translated the poem with these ideas in mind (for instance, keeping the graphic distribution of words on the paper is essential here). Yet, when I sent the paper to him by e-mail, Carter explained a very important mistake I had made. The explanation of the mistake did not change the translation but it helped me re-read it and correct it keeping certain details in mind. Now I knew that I could have made a deep mistake in the handling of the tone of the poem. The mistake itself is symbolic of the gap between Carter's culture and mine and therefore, between any two readings and between the original text and its translation, which come obviously from two different cultures.

I had thought the man in the car had hit the bird; I had made the bird's death a price for the man's epiphany. There is something personal in the mistake: the poem had reminded me of one time I was on a highway and a bird crossed the road flying too low; I could not stop the car in time. I haven't been able to forget the moment. But there is also a cultural bias here: I come from a culture where the death of a bird is generally not thought as too big a price to pay for a man's epiphany. Carter Revard, who comes from a completely different culture, pointed me to an evident truth I had not seen: there is no sadness in the poem, no loss (here, tone is essential); and therefore, within Osage culture, the bird cannot be dead or even wounded. It has just crossed the road in front of the car. I had not seen that because of my personal and cultural biases. I did not really change the translation after Carter told me this, but I reviewed it with the explanation in mind before getting to a version I thought I could feel happy about.

Driving in Oklahoma

On humming rubber along this white concrete
    lighthearted between the gravities
of source and destination like a man
    half way to the moon
  in this bubble of tuneless whistling
at seventy miles an hour from the windvents,
   over prairie swells rising
  and falling, over the quick offramp
that drops to its underpass and the truck
    thundering beneath as I cross
with the country music twanging out my windows,
    I'm grooving down this highway feeling
technology is freedom's other name when
        - a meadowlark
   comes sailing across my windshield
      with breast shining yellow
    and five notes pierce
      the windshield like a flash
        of nectar on mind
gone as the country music swells up and
     drops me wheeling down
  my notch of cement-bottomed sky
    between home and away

            and wanting
to move again through country that a bird
    has defined wholly with song
            and maybe next time see how
    he flies so easy, when he sings.

En auto en Oklahoma

Sobre goma que susurra a lo largo de este cemento blanco
    el corazón leve entre las gravedades
    de origen y destino como un hombre
        a medio camino de la luna
    en esta burbuja de silbido sin canción
a cien kilómetros por hora desde los ventiletes,
    sobre olas de praderas que suben
    y bajan, sobre la rampa rápida, lateral
  que cae hasta la ruta inferior y el camión
        que truena por debajo cuando paso
con la música country que sale, vibrando, de mis ventanillas,
        voy trazando un surco en esta autopista y siento
    que la tecnología es el otro nombre de la libertad cuando
                                                        -una alondra
        cruza navegando mi parabrisas
            con el pecho brillante amarillo
        y cinco notas perforan
            el parabrisas como un fogonaz
                de néctar en la mente
que se fue mientras la música country hace una ola y sube y
    y me deja caer rodando abajo
  por mi desfiladero de cielo con fondo de cemento
    entre mi casa y lejos
            y hace que quiera
moverme de nuevo a través de campo que un pájaro
    definió totalmente con canción
        y quizás la próxima vez ver cómo
    vuela tan fácil, cuando canta.

"Postcolonial Hyperbaggage"

The translation of "Postcolonial Hyperbaggage"[4] is an example of how collaboration with the author for certain poems can help understanding and translating other texts by the same author. I did not write to

---

4 "Postcolonial Hyperbaggage" was unpublished at the time of this translation; different versions appeared later in *The American Oxonian* (LXXVIII.2 [2001]: 192) and in *Studies in American Indian Literatures* (15.1 [2003]: 1–2).

Carter about this poem in particular. I chose it myself and translated it because I felt it touched not only on relationships between the USA and Native American cultures, but also between white and aboriginal cultures in the rest of what we, in my country, call América, meaning the whole continent, as well as between our Latin American countries and their cultures and the United States.

There are words that acquire new meanings when translated into the specific Spanish dialect we use in Argentina. I translated the word "tucked"—used by Carter Revard to describe how the Reservations could be put away behind a certain icon (the Sacajewea dollar, where Carter is also symbolizing the use of Indian images on the part of the Empire, and the problem of Indian "mascots" in white society)—as "desaparecer." I had my doubts, of course. "Tucked" could be translated literally as "almacenar," and the word would imply turning persons into things, commodifying Reservations and their inhabitants. Yet, for us, a country which made the word "desaparecer" famous after 30,000 "desaparecidos" were tortured and killed by a terrible military dictatorship between 1976 and 1983, the word "almacenar" would mean less from the point of view of politics and even emotion than "desaparecer," and I felt "desaparecer" was something similar to the "tucked" Carter had chosen for his poem. The poem, like the word in Spanish, is talking about *erasing* the Reservations (and the Nations) from the mind of the country, about turning them into "vanished" (another telling word) Americans, as the military wanted to erase the 30.000 persons from Argentina's mind during the dictatorship and even today. A choice between "almacenar" and "desaparecer" can change the translation of a poem, and both choices can be correct, I think. Yet, what is most important for me is that both are possible and the process of chosing makes us think of new meanings for the original.[5]

---

5   Interestingly, in the version of this poem that appears in *SAIL*, Revard changed the word "tucked" to "desaparecidos," adding this note to the poem: "In this poem I use a Spanish word that may be unfamiliar to readers in the United States: *desaparecidos*. It means 'disappeared,' and was applied especially to those citizens seized, tortured, and murdered by the Chilean, Peruvian, Argentine and other secret police—aided and abetted by the United States, during the Nixon and Reagan and Bush One years . . . " (1). I asked Carter through e-mail about the addition of the word *desaparecidos*. I wanted to know whether it had occurred to him because of our conversations and this is what he answered: "I added it as a direct reference to the resemblance between what was done post-1492 and is still being done in 21st century to American Indian people in North America, and what was done to South American and Central American people under the Nixon, Reagan,

The translation of a rich poem like "Postcolonial Hyperbaggage" can lead to incredible ideas, because translating implies a very deep and careful *reading*: thus, the process of translation itself can open up roads of analysis. A last example will make this clear: in the last part of the poem, there is a reference to the "selling" of consumerism and the American way of life: the Satan of computers offers the "Apple" to a new Adam and Eve. This "selling of buying" as the way to happiness is constant in our Latin American societies, and it is done through television, cinema, and advertising. Here, I knew I could not translate "Apple" as "Manzana," because Carter is talking about both the apple in the Bible and the "trademark," the "Apple" computer. Because of what is generally called here "cultural colonialism," my readers in Argentina know what "Apple" is, because computers are also sold to us as the way to Eden, the solution to all problems. Therefore, not translating "Apple," also points to the fact that through postcolonialism, English as a language and American trademarks are also our conquerors. Here too, the symbol of temptation is no longer "la manzana de la Biblia" (The Bible's apple) but "Apple," the computer, which promises us Eden and is taking us to Hell, as we (Argentinians) should know already after December 2001, when the deep economical crisis caused by the external debt to the Northern countries began. If the poem were to be published, I would like to add a footnote to the word "Apple" including the trademark logo.

Postcolonial Hyperbaggage	Hiperequipaje poscolonial
Oh, if Vuitton made a suitcase with modem and hypertext—or at least windows to let us put new folders in, where jackets won't wrinkle and all the smelly socks can be hung with care in the hyperspace herb-drawer—and with still cooler files whose chocolate	Ah, si Vuitton hiciera una valija con hipertexto y módem . . . o por lo menos ventanas para que pusiéramos ahí nuevas carpetas, donde las solapas no se arruguen y todas las medias llenas de olor puedan colgarse con cuidado en el cajón de hierbas del hiperespacio y con

and Bush regimes—I thought the word would carry over strongly. I hope you also may feel the kinship, as I think from your posts at different times about the Pampas and the Indian people you know of in your part of the world, and of course the struggle you have gone through in Buenos Aires and other parts of Argentina" (6 March 2005: E-mail to Márgara Averbach).

truffles would never melt
into a cashmere sweater. We need these
neat reversible black holes for crossing
Borders,
things we could pack and close
at a single touch and never pop a seam
or rip a zipper. They'd make the
Eurodollar
   zoom up in value—
and hey, just think,
Stealth Bombers could be replaced
  By diplomatic pouches full
of virtual assassins,
used terrorists could be dumped
  out of the Trash Can, leaving
    a Virtuous Reality.
All Indian Reservations could be tucked
Into Death Valley, accessible through
its golden icon, the Sacajawea Dollar.
Such a Pandora's Apple, I think,
Even the seediest Satan could have sold
to the smartest Adam and Eve, just by
saying
one taste of this, my dears,
and you're back in Eden.
	archivos todavía más frescos cuyas
	trufas
	de chocolate nunca se derritan
	en el suéter de cachemira. Necesitamos
	esos
	agujeros negros prolijos reversibles para
	cruzar Fronteras,
	cosas que podamos empacar y cerrar
	en un solo roce y nunca abrir una
	costura
	o desgarrar un cierre. Harían que el
	eurodólar
	   subiera como un cohete
	y ey, piensen solamente,
	se podría reemplazar a los bombarderos
	invisibles
	  por equipajes diplomáticos llenos
	de asesinos virtuales,
	se podría descartar a los terroristas
	usados
	  en el Cesto de Basura, para que
	quedara
	    una Realidad Virtuosa.
	Todas las Reservaciones Indias podrían
	almacenarse
	en el Valle de la Muerte, accesible a
	través
	de su ícono de oro, el dólar Sacajawea.
	A esa Apple de Pandora, creo yo,
	podría haberla vendido hasta el Satán
	más sórdido
	a los más inteligentes Adán y Eva, sólo
	con decirles
	un poquito de esto, mis queridos,
	y ahí están, en el Edén de nuevo.

Some Conclusions

In "Driving in Oklahoma" it is obvious that the relationship between Nature and human beings is not read in the same way in Western and Osage cultures, and this is one of the more important problems in translating poems that stand in a crossroads between cultures and languages. The crossing of culture-language characteristics is very important already in the original Native American texts. Carter Revard writes in English, and English is probably *the* language of Empire in the Twentieth century. Yet, his poetry transmits an Osage worldview—somewhat modified by life in close contact with EuroAmerican culture—and a defense of that world view against colonialism and cultural domination. The result is obviously hybrid, complex and dialogical.

When translating this piece of hybrid culture into Spanish, I am using another Imperial language and my choices (in words, structures, and even meanings) come from another mestizo culture, the Argentinian culture. This makes the bridging always present in translations a very complex operation, in which cultures and languages are difficult to control.

There are well-known and very good translators in Argentina who think that contact between author and translator is always negative. They believe (and this can be sustained through theory) that the reading has to come from the translator alone, that once the text is published, the translator becomes another reader, with power to make his or her own readings of the text obvious in the translation.[6] Yet, I believe in cases such as the ones described here, contact between author and translator can be very useful. The author can help the translator avoid misreadings that come from cultural differences and from the difficulty of interpreting (when interpreting is necessary) against and over the crossings of languages and cultures.

The same can be said about footnotes and author explanations. If the author has explained something and the explanation helps to bridge languages and cultures, I feel the explanation should become part of the translation in a footnote, especially when it cannot be inserted easily in the text without changing the rhythm of the original. The footnote can be of help to the reader of the translation; it can give him or her an essential knowledge of the original culture that the reader of the original text may not need. And as translation forces the reader of the original—as it has forced the translator before—to reflect on the different meanings, on the tones and connotations of words in one language and in the other, the reading of a commented translation is always a way to open the mind to different readings of the poems. In reading translations and the comments on translations, certain interpretations one did

---

6   The well known Konex Prize winner Rolando Costa Picazo (translator of Raymond Carver and William Faulkner, among other well known American authors) is of this opinion, as he has stated in interviews and personally to me in conversation.

not even think about become not only possible but serious and challenging, and they do so because of the quality of the process of translation. The translator always feels he or she understands the poem better after translating it, and the same could be said of the person reading the translation and the comments made either by the author or by the translator, or better still, by both of them joined in this disputed, fertile, always changing collaboration that translation really is.

Works Cited

Averbach, M. 2001. "Technology, 'Magic,' and Resistance in Native American Women's Writing." *Femspec* 2.2: 7–17.
Barthes, R. 1995. *El grado cero de la escritura*. Argentina: SXXI.
Dickinson, E. 1985. *Poemas seleccion y sraduccion de Silvina Ocampo*. Prólogo de J. L. Borges. Buenos Aires, Argentina: Tusquets.
Foucault, M. 1985. *Las palabras y las cosas: Una arqueología de las ciencias humanas*. Barcelona, Spain: Planeta.
Revard, C. 1980. *Ponca War Dancers*. Norman, Oklahoma: Point Riders Press.
———. 1997, 6 June. "Message from Argentina." E-mail to M. Averbach.
———. 1998, 14 October. "Indians Sightings Project/India [sic]." E-mail to M. Averbach.
———. 1998. *Family Matters, Tribal Affairs*. Tucson: University of Arizona Press.
———. 2001. "Postcolonial Hyperbaggage." *The American Oxonian* LXXVIII.2: 192.
———. 2002, 7 October. "Magic Realism." E-mail to M. Averbach.
———. 2001. *Winning the Dust Bowl*. Tucson: University of Arizona Press.
———. 2003. "Postcolonial Hyperbaggage." *Studies in American Indian Literatures* 15.1: 1–2.
———. 2002, 7 October. E-mail to M. Averbach.

An earlier version of this essay, "Translating Carter Revard: An Adventure among Mixed and Fertile Worlds," appeared in *Studies in American Indian Literatures* 15.1 (2003): 74–88.

Scholarship and Stories, Oxford and Oklahoma, Academe and American Indians: The Relational Words and Worlds of a Native American Bard and Storytelling Medievalist—Carter Revard

Susan Berry Brill de Ramírez
Peter G. Beidler

What happens when a reservation-raised boy from a mixed white-Indian family becomes one of the foremost scholars of medieval literature? Does he lose his down-home love of the everyday, of nature, stories, and humor once he enters the staid walls of the academy and confronts the establishment disapproval of all that is not strictly ratiocinative? Why would a young man from Indian country become a medieval scholar? Is not the world of medieval England far removed from the realms of rural poverty, Ponca storytelling, Osage dancing, and Oklahoma dust bowls, or are those distances across different centuries, histories, lands, cultures, and nationalities actually traversable in a storytelling heartbeat? Carter Revard left his rural and tribal communities in Oklahoma, traveled to the esteemed ivory towers of Oxford University, and in his study of medieval literatures found an early English language literature deeply informed by its own oral roots. Since his earliest childhood, Revard knew how to listen to stories. He had been raised doing that and was to become a remarkable storyteller in his own right. He brought those gifts and skills to bear along with his rigorous scholarly training to open up medieval texts in ways that traditional literary critical methods could not. We would like to offer our insights into Revard's distinctive scholarly methodology, for we feel that there is much in that methodology that would be of value for other scholars. We are both scholars of Native literatures: Beidler is a trained medievalist, while Brill de Ramírez is trained in literary theory and criticism. These areas of specialization give us a particular appreciation and understanding of Revard's scholarship which we see as an important alternative model for future literary scholarship.

In the introduction to *Family Matters, Tribal Affairs*, Revard offers his assessment of contemporary literary critical evaluations of literature and scholarship, commenting that much important new work is often overlooked because of scholars' critical biases. Revard writes, "My preference is for novels with plots, poems with stories, and writers with a sense of connection to the people reading" (1998: xvi). Revard is a poet, a storyteller, and a literary scholar, and whether his writing is literary or critical, there is in his work a deep sense of the writer's commitment to and relationship with readers. This sense comes in part from Revard's familiarity with Native American storytelling traditions, both from his own study and from his own lived experience growing up within his tribal communities—Osage through his stepfather and siblings, Ponca through his aunt and cousins. This is important in at least two ways: for one, Revard is a poet and storyteller in his own right and understands the intricate complexities of poetry and storytelling from the vantage point of the creator; two, he has lived in communities and worlds in which stories are a part of the very fabric of everyday life. As anthropologist Dennis Tedlock writes, "A story is not a genre like other genres of verbal art, but is more like a complex ceremony in miniature, encompassing aphorisms, public announcements, speeches, prayers, songs, and even other narratives" (1983: 3). Tedlock notes that this is true across all oral cultures throughout time. This is important in literary scholarship for those literatures that are very directly informed by their oral roots, especially those transitional written literatures that appear in the midst of active oral cultures, such as medieval European literatures and twentieth century Native American literatures. Revard's intimate knowledge of his Osage and Ponca storytelling traditions gives him invaluable insights into the related literary realms of medieval Europe.

Laguna Pueblo poet and storyteller Leslie Marmon Silko explains that storytelling is a co-creative process and that "storytelling always includes the audience and the listeners, and, in fact, a great deal of the story is believed to be inside the listener, and the storyteller's role is to draw the story out of the listeners" (1981: 57). In Native American storytelling, all involved are understood to be equally part of the storytelling event. The storyteller, the listeners, and the characters in the stories all come together as fellow participants within the unfolding story. This triple-woven fabric is different from the textualized presentations of the more dialogic, or even monologic, work of contemporary professional storytellers, lecturers, and comics. Within the framework of the storytelling circle, what holds everything together within that framework are the developing relationships among all involved. The words of the story serve the larger purpose of furthering those relationships—be they familial, tribal, or, in the case of Revard's scholarship, academic. In *Oral Poetry: An Introduction*, medievalist Paul Zumthor notes that "The listener while listening is completely present" (1990: 19). This relational presence and interactivity is also the case for listeners even when the act of co-creative listening is mediated by the written or electronic page.

Much like the work of a traditional storyteller, Revard's scholarship unfolds to his readers in a conversive (combining both senses of interpersonal conversation and transformative conversion) voice that welcomes his readers *into* the worlds within his books, essays, and notes. In this manner, readers are invited to become co-creative and interactive *listener*-readers who engage with and within the unfolding literary and scholarly stories and who, thereby, become transformed through the experiential and relational process of the storytelling event (even when textually mediated). Some of the conversive storytelling tools that Revard uses include voice shifts to the second person voice where he speaks directly to his listener-readers, episodic and associational shifts that bring the apparently unrelated together in new and unusual ways, an intermixing of diverse worlds and times (human, animal, mythic, historic, past, present, medieval British, and Native American), an interweaving of the expository and the narrative, and an informality of scholarly voice in which Revard speaks to his readers as comfortably and familiarly as if he was speaking with them over a cup of coffee at the Indian Center in St. Louis.

This congenial voice can be heard in Revard's remarkable essay about the central Indian character Injun Joe in Mark Twain's *Tom Sawyer*. In "Why Mark Twain Murdered Injun Joe—And Will Never Be Indicted," Revard focuses his essay around two central questions: "why Twain hated Indians so fiercely" and why there has been such critical "silence about his hatred" (1999c: 643). Combining a conversive storytelling strategy with extensive scholarly rigor, Revard fleshes out vignettes and passages, bringing them to storytelling life as a means of considering various interpretive possibilities to help us understand Twain's hatred of Indians. That hatred implicates not only Twain, but also America and us all. Revard concludes his essay by noting that at the end of Twain's life, when he traveled to Europe, he finally began to look at Euroamerica's continued conquest of Native peoples in relation to the American empire-building that he saw in the annexation of lands that had been part of Spain's colonial land-holding:

> Only when Twain left America for a trip round the world by which he hoped to pay off the creditors he owed, did he make his great discovery that the American takeovers of Indian Territory and of the Spanish Empire were closely related, which led him to realize that what he thought he hated about Indians was what he actually hated about Americans, and still more what he hated about "the damned human race." (660)

Revard neither whitewashes Twain's racism after the fashion of critics who attempt to "re-categorize Injun Joe not as historical Indian, but as mythic or psychic scapegoat" (647), nor does he brandish an essentializing critique that damns Twain and his writing as hopelessly racist. Rather, Revard grounds his response to Twain within the history and historicity of late nineteenth-century America—a land of Manifest Destiny, Reconstruction, and Indian removal. Revard sheds new light on the character of Injun Joe by bringing the character to life within the framework of Twain's own history and the real life stories of Native people at the time. Drawing on his own Osage cultural connections, Revard begins his essay with a story about an Indian-hating student at the University of Iowa in the 1860s. Revard fleshes out the racist portrayal of Injun Joe by including another story from the same time and region to help his listener-readers to more fully understand the times, the context, and, thereby, Twain's unexceptional views.

Traditional Native American storytelling, like traditional storytelling around the world, takes an episodic form with stories leading into other stories that circle back upon the first story much like the interwoven threads of a tapestry or rug. Revard's analysis of the Twain character takes this very form with diverse stories and histories interwoven to bring into focus the larger and much more complex story of the real people from which Injun Joe and Tom Sawyer emerged. This analysis combines with Twain's storytelling voice to invite his listener-readers into the unfolding story of the essay, including his uses of a colloquial first plural voice ("But let's turn from such deplorable omissions to the questions with which we began" [1999c: 649]), of the conversive strategy that brings Twain's writing and times into the contemporary world of the reader ("*Tom Sawyer* as a Stephen King Novel" [655]), and a traditional storytelling frame around the horrific that both begins and ends on a positive note (643, 660). Of course, the leap from Ponca and Osage country to the world of Twain's character Injun Joe is not as great as that from dust bowl Oklahoma to medieval England, but Revard's Native American storytelling voice pervades even that scholarship as he brings worlds and times, apparently distant from us today, into a conversive scholarship that opens up texts as he transforms those texts into fleshed out and living stories.

Another example of the way Revard's literary analysis begins to read like something other than a more traditional literary analysis can be found in one of his most recent scholarly articles. It is not about Joe but about Gilote this time, and it appears in the peer-reviewed *Chaucer Review*, one of the most respected journals devoted to research in medieval literature. Even the title is typical of Revard's genial nose-thumbing at the stuffiness of literary scholarship: "*The Wife of Bath's Grandmother*: or, How Gilote Showed Her Friend Johane that the Wages of Sin Is Worldly Pleasure, and How Both then Preached This Gospel throughout England and Ireland." The article is absolutely serious scholarship, and it is absolutely a bit of funny storytelling. Just as Revard brings both Injun Joe and Twain alive for us, so he here brings both Gilote and an anonymous medieval writer alive for us.

The subject of Revard's article is *Gilote et Johane*, a 349-line rhymed tale that appears in the Harley 2253 manuscript, dated around 1340, now in the British Library in London. The tale, written in a branch of Old French known as Anglo-Norman, begins as a spirited dialogue between two pretty young women about whether it is good to be a virgin. Johane (Joanne), a virgin still, praises the virgin state for all the usual reasons, such as that fornication is both sinful and unlawful while virgins emulate Mary. A central part of Revard's article is his own delightful translation of the Anglo-Norman poem. Here is his rendition of the chaste Johane's response after Gilote brags of what a fine lover her knight is:

> "Is that the truth?" Joanne said, "*I'm* a virgin—
> I keep my body pure, despite men's urging,
> And all the decent men will tell you so.

> But Jill, one thing I think you ought to know—
> The way you're living's really, truly, awful:
> Sleeping around like that is—well, unlawful. (2004: 125, lines 14–19)

Revard then translates a passage that refers to Gilote's multiple lovers as "this one" and "that one." Notably distinctive is the rhyme scheme where Revard rhymes "that one" ("that'n") with Gilote's promiscuous "alley-catting" ("cat'n"): "You bed with this one, then you ball with that one—/ Why don't you give up all that alley-catting / And take a husband?" (125, lines 20–22). In Revard's translation, he recognizes the colloquialisms in the Old French of the original and then presents a translation that parallels the original poem's bawdy light-heartedness. To rhyme "that one" with "catting" is a bit of a stretch until the reader as listener-reader hears the rural Oklahoman and reservation voice of storyteller Revard in what actually turns out to be a very close rhyme with "that'n" and "cat'n." At this early point in the poem, Revard brings out the bawdy humor that pervades the entire poem. As Johane presents her position of moral rectitude with her very un-Christian judgment against Gilote, in the contemporary version produced through the interwoven storytelling of the medieval writer and Native storyteller Revard, Johane's position is undercut by her colloquial diction and the hesitancy of her argument (evidenced in the pausal dashes inserted by Revard). The rhyme of "that'n" ("that one") with "cat'n" ("alley-catting") brings Johane down to Gilote's level and gives the poem's listener-reader an early indication of the direction the poem will take as Johane finds that she is really not so different from Gilote after all.

Gilote responds to Johane, telling her that she is all wrong about the virtues of virginity. It is good, Gilote insists, to go forth and multiply to increase the number of Christians worshiping God. Going even further, Gilote argues that to do so means that married women need not be bounded by their marriage vows and that a life of pleasure demands broader interests. While Gilote is quite pleased to advocate the sensually promiscuous life, she grounds her position with arguments that are solidly based in the harsh realities of medieval matrimony. Much like Chaucer's Wife of Bath, whose multiple marriages and husbands underlie the gritty reality of abuse, Gilote explains that women must be unfaithful to their husbands, for it is only outside of marriage that women will find any pleasure:

> "But as for marriage ... Joanne, *what* a crime
> To waste in wedlock all our best bed-time!

> Or if I married badly—as most *do*—
> He'd make my home a prison, beat me too,
> Keep me in strict confinement night and day,
> One brat at breast, another on the way!
> Sentenced to life, with such a thug for jailer,
> Who'd wonder if I found some wealthy bailer?
> Of women I've known, every single wife
> Repents her having chosen married life." (126, lines 53–62)

Gilote's arguments are successful, convincing Johane to give up her virginity. Notwithstanding her accuracy regarding the abuse of women within marriage (e.g., in medieval London, it was legal for husbands to beat their wives, but not to the point of permanent disfigurement or death), Gilote makes it very clear that her primary argument is not so much to denigrate marriage, but rather to privilege sexual activity outside of marriage. This primacy is evident at the outset of her critique of marriage which begins with Gilote lamenting that women's "best bed-time" is "waste[d] in wedlock." Further, in her criticism of abusive husbands who are "thugs," her remedy is to be found, not by any effort to reform husbands nor to improve marriages, but instead by means of each woman's recourse to "some wealthy bailer." The tale continues as the raucous Gilote and her fresh young convert Johane become a pair of advocates for "women's rights," spreading the good word about taking lovers out of wedlock. When a distraught young wife comes to Gilote and complains that her lordly husband is impotent, Gilote counsels her to take a lover for her own pleasure. Gilote and Johane make more and more converts to their doctrine of non-marital sex and soon travel throughout England and even Ireland preaching their message and gaining even more converts.

Revard's poem is faithful to the original—sort of. Will anyone really complain if his version has just a bit more life, just a bit more humor, just a bit more wit than its Anglo-Norman predecessor? In telling the tale of Gilote and Johane in his own way and, thereby, updating the telling for a contemporary audience, Revard is being entirely true to his Native American oral storytelling roots, and also true to many traditional storytelling strategies that are evident across all oral cultures (Brill de Ramírez 1999). The conversive nature of storytelling meant that each storyteller retold stories in his or her own way, adding this, subtracting that, altering the other, to suit a particular audience or a particular family, tribal, or cultural situation. In both Native American and medieval storytelling traditions, each telling is *supposed* to be new and different, while also remaining true to the essence of the story being told. Hence the different versions of the medieval French story about Little Red Riding Hood; details may shift from version to version, but the centering elements of the story are consistent across the diverse tellings. We see this conversive strategy that molds stories to fit with each telling throughout Revard's own translation of *Gilote et Johane*. Illustrating at least one Revardian expansion of the original poem, one passage includes the lament of the distraught young wife who comes bashfully to complain to Gilote of her husband's impotence:

> "It's hard to *talk* about such things . . . however,
> I've *got* to get some help, and you're so clever . . . .
> I married—young!—a well-connected lord
> Who's wealthy, titled, but . . . he can't afford
> To . . . pay his . . . marriage debt—his IOU's
> Date from the wedding night, and . . . (129, lines 224–229)

At this point, the poem becomes rather specific as the young wife notes the exact failings of her husband's diminutive physiology and inadequate performance. We can be sure that the Anglo-Norman poet never literally talked about IOU's, but Carter Revard does, and by doing so he connects the story to the twentieth-first century and familiarizes it into the world of his own listener-readers. In Revard's easy and colloquial translation of this decidedly bawdy tale, he reminds us all that literature throughout the ages has its roots in everyday storytelling and that those stories run the gamut from the bawdy and erotic to the more formal and sacred.

Revard's scholarly method in discussing this poem is entirely legitimate. He refers to the thematic connections, not explored by previous scholars, between *Gilote et Johane* and the wonderful 800-line prologue to Chaucer's *Wife of Bath's Tale*. In that prologue Alisoun of Bath brags about her own life, her loves, her right to as many men as she wants, and her ability and right to dominate her husbands—all within the frame and scope of her past abuse at the hands of at least one of her husbands, leaving one of her ears deaf. Commenting on the possible connections between the two poems, Revard asserts that the earlier Anglo-Norman tale may have provided Chaucer with part of the inspiration for his own tale: "Gilote, though not the marrying kind, is otherwise quite like the Wife of Bath—a clever and resourceful sensualist, alert to every opportunity for pleasure and heedless of any moral or ethical restraint in pursuing her opportunities" (2004: 119). Revard admits that Gilote is less complex than the Wife of Bath, but "like the Wife of Bath, she is every cleric's nightmare, voracious and insatiable and uncontrollable—and worst of all, more eloquent and better in debate than they are" (120).

As a scholar, Revard is interested not only in the literary similarity between Gilote and the Wife of Bath, but also in the literary context provided by the works surrounding *Gilote et Johane* in the Harley manuscript. He sees the Harley scribe not as a mere copyist but as an anthology-maker whose oral culture appreciated the meaningful importance of episodic and relational ordering. Revard does not approach *Gilote et Johane* alone; instead he recognizes that the poem's placement is crucial to its readers' deeper understandings. The scribe tellingly placed *Gilote et Johane* next to other poems that offer meaningful contrast with and implied comment on its characters, themes, and values. In contrast to those later literary traditions that provide a more tightly focused textual structure in terms of chronology, attention to place, and development of the individual psychology of the primary characters, Native American storytelling (like the early literature and storytelling of medieval Europe) is less textually developed in that listeners (and listener-readers) are expected to conversively complete the stories by acting as co-creative listener-participants in the interwoven storytelling/storymaking and, thereby, as actual participants (and fellow characters) in the unfolding story (Silko 1981: 57; Ortiz 1984: 57–69; Blaeser 1996:17–29; Brill de Ramírez 1999:129–135). The nature of oral storytelling is such that listeners and storytellers (along with the stories' characters) come together in the larger rubric of the storytelling event. The episodic structuring that occurs both within and across orally told stories invites listeners (and listener-readers, in the case of those conversively structured literatures) to stitch together meaningful linkages between characters, events, places, times, even repeated words and phrases. Revard clearly understands the intricate process of such semiotic interweaving. He grew up within the tribal worlds of Ponca and Osage storytelling—worlds that have provided important pathways into the stories of those other oral cultures distanced by an ocean and nearly a millenium: those of medieval Europe.

In Revard's analysis of this one Anglo-Norman poem, he brings to bear his familiarity with Native American storytelling, his education as a medieval scholar, and his conversive skill as a storyteller to assist the rest of us in recognizing and understanding those meaningful relationships that extend beyond the textual limits of the poem. Were our analyses limited by the textual boundaries of one poem like *Gilote and Johane*, we would miss the more intricate interwoven meanings evident in the episodic and associational structures of traditional oral storytelling (Native American and medieval) where one story or episode builds on, develops, and refers back to other stories or episodes. As Harold Scheub, a specialist in African oral traditions, notes regarding the broader contextual lineage behind each story, "Story is thus a very complex emotional, historical, and cultural experience, and is never centered on a single, isolated storytelling event; it involves the totality of one's storytelling experience.... There is therefore no canonical interpretation of story, just as there is no ur-version of a tale" (1998: 276). In contrast to the tendency of literary criticism and theory to posit correct and incorrect approaches to and readings of texts, in the conversive tradition of oral storytelling, Revard produces erudite scholarship that is, nevertheless, offered to his listener-readers with the inclusive and inviting familiarity of an oral storyteller who welcomes each listener personally to experience and learn from the story in community with others. Revard's readers are welcomed into the larger unfolding stories of medieval literatures that we approach through the interpretive pathways of indigeneity and orality.

As Paul Zumthor has noted, "For more than a century and a half, the study of oral culture has been left to the experts—ethnologists, sociologists, folklorists, and linguists.... At the same time literary criticism has either ignored or disdained the field" (1990:13). While our skills in close reading were finely honed through the decades of the American New Criticism, much was lost in not appreciating the extent to which each poem, like one thread, is part of a larger literary and cultural fabric. Scheub reminds us that this is inherent to stories (written or oral), "Story therefore is always more than the unique story: always in the process of becoming" (277). Rather than focusing on the surface elements of a poem's text, nor by telling us how we are to *read* the poem, Revard offers us storytelling guideposts (interconnections, related stories, signifying language, parallel characters) and invites his fellow medievalists to weave those together (with his guidance) and discover on our own the ever-widening richness of the poem's varied meaningfulness. Regarding the interwoven stories in the Harley manuscript, Revard points out that the medieval scribe, as storyteller, concludes *Gilote et Johane* with the two women going on a pilgrimage of sorts, far and wide to preach their libertine sexual doctrine. The scribe places this poem immediately before a quite different and entirely serious poem about the pilgrimages that true Christians make to the Holy Land; and right after that, the scribe places a poem describing the acts of penance that will earn pilgrims respite from some of the pains of purgatory. This juxtaposition, Revard says, makes readers less sympathetic to the delightful but aberrant and dangerous values of Gilote and her convert Johane. Revard continues his discussion of the poems surrounding *Gilote et Johane*. Among these poems is *The Old Man's Lament*, in which a man thinks about how he was once just the sort of eager lover whose actions are described so joyfully in *Gilote et Johane*, but now he is old and weak, sitting by the fire and waiting for death. In the context of those poems, *Gilote et Johane* seems less joyous, less funny, and more dangerous in its implications.

Revard's literary analysis of the possible connections of *Gilote et Johane* with, on the one hand, the work of Chaucer and, on the other, the poems surrounding it in the Harley manuscript is stimulating, original, and solid. In a related essay, Revard notes that "misuse of the label 'miscellanies' has blocked scholars from looking carefully at what medieval readers saw when they picked and read, or dipped into, many of the manuscripts so labelled" (2001: 262). He further explains that the episodic construction of medieval manuscripts (paralleling similar episodic oral storytelling methods) demonstrates that poems and stories were "deliberately placed within the manuscript so as to highlight oppositions and encourage intertextual readings" (262). There is no question that Revard is a careful scholar of medieval literature. He knows how to make his extensive footnotes legitimize his argument and place it within a framework provided by other scholars. His method as a scholar is refreshingly light in touch, humorous in tone, and modest, but there is no question that behind the informal tone is the voice of a confident scholar. Nevertheless, Revard is less concerned with the literary and contextual relations of *Gilote et Johane* than with the poem itself. He says little about the kinds of issues that would concern most scholars working on the poem—its movements, its plot, its characters, its themes, its humor. As a poet and a storyteller, he wants to let us read the poem and hear its story and then figure out for ourselves its movements, its plot, its characters, its themes, and its humor. It is entirely consistent with the storyteller in him that Revard wants to let the poem speak to us directly, not just through the medium of a scholar's interpretation. But how can a poem written in medieval Anglo-Norman speak to twenty-first century readers? Revard knows the power of conversive orality, and in his scholarship on this poem, he offers the poem to us in a storytelling manner that invites his readers as listener-readers to engage with and within the poem and its story.

In its original form in the Harley manuscript, *Gilote et Johane* speaks to none other than the very few who have taken the trouble to learn the language of northern France as it was written more than six centuries ago. Revard is scholar enough to be one of those very few, but poet enough and storyteller enough that he wants us to engage with and enjoy the poem rather than solely plodding through pages of analysis that in the end may disappear the very poem that is being critiqued. Revard's scholarship is especially notable in his commitment to keeping the literary work at the center, with his own words serving as guideposts for readers' deeper understandings of the poem. We can see this even in his English language rendition of the poem, for at the center of his essay "The Wife of Bath's Grandmother" lies Revard's translation of *Gilote et Johane*. Being a poet in his own right, Revard is not content to be just a translator. Instead, he recrafts the Anglo-Norman poem into something fresh and new while still being reasonably faithful to its original (both in language and essence). He is the first to acknowledge that his translation is not exact. He admits this with typical modesty, honesty, and wit:

> For the most part, the translation is fairly close, but it is—as Friar William Herebert once said of his own translation from Latin or French into his Herefordshire dialect of Middle English—*non semper de verbo ad verbum, sed frequenter sensum aut non multum declinando* ["not always word for word but often giving the sense, or not deviating greatly"]. Here and there I have added a bit and sharpened a point, in the fashion, though hardly with the brilliance, of Dryden's or Pope's "translations" of Chaucer: in their rococo sunlight, my couplets fade into Las Vegas neon. Nevertheless, they are not so far from the original poem, whose outrageous women (I hope) are alive and dancing even behind its veil. (2004: 117–118)

Carter Revard's original translation of the medieval *Gilote et Johane* is, then, a composite work that derives from his love of medieval poetry, from his skill as a scholar and a poet, and from his storytelling roots back in Oklahoma. His scholarly discussion of the literary relationships of *Gilote et Johane* is a storytelling event; his poetic retelling of *Gilote et Johane* is a scholarly event. In his essay "History, Myth, and Identity among Osages and Other Peoples," Revard explains that language reflects the values of a people, and that contemporary English has moved far away from its earlier more figurative roots: "In short, our system of naming has been impersonalized, demythicized, disfigured" (1980: 91). Throughout his scholarship, Revard is committed to resurrecting the figurative meanings that lie within the language of the literatures he studies, and he does so by drawing on his deep knowledge of orality and of the complex ways that words *mean* once they are infused with the life of interpersonal engagement.

Wittgenstein taught us over a half century ago that language use involves more than one person (e.g., in his arguments against the existence of private language) and that language becomes meaningful in actual practice—when a language game is played (1968: 11). Perhaps the most important common denominator that runs throughout Revard's scholarship is his awareness of the interactive storytelling spirit inherent in any literary work. The scholarship displayed in Revard's essays offers us all a model of profound rigor that is nonetheless engaged and engaging as it brings those literatures to scholarly storytelling life. This rigor is especially evident in a number of intriguing essays in which Revard explicitly interweaves his Native American cultures with his medieval scholarship. In the subsection "Old English, New English: Unriddling America" of his longer essay "Herbs of Healing: American Values in American Indian Literatures," he brings both worlds and times together in a conversive approach to Old English riddle poems. Much like his translation of *Gilote et Johane*, here Revard translates Old English riddles in ways that breathe life into them as if they were contemporary oral stories. He explains his approach as follows: "I want to show that this old Anglo-Saxon form is still alive, will still blossom and fruit if planted deep and watered from Indian springs" (1998: 179). A parallel essay entitled "Beads, Wampum, Money, Words—and Old English Riddles," which appeared in *American Indian Culture and Research Journal*, looks at Old English riddles within the conversive storytelling framework of oral cultures, and specifically draws on Revard's indigenous background. Revard brings all of this to a head in his most well known essay "Report to the Nation: Claiming Europe" in which he crafts an ironic piece in the tradition of Swift that rereads British and continental colonial history through an indigenous lens: "It may be impossible to civilize the Europeans" (1983: 166).

Revard understands the place of songs, chants, prayers, and poetry within living oral cultures, and he brings that knowledge to bear in his analyses of those other oral literatures that come to us from nearly a thousand years ago on the other side of the Atlantic Ocean. The disassociated presence of songs and poems on paper deceives readers into reading them as distinct from the larger realm of their respective cultural contexts. As Revard notes, the Europeans have separated songs from other word forms so that now what they call poems are put into books, not usually to be sung but to be read silently and alone. Even so, the lone and silent reader is finding a way through these poems to join a phantom community of other readers. They sit, or lie, or stand, far apart from each other, unable to see or hear or feel each other's presence except through the words they share, which creates this community of writers and readers. Usually they do not know each other, and they may be separated in time as well as space. (1999b: 180)

While Stanley Fish would have us recognize the interactive groupings of such interpretive communities, Revard reminds us that since the beginning of time people have been coming together in storytelling communities. The mediative distancing that is inherent in textual storytelling (what we refer to as literature) broadens the storytelling/literary circle almost to the point of absence in which geography, culture, language and time impede readers' abilities to *hear* the living co-creative stories that are being told behind the textual skeletons of the words on the page. Paul Zolbrod explains this textual dilemma in regards to orally informed Native literatures, noting that, "Because these works are stored only by way of print, however, readers overlook their origins as oral poems once produced in tribal or tribelike communities" (1995: 18). In his essay on the poem "Annote and Johon," Revard notes that scholars criticize that poem's co-creative minimalism, "complaining that it needs less art and more matter" (1999a: 5). Revard explains that the critics' lack of understanding of interactive orality demonstrates "not what is lacking [in the poem] but what they [the critics] are missing" (5). Revard provides in his scholarship models that flesh out textual skeletons and invite us all to step into the re-woven fabric of literary storytelling worlds. He does this to bring us all together, even though as different readers, "[W]e answer with some other word patterns, not so beautiful maybe, but stepping to the same drumbeat, hearing the same song, as if we were still together" (1999b: 181).

Like a drummer or community storyteller who welcomes us all as fellow dancers or story-listeners, Revard presents us with music that we are invited to dance to and stories that we are invited to become part of. As he explicitly notes, what this medievalist does is like a drummer and singer of a Native American drum circle: "[W]hat I can do is like that, if not so important or so useful. I can show a little of how the European elders worked in words... I take English words and beat them, or bead them, into patterns... putting words together to locate ourselves, to reach across time and space as the elders do, keep a community alive for us where our nations can come and go around the drum at the right time and in the right way" (1999b: 181). As scholars, all too often we get lost in words and texts to the extent that Jacques Derrida writes that there is nothing that is not part of a text ("Il n'y a pas de hors-texte" [158]). Revard, in contrast, affirms that within texts lie stories—what he refers to as "giving the poems their stories" (2001: xiv). Remembering that at the center of storytelling lies the relationality that defines and strengthens the community bonds out of which the storytelling emerges, Revard reminds us all that literary scholars are indeed storytellers retelling stories that we have read in new ways for new audiences. As classicist and folklorist John Miles Foley encourages scholars to approach orally informed literatures with greater understanding of the significance of their oral roots: "We must be ready to suit our thinking and frame of reference to oral poetry, rather than demanding that oral poetry suit our tried-and-true (but very parochial) ways of transacting the business of verbal art" (2002: 80). More than anyone we know, Revard does this by bridging the gap between literature and scholarship through their connective heritage in relational storytelling. In this way, we all are invited to come together in community through language and story. For Revard, this is a healing activity, vital to the health of our communities: "One way to survive is to keep a sense of hope, of being able to find what works, what helps, the laughter and shared strength and awareness of good things and good ways. . . For my part I hope it is true that good language, in both talk and writing, builds a small community in which people can live a little more completely and joyously than solitude allows—words are not poems until that happens" (2001: xvi). Especially now during the early years of the twenty-first century when it seems that the global tendencies are so horrifically towards disunity, discord, and dispute, Revard's scholarly model of relational knowing that bridges worlds, times and cultures is that much more needed and valuable to us all.

Works Cited

Blaeser, K. M. 1996. *Gerald Vizenor: Writing in the Oral Tradition.* Norman: University of Oklahoma Press.
Brill de Ramírez, S. B. 1999. *Contemporary American Indian Literatures and the Oral Tradition.* Tucson: University of Arizona Press.
Derrida, J. 1976. *Of Grammatology.* Trans. G. C. Spivak. Baltimore: Johns Hopkins University Press.
Foley, J. M. 2002. *How to Read an Oral Poem.* Urbana: University of Illinois Press.
Ortiz, S. J. 1984. "Always the Stories: A Brief History and Thoughts on My Writing." *Coyote Was Here: Essays on Contemporary Native American Literary and Political Mobilization.* Ed. B. Schöler. Aarhus, Denmark: Seklos. 57–69.
Revard, C. 1980. "History, Myth, and Identity among Osages and Other Peoples." *Denver Quarterly* 14.4: 84–97. Revised in *Family Matters, Tribal Affairs,* 126–141.
———. 1983. "Report to the Nation: Claiming Europe." In *Earth Power Coming: Short Fiction in Native American Literature.* Ed. S. J. Ortiz. Tsaile: Navajo Community College Press. 166–181. Revised in *Family Matters, Tribal Affairs,* 76–91.
———. 1998. *Family Matters, Tribal Affairs.* Tucson: University of Arizona Press.
———. 1999a. "'Annote and Johon,' Ms. Harley 2253, and *The Book of Secrets.*" *English Language Notes* 36: 5–19.
———. 1999b. "Beads, Wampum, Money, Words—and Old English Riddles." *American Indian Culture and Research Journal* 23.1: 177–89.
———. 1999c. "Why Mark Twain Murdered Injun Joe—And Will Never Be Indicted." *The Massachusetts Review:* 643–670.

———. 2001. "From French 'Fabliau Manuscripts' and MS. Harley 2253 to the *Decameron* and the *Canterbury Tales*." *Medium Ævum* 69.2: 261–278.

———. 2004. "The Wife of Bath's Grandmother: or, How Gilote Showed Her Friend Johane that the Wages of Sin is Worldly Pleasure, and How Both then Preached This Gospel throughout England and Ireland." *The Chaucer Review* 39: 117–136.

Scheub, H. 1998. *Story*. Madison: University of Wisconsin Press.

Silko, L. M. 1981. "Language and Literature from a Pueblo Indian Perspective." *English Literature: Opening Up the Canon*. Ed. Leslie A. Fiedler and H. A. Baker, Jr. Baltimore: Johns Hopkins University Press. 54–72.

Tedlock, D. 1983. *The Spoken Word and the Work of Interpretation*. Philadelphia: University of Pennsylvania Press.

Wittgenstein, L. 1968. *Philosophical Investigations*. Ed. G. E. M. Anscombe and R. Rhees. Trans. G. E. M. Anscombe. 3d ed. New York: Macmillan.

Zolbrod, P. 1995. *Reading the Voice: Native American Poetry on the Written Page*. Salt Lake City: University of Utah Press.

Zumthor, P. 1990. *Oral Poetry: An Introduction*. Trans. K. Murphy-Judy. Foreword W. J. Ong. Minneapolis: University of Minnesota Press.

Trail-Tracking the Ludlow Scribe: Carter Revard as Translator-Scholar-Sleuth of Medieval English Poetry

Susanna Fein

To capture Carter Revard's range as a writer and as a human being, one needs to include and embrace the medievalist in him. Like J. R. R. Tolkien, one of his teachers at Oxford, he loves words and languages. And having imbibed already in college what is a revered tradition among medievalists—that to profess this field is to venerate those who precede us, those who studied much and taught us well—Revard fittingly lauds his Tulsa mentors. He writes of how he met Professor Franklin Eikenberry on his first day at the university, when he was too green even to know how to use a telephone or find a place to live (Revard 2001a: 133), and Professor Eikenberry sent him to young Assistant Professor Don Hayden, who drove him around Tulsa that very day until a place had been located, and only *then* brought him back to campus: "He did this like an English gentleman: as if it were simple, natural, and no trouble" (2001a: 137). He writes of how Professor Hayden later introduced him to the astonishing verse of Shelley and Keats, and also of Chaucer read aloud: "[W]hen I got to Oxford I stood in there with those Brits, bright as they were, and was able to read the Middle English aloud as well as they did" (2001a: 137). And he recalls with awe and gratitude the interest Professor Eikenberry took in him, and the way this man led Revard to apprehend Shakespeare on his own terms, by way of an epiphany that came, not surprisingly, upon reading a speech of supreme verbal absurdity—the monologue of Launce in *Two Gentlemen of Verona*, act 2, scene 3, in which a recalled scene of family hysteria was dampened only by Launce's unfeeling dog—during which, and in Professor Eikenberry's living room, student Revard fell apart laughing (2001a: 210–11). The professor responded by going to the kitchen and bringing out "a quart of milk and a half-dozen glazed doughnuts, after which we got back to the play." This anecdote nourishes Revard's closing words of tribute to his mentor:

> The teaching was being done by someone with the deepest respect for text and poet, with the most careful and thorough reading and rereading behind him, and with a great store of knowledge not only of Shakespeare's plays but the history and society around and within them. . . [T]his was a man, take him for all and all, I would not look upon his like again. (2001a: 212)

Professor Eikenberry was, for Revard, "like having an Indian uncle to train me, but this time in the literary 'wilderness'" (2001a: 208).

Reverence for forefathers and foremothers—those who lovingly pass lore to their descendents and their descendents' descendents—is, indeed, a common thread for both medievalist and Native American cultures. After graduating from the University of Tulsa, Revard won a Rhodes Scholarship and found himself at Merton College, Oxford, studying literature with "Inkling" Hugo Dyson in the heady days of Tolkien and C. S. Lewis (1952–53). Later he attended Yale, where he wrote a dissertation (completed in 1959) on the Middle English comic monologue in which a grumbler over actual social ills happens to reveal, unwittingly and quite satirically, his own massive foibles. In pursuing this subject, Revard unearthed a rich body of important yet neglected verse, and his efforts flourished under the guidance of the great medievalist critic, editor, and translator E. Talbot Donaldson. Like Eikenberry, Donaldson was driven to find the enduring human and social core in what is historically past yet textually present, and in their scholarly examples Revard found kindred spirits. Beyond this venerable respect for the past, there are further threads that entwine the medievalist in Revard with his Indian heritage: a keen appreciation for humor tinged with wry authorial wisdoms; a fascination with human complexities rendered in colloquial, emotionally true, clever, and often earthy diction; and an interest in dramatic monologues that erupt from the edges of society—the outlaw, the trickster, the bawdy woman—that is, from characters who operate from the outside, as did much of the

Indian culture of Revard's upbringing. Just so was displayed Shakespeare's profundity of feeling in Launce's comic monologue. And, holding to this interest in the funny, the low, the tricky, Revard's sensibilities often recall those of Mark Twain, to whom Revard alludes more than once in *Winning the Dust Bowl*. Even more, a medievalist will recognize in his account of his dashing Uncle Carter the bank robber, of a defiant Indian standoff during the Nixon era, and of the wonderful Coyote Trickster stories (Revard 2001a: 145, 158, 170), the same elements and talents that gird Revard's very important activities as a scholar of manuscripts, scribes, Middle English verse storytelling, and medieval social history.

I first met Carter Revard in the fall of 1985 when I had just graduated with my doctorate and appeared at my first conference as an assistant professor from Kent State University in Kent, Ohio. It was a meeting of the Midwest Modern Language Association in St. Louis. I had prepared a paper displaying my skills as a novice (which I was) on two Middle English alliterative poems, and Professor Revard of Washington University was scheduled to give the response to my work and that of two other fledging scholars. I recognized his name and I had read his articles; there were not a lot of people publishing then on alliterative verse, and his 1967 piece in a *festschrift* for F. J. Eikenberry (edited by D. E. Hayden) had explicated three "Middle English Confessional Satires in Harley 2253 and Elsewhere," the most interesting one, for me, being *The Papelard Priest*, which demonstrated that Professor Revard was a person interested in digging raw, long-buried literary gems directly from manuscripts. This was work I found admirable, and I had begun to do it too. I remember him then, in his response to my paper, as both kind and informative, courteously correcting an infelicitous translation of a word, suggesting rightly that it denoted a type of cloth rather than a color. Afterwards he spoke to me informally in a manner that assured me my work was inherently interesting and worthwhile. He took care to be a gentleman "as if it were simple, natural, and no trouble," and I, having experienced wise mentors in my own medievalist training, understood that here was another model of generous erudition with whom I could share common interests. Several years later, at the International Congress on Medieval Studies—the huge meeting for medievalists held annually on the campus of Western Michigan University in Kalamazoo, Michigan—I listened to Revard speak on the scribe of London, British Library Manuscript Harley 2253, and then I began to understand the innovative scholarship that has most distinguished Revard's career as a medievalist, because of which our professional paths would again cross.

As for his authoritative knowledge of that word I had misconstrued (it was *rosset* in *The Parliament of the Three Ages*), this degree of semantic learning fits with the lexicographical bent one sees in Revard's early scholarship, when he was publishing linguistic essays, some with such playful titles as "How to Make a NUDE (New Utopian Dictionary of English)" (1972), and "Why Shakespeare and Chaucer, Though Not Unselfish, Could Never Have Fun" (1978). In a personal e-mail exchange I had with Revard years later, he fretted over an Argentinian translator of his poetry getting a word wrong through no fault of her own: "[H]er translation of one poem has made a considerable mistake, the sort of mistake one makes when the original English uses a term from the past which is not going to be in the Spanish dictionaries—I spoke of constructing a cow-pond in Oklahoma by use of a 'slip,' which was our term for a kind of mule-drawn digging 'shovel,' the sort of thing we now use backhoes and Caterpillar diggers for" (20 June 1997: E-mail to author). Of course, this concern for getting words just right goes with Revard's own prose and verse style, which is as precise as it is unforced. In his medieval scholarship it surfaces in how easily he explores complex archival materials written in a range of dialectal variants of English, French, and Latin, languages that in medieval England and France would change by locale and by occupational usage (legal, courtly, mercantile, literary, and so on). Revard is also a fine translator of medieval texts, one who, when faced with poetic comedies of the fourteenth century, lifts his own art from mere academic expediency to heroic heights. To render the rollicking Anglo-Norman poem *Gilote et Johane* into English for the first time, he adopts its couplet style, which opens with "En May, par vne matyne, s'en ala juer / en vert bois rame, vn jeuene cheualer," and takes off:

> On a May morning, through the new-green trees
> A brisk young knight was strolling at his ease,
> When not far off he heard two women talking.
> He listened, smiled, then carefully went stalking
> Among the shrubberies till he spied a pair
> Of young and pretty women sitting there ... (Revard 2004: 125)

When I first met Carter Revard, his name as a medievalist was established, though in a somewhat unorthodox way. He had published philological notes on Chaucer's *Miller's Tale* (1980), on the beautiful elegaic allegory *Pearl* (1964), and on the well-known lyric "Foweles in the Frith" (1978). He had also published an analysis of three confessional satires in the *festschrift* item mentioned above (1967), an article that demonstrated his keenness to uncover and connect neglected Middle English works whose survival sometimes depended on the most tenuous of circumstances. *The Papelard Priest* is an alliterative satire that had dropped virtually out of scholarly sight, having been preserved only on a legal document roll, which, when it was discovered in 1941 in an abandoned safe, was edited and photographed, but then misplaced or lost by 1951, so that any further study of it can rely only on twentieth-century records (Revard 2001b: 361). The speaker in this funny piece is, in Revard's blunt epithet, "a sensual, vain, lazy, bumbling and brainless nincompoop" (Revard 1967: 67–68). Stylistically, the poem has its share of alliterative *tour de force*, quite notably in a list,

> . . . where the priest names all the tools and trappings he must care for. It is *rum-ram-ruf* with a vengeance, but the sound-explosions are as controlled as a fireworks display . . . [or] a conveyor-belt bringing past the reader the innumerable rusty, broken, and gremlin-infested tools of the parsonage: . . . they flow past in their jostling yet consonantally ordered stream, alliteratively clinking in time. (1967: 68)

Revard shows how such confessional poems develop and satirize a speaker's lack of self-awareness while exposing his self-rationalizing duplicitous behavior. The fun is in the trickster being verbally exposed, in his own words and in spite of himself. As a scholar, Revard is intrigued by such social drama, and he is ever-inquisitive about where such performance pieces were enacted and for whom. In this essay he suggests that they "were being recited in taverns and dininghalls, as well as being anthologized by such ecclesiastics as those who, I believe, put together the Harley 2253 manuscript" (1967: 69). He also asserts that such popular songs—now rare and mostly vanished—fed the creation of the many remarkable characters inhabiting *The Canterbury Tales* and *Piers Plowman*.

The desire expressed here about how we may use writings to track—or at least *try* to track—the living presence of what is gone is not so very different from Revard's exquisite image of the flitting swallowtail in "*Over by Fairfax, Leaving Tracks*":

> Makes me wonder—
> if archaeologists should ever dig our prints

> with Possum's here, whether they'll see
> the winged beings who moved
> in brightness near us, leaving no tracks except
> in flowers and
> these winged words. (2001a: 124)

Recalling the event that led to this poem's making, Revard reflects upon the ephemera of daily event and the fragile legacies to be found in words:

> As I followed Lawrence and Wesley (Mi-ka-si), I saw that they were leaving tracks right alongside those of last night's possum, and I noticed off to the side, in the tall bluestem, some brilliant orange "butterfly weed" with a tiger swallowtail on them, a huge gold and black-striped being with rainbow spots, saw it lift up from those orange flowers and float over to some blue morning glories draping a bank. So later I got to thinking about these things, and I thought I would try to put something into words that might get across to our children when we have gone ahead far enough that this would be our best chance of being heard. (2001a: 122–23)

Revard's fascination with the popular songs sung in the taverns and dininghalls of medieval England—songs that draw pointed, recognizable, and funny sketches of those who were like the audience's own neighbors—is a fascination with the trackless swallowtail, its trace drawn only in poetry that may catch a snippet of the living essence of a time and community gone ahead.

What had made Carter Revard's name well known among medievalists before 1985—and what qualifies as creative and unorthodox research—was his tracking of words made by a particular man, namely, the words scrivened professionally by the scribe responsible for the poetry and prose found in MS Harley 2253. The two other confessional satires analyzed in the *festschrift* piece—*Man in the Moon* and *Satire on the Consistory Courts*—are from this famous book, which is critical to our concept of pre-Chaucerian English poetry. Most important and best known among its contents is a rare group of early English secular and political lyrics. Overall, the Harley manuscript comprises a library of eclectic reading material in three languages—English, French, and Latin. Its trilingualism reflects the way England was in the 1330s and 1340s, when the aristocratic prestige language was Anglo-Norman, the language of church and law was Latin, and the common people spoke and dealt in English. The Harley scribe acquired a book of French saints' legends and biblical paraphrases written by someone else. He then chose to extend it by filling up 92 more parchment leaves with an array of mixed material, some bawdy, some pious, and some political. All told, his portion of the Harley book portrays a cross-section of what was edifying, or entertaining, or both, for English folk of the early fourteenth century. The main element unifying this collection is the single hand that copied it—and, more so, the discerning literary intelligence behind that hand. The driving force behind Revard's best medieval scholarship has been a dogged certainty that more records survive to tell us whose hand this was, what were the man's training, occupation, and proclivities, and what was his life story. Few medievalists, and fewer still of a literary ilk, would or could have pursued the clues—physical traces in old documents and their social reconstructions—the way Carter Revard has tracked them down to permit us to recover many local circumstances of the unnamed Harley scribe.

It is this pursuit that makes Revard's work unusual and the stuff of legend. And news of his first results broke in a *footnote* to a *note*! There are scholars, and many medievalists, who compose footnotes more lengthy than the very articles they accompany. Sometimes, when read continuously, the notes themselves recount their own story of scholarly sleuthing, that is, they provide a supporting, nearly self-standing narrative of research related to the main argumentative thread. The footnotes in Revard's 1979 *Notes and Queries* note entitled "Richard Hurd and MS. Harley 2253" are of this sort. The main text proposes historical correspondences between first names given in a Harley lyric and particular persons in the market town of Ludlow in the early fourteenth century. Footnote Number One drops the bombshell. Toward the beginning of the essay, after writing the phrase, "In the course of research which has established that the scribe of MS. Harley 2253 actually worked in and around Ludlow during the years 1314–1349," Revard inserts this sentence at the foot of the column: "Evidence proving this is a series of 34 dated legal documents in the hand of the main scribe of Harley 2253: 4 in the British Library . . . and 30 in the Salop Record Office in Shrewsbury . . . listed here in chronological order from the earliest . . . 17 December 1314 to the latest . . . of 13 April 1349" (1979: 200). To the text he adds a caution: "I must emphasize immediately that the evidence needs very gingerly handling" (1979: 200). For the community of English medievalists, this footnote generated great excitement. The still-anonymous Harley scribe had been located to a particular site within an exact window of time! A few clues in the manuscript had suggested that there might be a connection with the Hereford bishop Adam Orleton or with warlord baron Roger Mortimer of Wigmore, but these traces could now be identified as unrelated to the scribe's occupational identity and lines of patronage because he had definitely operated in the Ludlow area. Further clues for his sources of employment were to be sought there. Revard closes his final footnote (Number Nine) with two apt figures for the fragile effects of his research:

> But I cannot forbear, to show how delicate are the houses of cards that one builds in connecting personal names to ME lyrics, giving a final tap to the one I have just built. . . . And perhaps the figure for this dilemma ought not to be that we are building card-houses, but that we are turning a kaleidoscope in which the scattered and colourful bits of information insist on making lovely patterns—which we ought not to mistake, too readily, for portraits of actual persons. (1979: 202)

A house of cards and a kaleidoscope. Revard's figures nicely encapsulate the tenuousness of historical conclusions drawn from accidental fragments, and yet they modestly understate the impact when new primary evidence arises on a subject about which there has been much curiosity, speculation, and misdirected surmise.

In short space Revard followed up the 1979 article with two brief notes, also published in the Oxford-based journal *Notes and Queries* (1981, 1982), which reported that he had located three more Harley scribe documents in Shropshire and one more in Salop, respectively, for a total of 38 previously unknown legal writs in the hand of the Harley scribe. In 1982, too, he extended his research upon the Harley scribe's portion of MS Harley 2253—a book deemed so important to English literary history that it had been preserved and replicated for scholars in a facsimile edition (Ker 1968)—by looking more closely at its French contents. The amalgamation of texts collected in the Harley manuscript are unusual to say the least. Many items copied by the scribe provide the *only* surviving traces of that work's existence, and this is true for texts in each of the three languages. The scribe seems to have been pursuing an unusual hobby of collecting literary materials that passed his way, perhaps to please an employer. What we know of literature in the generation before Chaucer is notably fuller on account of the Harley scribe's idiosyncratic efforts. Because other books from the same period display nowhere the same variety and richness, it is quite lucky for us that this particular book happened to survive the accidents of time.

It may seem strange to those outside medieval studies that scholars do not yet have a full grasp on all that the Harley manuscript holds between its cover-boards. But this is indeed the case as I write this essay in 2005. The reason rests in the hurdle posed by the necessity to transcribe handwritten medieval texts and, even more so, in the learned effort involved in editing those texts and translating them from their older languages into modern English, the medium that would render them readily accessible to present-day readers. The technical complexity of such work means that current scholarship is confined primarily to specialists who can consult the facsimile and find the specialized editions. In general, the Harley poems in English can be located by the nonacademic reader in various student anthologies, but the French works are not available except in scattered, remote French-language editions, and many of the Latin works have never even been printed.

Carter Revard is one of the pioneers at work on the Harley manuscript, and he has done much to make its contents and its organization better known to the scholarly community. He has also worked to see that its texts become accessible. It is with the French works—many of them lively and irreverent—that he has made considerable headway. In 1982 he published a landmark article in Harley studies, which appeared in *Studies in Philology*, on the comic, bawdy Anglo-Norman piece known as *Gilote et Johane*. Here Revard characterizes the Chaucerian licentiousness of this lively poem (where the characters resemble the Wife of Bath), delineates its free-form mix of medieval genres—pastourelle, debate, fabliau, dramatic interlude, and parody—and proposes an organizing principle for the Harley manuscript as a whole. The book is, he declares, a deliberately planned *anthology*, with its scribe constructing sequences and arrangements of texts throughout. Revard demonstrates by means of several meaningful juxtapositions of texts that the scribe used, in his words, a "principle of selection" of "not mere variety but contrariety" (1982: 129). Such a theory helps to explain why it is that the Harley manuscript preserves such a wildly various assemblage of items. Subsequent scholars have largely corroborated Revard's assessment as Harley studies have proceeded in subsequent decades with further and further refinement (for example, Turville-Petre 1996: 190–98, 219; Nolan 2000: 291; Fein 2000: 8; Scahill 2003: 18–32; Hines 2003: 78, 88).

In recent years Revard's scholarship has further popularized the fact that Harley 2253 preserves a big percentage of our surviving Anglo-Norman literature, including the largest number of French fabliaux found in any English medieval manuscript. Assessing all the books bearing traces of the scribe's hand (there are three in all), Revard once observed to me how these facts had been overlooked:

> You know, when I looked back at the list of Anglo-Norman texts so wonderfully provided by Ruth Dean [1999], I observe that out of 986 items she numbers, about 108 of them are found in the Harley 2253 scribe's three manuscripts—have not got the math precisely right, but something like this: 57 items in Harley 2253, 34 items in Harley 273, 17 items in Royal 12.C.xii. More than one in ten of known AN texts were gathered, and many of them copied, by this one man over the years 1314–49. Not only the M[iddle] E[nglish] lyrics picture would be very different without his compilations. (19 November 2003: E-mail to author)

Very recently in the journal *The Chaucer Review*, Revard has published a much-needed edition of *Gilote et Johane* with (set alongside its French verses) his own effervescently funny translation in English heroic couplets, on which he avers that, "Here and there I have added a bit and sharpened a point, in the fashion, though hardly the brilliance, of Dryden's or Pope's 'translations' of Chaucer: in their roccoco sunlight, my couplets fade into Las Vegas neon. Nonetheless, they are not so far from the original poem, whose outrageous women (I hope) are alive and dancing even behind its veils" (2004: 117–18). Revard has also brought the French fabliaux found in Harley 2253 to modern light. Fabliaux are bawdy stories of sexual antics told for amusement and often to mock social pretensions. Our most well-known example in English is Chaucer's *Miller's Tale*. In creating this and other fabliaux, Chaucer crafted in English a type of tale that is essentially French. A more recent issue of *The Chaucer Review* (2005) features Revard's editions and translations of the four Harley poems that are most thoroughly of the fabliau type, thus presenting them to the English-speaking world with every bit of their shocking rambunctiousness intact as they are rendered in an earthy American idiom. In another recent letter, Revard wrote coyly that he was delighted that I and my co-editor of *The Chaucer Review* "are still willing to put the naughty things between the sheets with all those footnotes sniffing at their toes" (7 February 2005: E-mail to author).

In other French-to-English translation work, Revard has published his version of a political outlaw poem found in Harley, *Trailbaston* (1998). And currently in press is the translation of another Harley text, a comic poem on gluttony. By a blend of scholarly acumen and poetic creativity, Revard is thus bringing these important texts into the canon of works to be read by medieval English scholars and students. This is as it should be, for these narratives were promulgated and enjoyed in England in what was then an active, indigenous French dialect, Anglo-Norman. They are bold, funny tales that merit an ongoing audience. Now receiving the gloss of Carter Revard's incomparable style, they may even entice those who love Revard's poetry to discover these hilarious narratives if only because his verse renditions are delightful and exceptional in their own way.

At the same time Revard's exploration of the scribe's milieu in Ludlow has continued apace. In the earlier article on *Gilote et Johane*, he devotes the last footnote to a lengthy excursus upon several potential associates and identifications of the scribe, concluding that, "Among the local household clerics and chaplains and lawyers we may be sure the Harley Scribe moved as a peer, and the households of the Ludlow milieu would have provided a very lively and interested audience for such a piece as *Gilote et Johane*, as well as the rest of the richly mixed contents of Harley 2253" (Revard 1982: 145). Seeking to know more about what the households of Ludlow read and used for entertainment has led Revard to more precise discoveries. An extremely interesting article from 1997 uncovers the titles of books being circulated—and to whom they were circulated—in the English court during the "four years 1326-30 when Roger Mortimer of Wigmore, as Isabella's Minister of Courtly Love, held all but royal sway in England" (1997: 297). He finds in the records of John Fleet, First Keeper of the Privy Wardrobe, contemporary evidence on who actively read for enjoyment (both men and women) and by what ranks such activity took place (both the barons and their retinues). He uncovers not only that Mortimer and Isabella devoured books of political theory and practice, but that there was also a strong taste for romances, stories of the trickster fox Renart, and exotic tales of the Orient. Revard's research allows historians to glimpse how the political intrigues and alliances of court were entwined with regular reading activities: "[I]t appears that Fleet's evidence on books borrowed and—presumably—read by Mortimer and Isabella, and by the clerics, noblewomen and noblemen at court with them in 1326-30, points to a court with many readers of a wide range of texts—political, theological, legal, satiric, romantic, didactic, military, devotional, enigmatic and prophetic" (1997:308). Then, with a lyric wink more typically found in his creative work, scholar Revard delivers a final witticism (spiced with a dose of Dante and a touch of Irish poet Thomas Moore's lyric "The time I've spent in wooing") upon those long-ago dalliances of Isabella and Mortimer: "The time they spent in wooing was no doubt their undoing—but they certainly read in books as well as looks, whatever folly the looking, or the booking, eventually led them into" (1997: 308).

Carter Revard's accomplishments as a medievalist draw on a happy blend of talents: the keen ear of a writer who understands learned and popular tastes, the determined doggedness of a sleuth deciphering fragmentary clues, the cultural curiosity of an anthropologist, the respectful reverence for the past of a true historian, and the fluent play with language of a well-trained linguist. His long pursuit of the Ludlow scribe of Harley 2253 may yet turn up a name and an exact manorial environ for the man whose hand has uniquely preserved a treasure-trove of materials for current scholars of medieval English literature. But the legacy of Revard's years of research on the Ludlow scribe is likely to exist not so much in an identification as in the extraordinary example such scholarship gives to others. In 2000 Revard's work on the Ludlow scribe was the centerpiece of a lengthy collection of essays, entitled *Studies in the Harley Manuscript: The Scribe, Contents, and Social Contexts of British Library MS Harley 2253*, of which I was the editor. Here, in a ninety-page essay of remarkable discovery and deduction, "Scribe and Provenance," Revard delivers a magisterial portrait of the scribe, including the discovery of forty-one dated holographs (that is, all the known legal writs in the scribe's own handwriting), with an analysis of the script as it changed over time. Because the documents bear dates, Revard shows how we can now sequence the copying of materials in the scribe's three books, and most crucially, the copying of texts into Harley 2253. Revard accompanies this analysis with an investigation of the scribe's reading, education, and probable roles as secretary, chaplain, and master of entertainment in an aristocratic household, as revealed by his known library, as well as his role as legal scrivener in the vicinity of Ludlow. The picture we have of the man is now much more vivid, and the scholarly reaction to Revard's work has been electric. In the many positive reviews given the book, other scholars celebrate his accomplishment. Here are some sample responses:

> The most eagerly awaited contribution is undoubtedly Carter Revard's study of the scribe and provenance of the manuscript, which has been foreshadowed in several preliminary articles over the past two decades; it is by far the longest and most important piece in the book.... The minor documents all have precise dates and localizations and cover a period of thirty-five years, so Revard is able to show the development of the scribe's handwriting and to make plausible suggestions concerning his status as a secular cleric in the employment of one or more high-ranking landowners in the neighbourhood of Ludlow. Thanks to Revard's work a good deal is now known about the Harley scribe, and this gives us a clearer social context for the texts he copied. (Frankis 2002: 406–7)

One of [the volume's] main achievements is to have provided no less than ninety pages for Carter Revard (whose pioneering work on the manuscripts had previously been available only in scattered publications) to set out all he knows about Scribe B of Harley, the Ludlow scrivener whose hand is known in two other MSS, . . . and has also been found by Revard in 41 local charters. Revard's researches have uncovered a remarkable archive, and one that we must assume is representative of the opus of a professional provincial scribe—much routine copying, and occasional commissions that bring him within the ambit of the literary scholar. (Pearsall 2002: 402)

Carter Revard treats us to illustration and analysis of substantial new evidence about the main scribe of Harley 2253. . . . [T]hese documents offer us one of those rare opportunities to study the development of a literary scribe's hand over the course of his career. Revard demonstrates how the documents enable him to date changes in the handwriting over time and thus to date each manuscript or distinct portions of manuscripts. Here is concrete evidence of the variability of scribal handwriting over the course of a thirty-five-year career that all medieval paleographers will appreciate. (Mooney 2002: 912)

[I]n putting together the potsherds of history one cannot always tell whether the gathered pieces belong to the same pot. Perhaps decades of further research in archives will turn up more documents to complete the puzzle. It will require painstaking effort, and there are few who can match the skill that Professor Revard has brought to this endeavor. (Ransom 2003: 553; for other reviews, see Cannon 2001; Hanna 2002; Kemmler 2001; O'Rourke 2001)

The metaphor of putting together "the potsherds of history" is tellingly appropriate when applied to Revard's work, for one senses that his diligence in reviving the Harley scribe's human identity amidst the accidental remains and losses of history is indebted to a sense of the past as a living, colorful presence, a sense that owes as much to his American Indian roots as to his being privileged to grow and flourish on the ancestral tree of medieval scholars. Upon receipt of the first few reviews, Revard sent me a glowing e-mail: "Your volume is really a major achievement. Bloomfield and Robbins and Donaldson and Ruth Dean and all our grandparents must be cheering" (21 January 2003). "Bloomfield" refers here to my mentor, the late Morton W. Bloomfield, former distinguished professor of medieval English studies at Harvard. "Robbins" is Rossell Hope Robbins, late key scholar of Middle English lyrics and of MS Harley 2253, and a former professor of English at the State University of

New York at Albany. "Donaldson" is E. Talbot Donaldson, Revard's own mentor at Yale. And the late Ruth Dean finished her monumental *Anglo-Norman Literature* in 1999 when she was more than one hundred years old. Revard imagined a host of wise and revered elders—scholarly mentors, blood grandparents—cheering us through our endeavors and victory. It is a good thought.

Works Cited

Cannon, C. 2001. "Review." *Yearbook of Langland Studies*. 15: 230–34.
Dean, R. J., with M. B. M. Boulton. 1999. *Anglo-Norman Literature: A Guide to Texts and Manuscripts*. Anglo-Norman Text Society Occasional Publications Series 3. London: Anglo-Norman Text Society.
Fein, S. 2000. "British Library MS 2253: The Lyrics, the Facsimile, and the Book." *Studies in the Harley Manuscript: The Scribes, Contents, and Social Contexts of British Library MS Harley 2253*. Ed. S. Fein. Kalamazoo, Michigan: Medieval Institute Publications. 1–19.
Frankis, J. 2002. "Review." *Notes and Queries*, n.s. 49.3: 406–7.
Hanna, R. 2002. "Review." *Medium Ævum* 70.2: 328–30.
Hines, J. 2004. *Voices in the Past: English Literature and Archaeology*. Cambridge, UK: D. S. Brewer. 71–104.
Kemmler, F. 2 May 2001. "Review." *Medieval Review*. 25 June 2001. http://www.hti.umich.edu/t/tmr/.
Ker, N. R. 1968. *Facsimile of British Museum MS. Harley 2253*. Early English Text Society Original Series 255. London: Oxford University Press.
Mooney, L. R. 2002. "Review." *Speculum* 77.3: 910–12.
Nolan, B. 2000. "Anthologizing Ribaldry: Five Anglo-Norman Fabliaux." *Studies in the Harley Manuscript: The Scribes, Contents, and Social Contexts of British Library MS Harley 2253*. Ed. S. Fein. Kalamazoo, Michigan: Medieval Institute Publications. 289–327.
O'Rourke, J. 2001. "Review." *Journal of the Early Book Society* 4: 292–95.
Pearsall, D. 2002. "Review." *Studies in the Age of Chaucer* 24: 401–5.
Ransom, D. 2003. "Review." *Journal of English and Germanic Philology* 102.4: 552–54.

Revard, C. 1967. "The Lecher, the Legal Eagle, and the Papelard Priest: Middle English Confessional Satires in MS. Harley 2253 and Elsewhere." *His Firm Estate: Essays for F. J. Eikenberry*. Ed. D. E. Hayden. Tulsa, Oklahoma: University of Tulsa. 1967. 54–71.

———. 1972. "How to Make a NUDE (New Utopian Dictionary of English." *Lexicography in English. Annals of the New York Academy of Science* 211: 91–98.

———. 1978. "Why Shakespeare and Chaucer, Though Not Unselfish, Could Never Have Fun." *Proceedings of the Mid-America Linguistics Conference*. Norman, Oklahoma.

———. 1979. "Richard Hurd and MS. Harley 2253." *Notes and Queries*, n.s. 26.3: 199–202.

———. 1982. "*Gilote and Johane*: An Interlude in B. L. MS. Harley 2253." *Studies in Philology* 79: 122–46.

———. 1998. "*The Outlaw's Song of Trailbaston*." *Medieval Outlaws: Ten Tales in Modern English*. Ed. T. H. Ohlgren. Stroud, UK: Sutton. 99–105; 302–4.

———. 2001a. *Winning the Dust Bowl*. Tucson, Arizona: University of Arizona Press.

———. 2001b. "*The Papelard Priest* and the Black Prince's Men: Audiences of an Alliterative Poem, ca. 1350–1370." *Studies in the Age of Chaucer* 23: 359–406.

———. 2004. "*The Wife of Bath's Grandmother*: Or, How Gilote Showed Her Friend Johane That the Wages of Sin Is Worldly Pleasure, and How Both Then Preached This Gospel throughout England and Ireland." *The Chaucer Review* 39.2: 117–36.

———. 2005. "Four Fabliaux from London, British Library MS Harley 2253, Translated into English Verse." *The Chaucer Review* 40.2: 111–40.

Scahill, J. 2003. "Trilingualism in Early Middle English Miscellanies: Languages and Literature." *Yearbook of English Studies* 33: 18–32.

Turville-Petre, T. 1996. *England the Nation: Language, Literature, and National Identity, 1290–1340*. Oxford: Clarendon.

Appendix

Medieval Scholarship by Carter Revard

Revard, C. 1964. "A Note on *at the fyrst fyne* (*Pearl* 635)." *English Language Notes* 1.3: 164–65.

———. 1967. "The Lecher, the Legal Eagle, and the Papelard Priest: Middle English Confessional Satires in MS. Harley 2253 and Elsewhere." *His Firm Estate: Essays for F. J. Eikenberry*. Ed. D. E. Hayden. Tulsa, Oklahoma: University of Tulsa. 1967. 54–71.

———. 1978. "'Sulch Sorw I Walke With': Line 4 of 'Foweles in the frith.'" *Notes and Queries*, n.s. 25.3: 200.

———. 1979. "Richard Hurd and MS. Harley 2253." *Notes and Queries*, n.s. 26.3: 199–202.

———. 1980. "The Tow on Absalom's Distaff and the Punishment of Lechers in Medieval London." *English Language Notes* 17.3: 168–70.

———. 1981. "Three More Holographs in the Hand of the Scribe of MS Harley 2253 in Shrewsbury." *Notes and Queries*, n.s. 28.3: 199–200.

———. 1982. "Scribe of MS Harley 2253." *Notes and Queries*, n.s. 29.1: 62–63.

———. 1982. "*Gilote and Johane*: An Interlude in B. L. MS. Harley 2253." *Studies in Philology* 79.2: 122–46.

Cox, D. C., and C. Revard. 1985. "A New ME O-and-I Lyric and Its Provenance." *Medium Ævum* 54.1: 33–46.

Revard, C. 1987. "*Title* and *Auaunced* in *Piers Plowman* B.11.290." *The Yearbook of Langland Studies* 1: 116–21.

———. 1997. "Courtly Romances in the Privy Wardrobe." *The Court and Cultural Diversity*. Ed. E. Mullally and J. J. Thompson. Cambridge, UK: Boydell and Brewer. 297–308.

———. 1998. "*The Outlaw's Song of Trailbaston*." *Medieval Outlaws: Ten Tales in Modern English*. Ed. T. H. Ohlgren. Stroud, UK: Sutton. Pp. 99–105, 302–4.

———. 1999. "Beads, Wampum, Money, Words—and Old English Riddles." *American Indian Culture and Research Journal* 23.1: 177–89.

———. 1999. "'Annote and Johon,' MS. Harley 2253, and *The Book of Secrets*." *English Language Notes* 36.3: 5–19.

———. 2000. "Scribe and Provenance." *Studies in the Harley Manuscript: The Scribes, Contents, and Social Contexts of British Library MS Harley 2253*. Ed. S. Fein. Kalamazoo, Michigan: Medieval Institute Publications. 21–109.

———. 2000. "From French 'Fabliau Manuscripts' and MS Harley 2253 to the *Decameron* and the *Canterbury Tales*." *Medium Ævum* 69.2: 261–78.

———. 2001. "*The Papelard Priest* and the Black Prince's Men: Audiences of an Alliterative Poem, ca. 1350–1370." *Studies in the Age of Chaucer* 23: 359–406.

———. 2001–02. "Was the Pearl Poet in Aquitaine with Chaucer? A Note on *Fade*, l. 149 of *Sir Gawain and the Green Knight*." *SELIM: Journal of the Spanish Society for Medieval English Language and Literature* 11: 5–26.

———. 2004. "*The Wife of Bath's Grandmother*: Or, How Gilote Showed Her Friend Johane That the Wages of Sin Is Worldly Pleasure, and How Both Then Preached This Gospel throughout England and Ireland." *The Chaucer Review* 39: 117–36.

———. 2005. "Four Fabliaux from London, British Library MS Harley 2253, Translated into English Verse." *The Chaucer Review* 40.2: 111–40.

———. Forthcoming. "*A Goliard's Feast* and the Metanarrative of Harley 2253." *Revue Belge de Philologie*.

———. Forthcoming. "MS Harley 2253 as Anthology: Oppositional Thematics and Metanarrative." *Manuscripts of the West Midlands*. Ed. W. Scase and R. Farnham. Turnhout, Belgium: Brepols.

Author Notes

Ellen L. Arnold is Associate Professor of English at East Carolina University in Greenville, North Carolina, where she teaches Native American literatures, ethnic American literatures, and women's literature. She has published essays, book chapters, and reference entries on the work of Leslie Marmon Silko, Linda Hogan, and Carter Revard. She edited *Conversations with Leslie Marmon Silko* (University Press of Mississippi, 2000), as well as a special issue of *Studies in American Indian Literatures* in honor of Carter Revard (2003).

Márgara Averbach teaches U.S. Literature in the Universidad de Buenos Aires and Literary Translation in the I.E.S. Lenguas Vivas J.R. Fernández. She has translated 51 novels from English into Spanish and has published 15 books on literature for children and adults. She has published one academic book on slavery, *Memoria oral de la esclavitud*, and and another on Native American testimony, *Historias orales de nativos estadounidenses contemporaneous*, both published by Programa de Historia Oral de la Universidad de Buenos Aires, Argentina. She has 21 journal articles, including *American Quarterly*, *Feminine Speculation*, *American Indian Quarterly*, and *Studies in Native American Literatures* (U.S.). She also has a chapter on *Dances with Wolves* in *Screening Culture*, edited by Heather Norris Nicholson (Lexington Books, Canada).

Peter G. Beidler is the Lucy G. Moses Professor of English at Lehigh University, Bethlehem, Pennsylvania. Like Carter Revard, he is a medievalist by academic training. He has also, however, been teaching and publishing on Native American literature for the last quarter-century. Although he has published on Silko, Welch, and other Indian writers, he has a special interest in the work of Louise Erdrich. A new and expanded edition of the book he wrote with Gay Barton, *A Reader's Guide to the Novels of Louise Erdrich*, is just out (2006) from the University of Missouri Press.

Robert Bensen is the editor of *Children of the Dragonfly: Native American Voices on Child Custody and Education* (Univeristy of Arizona Press, 2001), for which Carter Revard wrote the Foreword. He has published five collections of his poems, most recently *Two Dancers* (Woodland Arts Editions, 2004). His poetry and essays have appeared in journals in the U.K., U.S. and Caribbean. Bensen won the Robert Penn Warren Award for Poetry as well as a poetry fellowship from the National Endowment for the Arts. He, his wife and daughter live in Oneonta, New York, where he is director of writing at Hartwick College.

Susan Berry Brill de Ramírez, Professor of English, teaches Native American literatures, environmental literatures, and literary criticism and theory at Bradley University. Author of *Contemporary American Indian Literatures & the Oral Tradition* (University of Arizona Press, 1999), *Wittgenstein and Critical Theory* (Ohio University Press, 1995), and numerous scholarly articles, she is completing two book manuscripts for the University of New Mexico Press: *Native American Life History Narratives: Colonial and Postcolonial Navajo Ethnography* and *"A Spring Wind Rising": Native American Poet, Educator, Essayist, and Activist Simon J. Ortiz* (co-edited with Evelina Zuni Lucero). Brill de Ramírez's current projects include work on indigenous women storytellers and their women ethnographers, several collaborative research projects, and continuing work in environmental literatures and ecocriticism.

Robin Riley Fast teaches American literature at Emerson College in Boston. She is the author of *The Heart as a Drum: Continuance and Resistance in American Indian Poetry*, the co-editor (with Christine Mack Gordon) of *Approaches to Teaching Dickinson's Poetry*, and has published numerous articles on American Indian literature, poetry, and other topics.

Susanna Fein is Professor of English and Coordinator of Ancient, Medieval, and Renaissance Studies at Kent State University. Her scholarship focuses on medieval manuscripts and Middle English poetry, including the lyrics of London, British Library Manuscript Harley 2253 and the works of Geoffrey Chaucer. She is editor of the journal *Chaucer Review*, and has authored or edited many articles and books, including the volume of essays entitled *Studies in the Harley Manuscript* (2000), which features the research of Carter Revard. She is currently editing the poems and carols of John the Blind Audelay from a fifteenth-century manuscript housed in Oxford.

Jerry Harp's books of poems are *Creature* (Salt Publishing, 2003), *Gatherings* (Ashland Poetry Press, 2004), and *Urban Flowers, Concrete Plains* (Salt Publishing, 2006). He is currently working on a book about the poetry of Donald Justice. He teaches at Lewis and Clark College.

Patrice Hollrah is the director of the Writing Center at the University of Nevada, Las Vegas, and teaches for the Department of English. She has published articles on Native America literature and is the author of *"The Old Lady Trill, the Victory Yell": The Power of Women in Native American Literature* (Routledge, 2004).

Suzanne Evertsen Lundquist is a professor of English, Native American Studies, and Cultural Studies at Brigham Young University. She is the author of *Trickster: A Transformation Archetype* (Mellen Research University Press, 1991) and *Native American Literatures: An Introduction* (Continuum Press, 2004). Lundquist has also published numerous essays on Native American Literature as well as essays on Jewish American and Women's literatures. Lundquist spent ten years working among various Native tribes—the Tarahumara (Mexico), Quechua (Peru), and Aymara (Bolivia) Indians as well as among villagers in Central Mexico. Her central research interests surround the connections between ethnic/gender identity, politics, and cultural/human survival.

Janet McAdams' poetry collection, *The Island of Lost Luggage*, won an American Book Award in 2001. She edits Earthworks for Salt Publishing, a series of books by indigenous writers. She was named "Mentor of the Year" by the Wordcraft Circle of Native Writers and Storytellers. She teaches at Kenyon College.

Robert M. Nelson is a Professor of English at the University of Richmond, where he teaches a variety of courses in American Indian literatures. A former co-editor of the journal *Studies in American Indian Literatures*, he has published a number of articles on 20th century Native

American poets and novelists and is currently completing a book that addresses the origins and functions of the embedded texts in Leslie Silko's novel *Ceremony*.

Susan Scarberry-Garcia is Assistant Professor of English at Arizona State University, specializing in Native American literature. She is author of *Landmarks of Healing: A Study of House Made of Dawn* and of *Dancing Spirits: Jose Rey Toledo, Towa Artist*. She has published numerous articles on the literatures and arts of the American Southwest and, and since 2000, articles in Russia and English on the literatures and ritual arts of Native Siberians with whom she has collaborated on their Native grounds. Previously President of the Association for the Study of American Indian Literatures and Chair of the Executive Committee for the Division of American Indian Literatures of MLA, Scarberry-Garcia has the highest regard for Carter Revard's lifetime work.

Norma C. Wilson is Professor Emeritus of English at the University of South Dakota where she taught American Indian literature from 1978-2005. She met Carter Revard in the mid-1970s when she was writing her doctoral dissertation at the University of Oklahoma. Her articles on Native literature have been published in a numerous reference books and journals, including the *Cambridge Companion to Native American Literature*, *The Columbia Companion to the Twentieth Century American Short Story*, *Teaching American Ethnic Literatures*, *Studies in American Indian Literatures*, and *Phatitude*. She lives in the countryside near Vermillion, South Dakota, where she is currently writing poetry and prose about her life.

Index

Alexie, Sherman, 2, 111
Alfred, Taiaiake, on tradition and community 86–87
Allen, Paula Gunn, 38
allotment, 13. 17, 44, 50
American Indian Movement (AIM), 1, 7, 101–04, 105, 106, 107
Anderson, Eric Gary, on American Indian intelligence of travel 61
"Annote and Johon," 215
Armstrong, Jeanette C., on language and place 61–62
assimilation, 7, 13, 46, 98, 101, 103
Aunt Jewell, see Farmer, Jewell McDonald Camp
autobiography, Native American compared to Euroamerican 34–36, 146
autoethnography, definition 36–37, 39

Bachelard, Gaston, on the poetic act and the past 112, 113
Baptista, Luis F., on bird dialects 78
Barthes, Roland ("Zero Degree of Writing"), 184
Beowulf, 63, 65–66, 153, 155
Bevis, William, on "homing in" 60–61
Bhabha, Homi K., on hybridity 45; on "third space' 45–46

Biblical creation story, 47, 54, 165, 197
black holes, 23, 161, 177–79
Blake, William ("London"), 176
Bloomfield, Morton W., 231
Breughel, Pieter (*Adoration of the Magi*), 64, 65, 152, 153
Brown, Kurt (*Verse and Universe*), 166
Bruchac, Joseph (interview with Revard), 15, 116, 133, 147–49, 150
Bureau of Indian Affairs takeover, 1, 102
Burns, Louis F., 115

Cahokia, 28, 41, 54, 93, 132–39
Camp, Arthur (Revard's uncle), 49, 56
Camp, Carter (Revard's cousin), 26, 27, 79, 102, 104n10, 106, 106n14
Camp, Carter (Revard's uncle). 54, 56, 221
Camp, James Alexander (Revard's grandfather), 13, 41–42, 54, 56, 64, 69, 70, 130, 155
Camp, Thelma Louise, see Jump, Thelma Louise Camp
Camp, Roy (Revard's cousin), 13, 40
Camp, Woody (Woodrow, Revard's uncle), 13, 29, 56, 66, 104n10, 106
Carter Revard Scholarship (Washington University), 44
Charles, Jim, on *Helushka* 98

[241]

Chaucer, Geoffrey, 207, 209, 212, 213, 219, 222, 227–28; *The Canterbury Tales* 223; *The Miller's Tale* 222, 228; *The Wife of Bath's Tale* 207, 209
Cliff, Michelle, on interconnectedness 156
Close Encounters of the Third Kind (film), 23
Cole, Sally, on ethnography 36
Coleridge, Samuel Taylor, 112
colonization, colonialism, 15, 22, 23, 39, 44, 45, 50, 51, 52, 62, 73–74, 143, 176–77, 179, 196, 197, 199, 205, 214
Columbus, Christopher, 23, 46–47, 52, 55, 168, 180
community, importance of, 5, 6, 9, 12–13, 21, 24, 26, 28, 30, 42, 61, 72, 74, 85, 87, 89, 93, 94, 95, 101, 103, 134, 146, 211, 215–16
Crook, General George, 25

Dante (*Divine Comedy*), 29–30. 49, 229
Dean, Ruth, 228, 231–32
decolonization, 6, 62, 87
Deloria, Vine, Jr., 26
Derrida, Jacques, on text 216
desaparecidos (the "disappeared"), 196, 196n5
Dickinson, Emily, 49, 147, 187n2, 238
Dodge Dart, 104n9, 105
Donaldson, E. Talbot, 220, 232
Dust Bowl, 40, 41, 54, 62, 202, 206
Dyson, Hugo, 220

Eckhart, Meister, 63, 65, 152, 153
Eikenberry, Franklin J., 162, 219–20, 221
Einstein, Alfred, 36, 121, 162, 169; Einsteinian theory 168
Eliot, T. S., 113
Emerson, Ralph Waldo, 15–16
Eoyang, Eugene C., on subject-object relationship, 145, 146–47, 155
Erdrich, Louise, 2, 4, 38, 51, 184, 238

Farmer, Jewell McDonald Camp (Revard's Aunt Jewell), 6, 7, 13, 28–29, 30, 54, 66, 67, 70, 72, 79, 81, 85–95, 104, 104n10, 105n12, 130, 131, 133–35, 136, 137, 138, 139, 140
Fast, Robin Riley (*The Heart As a Drum*), 2, 7, 111
Fleet, John, 229
Fletcher, Alice and Francis La Flesche, on Osage myth 17, 20; on definition of "Wakonda" 100n4, 124–25
Foley, John Miles, on oral roots of literature 216
Forty-Nine song, 102, 102n6, 106, 108;
Foucault, Michel, 186
Frost, Robert, 4, 51

Geiogamah, Hanay, on 49s 102n6
gender roles, traditional 48, 51, 87, 99; in Wendy Rose and Robert Frost 51
General Allotment Act (1887), 17
Geronimo. 35, 57, 105, 146, 154
Ghost Dance, 55, 136, 138, 178
Gilote et Johane, 8, 9, 206, 207–14, 222, 227–28, 229
Glancy, Diane, 38
Going to College (radio quiz show), 1, 14, 147, 162
Gourd Dance, 21, 78

Harjo, Joy, 2, 61, 83
Harley Manuscript (MS Harley 2253), 9, 206, 210–13, 221–31
Harley scribe (Ludlow scribe), 9, 210, 211–12, 221, 224, 225–26, 227–229, 230–31
Hayden, Don, 219, 221
Helushka (Ponca men's society), 6, 98–99, 101, 106, 106n13, 107
Hilden, Patricia Penn, on "Tonto speak" 152n3
Hirsch, E. D., on genre formation 36
Ho-e-ga, definition 16–17

Hogan, Linda, 2, 80, 83, 160
hybridity, 45, 57

identity, 136; mixedblood 5, 37–40, 41–44, 57–58, 69n7, 144; myth, significance of to identity formation 47, 161; Native compared to Western conceptions 5, 35–36, 146–47; pan-tribal 4, 5, 6, 7, 28, 98–108,102n6; poetic voice and 147–48; traditional/progressive split 102, 103n7; tribal/cultural 25, 29, 35, 38–39, 41–44, 45, 47, 62, 67n6, 80, 100–01, 105–06, 107, 130, 131, 144, 146–47, 174
Il lonsha (Osage men's society), 106n13, 107
Isabella, Queen, 229

Jahner, Elaine, on metaphor and limits of culture 155–56
Joyce, James (*Finnegans Wake*), 163,
Jump, Addison Benjamin, Sr. (Revard's stepfather), 12, 13, 41, 56, 79
Jump, Jacob (Revard's Osage grandfather), 18, 56
Jump, Jim (Louis James, Revard's younger half-brother), 13
Jump, Josephine Strikeaxe (Revard's grandmother), 1, 18, 43, 54, 56, 69
Jump, Kenneth (Revard's uncle), 42, 56, 162
Jump, Thelma Louise Camp (Revard's mother), 12, 13, 53, 56, 69

Konkle, Maureen, 177
Krupat, Arnold, on Native American autobiography 35–36

La Flesche, Francis, on Osage cosmology and ceremony 16, 43, 46, 131
La Flesche, Susette, 108n18

language, performativity 72–73, 155, 171
Langston, Donna Hightower on women's roles 91, 93
Levinas, Emmanuel, 46
Lincoln, Kenneth, on cultural fusion 44–45

Manifest Destiny, 23, 205
marriage, Ponca customs 90
Mathews, John Joseph, 14, 15, 18, 21, 118, 123, 124, 128, 131–32
McAdams, Janet, 4, 64n2, 111, 167
McDonald, Gus ("Uncle Gus" or Shon-geh-ska, Revard's uncle), 6, 7, 26–28, 54, 78, 93, 99–101, 104, 105–08, 132, 134, 137–38
Medicine, Beatrice, on women's roles 87
Midgley, Mary (*Science and Poetry*), 160, 166
Milton, John, 4, 15, 46, 51, 55, 57
mixedblood identity, see identity
Momaday, N. Scott, 2, 38, 39, 83
Mortimer, Roger, 226, 229
myth/mythic imagination, 41, 47–49, 52–53, 57, 80, 82, 89, 160, 163, 166–68; relationship to science 49, 55, 166–68, 179–80. See also **Osage myth and cosmology.**

Nabhan, Gary, on cross-pollination of science and poetry 161, 164
names and naming, importance of 5, 6, 14–15, 35, 43, 47, 82, 83, 131–33, 151, 161, 170, 174–75, 179–8, 213
Native American cultures, similarities to Latin American cultures 196
Native American literature, characteristics of 3, 111
Native American poetry, critical approaches to 2; characteristics of 3–4,
Navajo cosmology, 46, 48, 180

neocolonialism in Latin America, 196
Niatum, Dwayne, 2

Old Man's Lament, The, 212
oral tradition, 3, 5, 6, 8–9, 49, 60, 62, 67, 79, 82, 106, 138, 164, 179, 202–221
Ortega y Gassett, Jose, on autobiography 36
Ortiz, Simon, 2, 4, 51, 62
Osage myth and cosmology, 14–15, 16–17, 20, 22, 24, 29, 43–44, 46, 47, 80–81, 117–18, 123–25, 132, 173, 174, 178, 179–80
Osage history, 17–20, 21–22, 114, 132; allotment 17; headrights 18; relocation 17
Osage language, 60
Osage Naming Ceremony, 1, 7, 14, 20, 42, 43, 47, 54, 70–71, 71n8, 80, 82, 131, 133, 161, 173–74
Osage-Ponca relationships, 24, 27–28, 85–86

pan-Indian/pan-tribal community, see identity
Papelard Priest, The, 9, 221, 223
Parini, Jay, on autobiography 36
Piers Plowman, 223
Ponca history, 24–26, 29, 86, 90, 98, 108, 140; relocation 24, 108, 140
Ponca language, 60, 91–92
Ponca-Osage relationships, 24, 27–28, 85–86
Porush, David, on Postmodernism 37
postcolonialism, 143, 197
Postmodernism, 8, 36, 37, 128
Pratt, Mary Louise, on autoethnography 5, 39; on contact zones 5, 7, 39, 143
Pryor, Antwine (Revard's older half-brother), 13
Purce, Stella Hill, see Revard, Stella Hill Purce

quantum mechanics, 49, 145, 160, 162, 175

Rader, Dean and Janice Gould (*Speak to Me Words*), 2, 3, 4, 7
Reagan, Ronald, 24, 176, 196n5
Revard, Carter, as community organizer 2, 44, 94, 101; as Gourd Dancer 2, 31, 44, 94, 124, 133; awards 2; binaries, disruption of 8, 57, 65, 143–51, 155–56, 161, 167; birds and birdsong in 4, 6, 13, 15, 20–21, 29–30, 31, 49, 54, 60, 72, 77–84, 89, 91–92, 93, 95, 114–15, 119–22, 124–25, 131, 140, 153, 155, 161, 165, 167, 168, 169, 192, 193–94; boundary transgression in 2, 7, 8, 34, 45–46, 51, 108, 111, 123, 130, 145, 156, 161, 175, 210; childhood 1, 12–15,18, 20, 31, 64, 68–70, 79, 147, 153, 171, 202; children and grandchildren 55, 57; conversive strategies in 204, 204–16 *passim*; "double vision" in 38, 57, 66; education 1, 13, 14–15, 32, 42, 44, 63–65, 147–48, 154–55, 162–63,190, 219–20; emic and etic perspectives on 6–7, 100–01, 104n9; ethnic identity, theory of 37, 43; family genealogy 12–13, 41, 55–57; home in 6, 19, 49, 78, 107, 152–56 (as source of community and language 60–69; as site of loss 69–73); holograms in 165–67; light, images in 12, 22–23, 64–65, 65n3, 95–96, 122, 131, 132, 137, 153, 161, 165–66, 167, 172, 178, 179–80; local-global relationships in 4, 5, 8, 63, 73, 143, 171, 177, 216; medieval scholarship 1, 8, 9, 44, 123, 152,

173, 202–16, 219–32; mixed heritage 1, 12–13, 19, 31, 41–42, 37–40, 41–2, 57–8, 69n7, 144; on literary theory and community 24; on Native American autobiography 35; on responsibility of non-Native scholars 94; on science 8, 22, 112, 160–182; on song as interspecies communication 77; on stars 5, 12, 16, 20–23, 29, 43, 46, 48, 94–95, 117, 131–32, 165, 167, 173–75, 179, 180, 188; on travel 62–63; Osage name (Nompehwahthe, Nompewathe, Non-peh-wa-the) 1, 14, 42–43, 132, 145,188; place, importance of in 41, 49, 55, 57, 60–67, 78, 115–116, 119, 122–23, 152–54, 156, 161, 174; poetic voice in 7,15, 37; 68, 95, 98, 115, 121, 125, 133, 144–51, 155, 156, 171, 188, 204–07, 212; poetics of 4, 5, 6, 7, 24, 31, 61, 73–74, 132; refiguration of language 161, 169, 175, 213; riddle form in 4, 31, 38, 74n10, 81–82, 124, 151, 172, 214; storytelling in 2, 5, 8–9, 38, 49, 60, 67, 98, 106, 138, 156–57, 164, 179, 202–16, 221; sonnet form in 15, 147–51, 188; survival, cultural in 28, 40–41, 48, 53, 54, 62, 72–74, 82, 85–93, 95, 118; transformation in 20, 82, 118, 145, 148–49, 150–51, 167, 180; **Books:** *Cowboys and Indians, Christmas Shopping* 2, 79, 86, 94, 144, 151; *An Eagle Nation* 2, 12, 14, 29, 49, 63, 72, 81, 144, 151, 170, 175; *How the Songs Come Down* 2, 5, 9, 85, 86, 89, 135, 170, 171; *Family Matters, Tribal Affairs* 1, 2, 12, 13, 21, 39, 46, 53, 60, 73, 77, 87, 88, 144. 154. 173, 177, 179, 190n3, 203; *My Right Hand Don't Leave Me No More* (chapbook) 2; *Nonymosity* (chapbook) 2; *Ponca War Dancers* 2, 6, 26, 49, 78, 86, 88, 104n10, 108n18, 129, 132, 144, 146, 186, 187n1, 158, 192; *Winning the Dust Bowl* 2, 7, 13, 15, 28, 30, 34, 37, 39, 40, 53, 62, 69, 70, 72, 86, 130, 135, 138, 144, 168, 171, 187, 190n2, 221; **Essays:** "'Annote and Johon,' MS. Harley 2253, and *The Book of Secrets*" 215; "Beads, Wampum, Money, Words—and Old English Riddles" 79, 82, 214; "Buck Creek Community" 60; "Buck Creek to Oxford by Birch Canoe" 37–38; "The Lecher, the Legal Eagle, and the Papelard Priest: Middle English Confessional Satires in MS. Harley 2253 and Elsewhere" 221; "A Giveaway Special" 114; "Going to College" 60; "Herbs of Healing" 4, 46, 51, 214; "History, Myth, and Identity among Osages and Other Peoples" 35, 146, 174, 213; "How to Make a NUDE (New Utopian Dictionary of English)" 222; "How Columbus Fell from the Sky and Lighted Up Two Continents" 46, 180; "Making a Name" 61, 66, 68, 70. 71. 73, 174, 179; "Report to the Nation: Claiming Europe" 46, 52–53, 73, 154, 214; "Scribe and Provenance" 230; "Some Notes on Native American Literature" 24, 172; "Traditional Osage Naming Ceremonies: Entering the Circle of Being" 1, 14, 71n8, 131, 161; "Walking Among the Stars" 34, 53, 60, 79, 82, 132; "Why Mark Twain Murdered Injun Joe—And Will Never Be

Indicted" 50, 204; "Why Shakespeare and Chaucer, Though Not Unselfish, Could Never Have Fun" 222; "The Wife of Bath's Grandmother" 8, 206–211, 213; **Poems**: "And Don't Be Deaf to the Singing Beyond" 49; "Another Sunday Morning" 49, 68, 73; "Aunt Jewell as Powwow Princess" 4, 6, 7, 28, 54, 86, 93–94, 130, 132–39; "Behind the Hill" 68; "Birch Canoe" 31, 34, 38; "Brothers" 79; "A Cardinal, New Snow, and Some Firewood" 7, 118–20; "Chiggers" 169; "Christmas Shopping" 55; "Close Encounters" 22–23, 65n3, 81, 161, 173–74; "Columbus Looks Out Far, In Deep" 4, 164–69; "Communing Before Supermarkets" 68–69, 171; "Coyote Tells Why He Sings" ("The Coyote") 4, 7, 15–16, 133, 147–51 (translation into Spanish 186–89); "Dancing with Dinosaurs" 20, 49, 78–79, 82, 160, 168; "Discovery of the New World" 23; "Driving in Oklahoma" 8, 198 (translation into Spanish 192–95); "Dragon Watching in St. Louis" 55; "An Eagle Nation" 4, 6, 7, 73, 85, 86, 90–92, 93, 130, 140; "Earth and Diamonds" 49, 114, 166–68; "ESP" 8, 162, 163–66, 167, 168, 169; "Geode" ("This Is Your Geode Talking") 49, 114, 166–68; "Given" 6, 65n3, 86, 87, 94–95; "Home Movies" 130; "Homework at Oxford" 6, 8, 42, 49, 63–66, 67, 68, 73, 74 n, 10, 143, 144, 152–56; "How the Songs Came Down" ("How the Songs Come Down") 6, 7, 86, 88–89, 130, 139, 177; "In Oklahoma" 63, 73; "Looking Before and After" 7, 129–31, 132, 137, 139; "Making Money" 4; "The Man Lee Harvey Oswald Missed" 55; "A Mandala of Sorts" 79; "My Right Hand Don't Leave Me No More" 6, 42, 69; "Nonymosity" 8, 174–75; "November in Washington DC" 4; "Over By Fairfax, Leaving Tracks" 55, 223–24; "Outside in St. Louis" 78, 114; "Paint and Feathers" 6, 30, 31, 70, 72, 73, 74, 80–81; "People from the Stars" 21–22, 132; "Planet of the Blue-Eyed Cats" 55; "The Poet's Cottage" 8, 172–73; "Ponca War Dancers" 6, 26, 78, 98–108; "Postcolonial Hyperbaggage" 4, 8, 23–24, 178; translation into Spanish 195–98; "Pure Country" 42; "Rock Shelters" 7, 18–20, 115–18; "Sea-changes" 49; "Songs of the Wine-Throated Hummingbird" 9, 55; "Starring America" 29, 49, 55; "A Sun Dance Story" 7, 110–11, 134–35; "That Lightning's Hard to Climb" 53–54, 69, 73; "To the Muse in Oklahoma" 6, 62–63, 74, 190n3 (translation into Spanish 190–92); "Transactions" 4; "Transfigurations" 4, 8, 176–79; "Wazhazhe Grandmother" 6, 16–17, 18, 20, 21, 54, 69; "What the Eagle Fan Says" 4, 31, 81, 123–25; "What the TV Said" 4, 7–8, 143, 144, 151–52; "Where the Frontier Went" 68; "Winning the Dust Bowl" 40; **Short Story**: "How the FBI Man Nearly Found God" 177–78

Revard, Charles E. (Revard's grandfather), 56

Revard, Maxine (Revard's twin sister), 7, 13, 42, 54, 104n10, 130, 147
Revard, McGuire (Revard's father), 12, 56
Revard, Stella Hill Purce (Revard's wife), 15, 55, 56, 57
Robbins, Russell Hope, 231
Rose Bowl, 40
Rosen, Kenneth (ed., *Voices of the Rainbow*), 163

Sangari, Kumkum, on hybridity 45
Scheub, Harold, on African oral tradition 211
Shakespeare, 44, 46, 221, 222; *Henry the Fifth* 47; *King Lear* 49; *The Tempest* 29; *Two Gentlemen of Verona* 219–20;
Silko, Leslie Marmon, 38, 99n1, 160, 203, 210
sovereignty, 6, 28, 92
Standing Bear (Ponca leader), 25–26, 107
Stevens, Wallace, 4, 51, 63
storytelling, see oral tradition
Sun Dance, 28–30, 72, 81, 92–93, 110, 111, 133, 134, 135, 137, 138, 140

Tapahonso, Luci, 61
Tedlock, Dennis, on story and ceremony, 203
Thatcher, Margaret, 176
"third space," 6, 7, 45–48, 49, 51, 57; as trickster pose 46, 51
Tibbles, Thomas Henry, 25
Tolkien, J. R. R., 219, 220
Trail of Broken Treaties, 1, 102
Trailbaston, 228

translation, problems in 184–85; issues across hybrid cultures 198–99; translator-author collaboration 199
trickster, 22–23, 44, 46, 51, 52, 53, 156, 220–21, 223, 229
Turner, Victor. on experience 37
Twain, Mark, 13, 44, 183, 221; racism in *Huckleberry Finn* 50–51; Indian hating in *Tom Sawyer* 204–06

Uncle Gus, see McDonald, Gus

Verse and Universe, 166, 169, 170
Vizenor, Gerald, 38, 160

Wakondah (Wakonda, Wah-kon-tah: Osage creator or life spirit), 15, 100, 100n4, 124–25
wa-thi'-gethon, definition 46; 49, 57
Wazhazhe, 21, 31, 52–53, 73, 85, 133
Welch, James, 2, 237
White Eagle (Ponca leader), 25–26, 107, 108, 108n18
Whitman, Walt, 15, 128
Wilson, Norma (*The Nature of Native American Poetry*), 2, 3, 5
Winter, Joysa M., on paradox 143
winter count, 21, 27, 107–08, 108n17
Wittgenstein. Ludvig, 214
women, traditional roles of 87, 91, 93
Wounded Knee massacre, 57, 102n5
Wounded Knee occupation, 1, 22, 26, 27, 28, 101–03, 102n5, 106, 108

Zepeda, Ofelia, 2
Zolbrod, Paul, 48, 215
Zumthor, Paul, on oral cultures, 204, 211

www.ingramcontent.com/pod-product-compliance
Lightning Source LLC
Chambersburg PA
CBHW021854230426
43671CB00006B/383